Mastering Salesforce Experience Cloud

Strategies for creating powerful customer interactions

Lillie Beiting

Rachel Rogers

Mastering Salesforce Experience Cloud

Group Product Manager: Aaron Tanna
Publishing Product Manager: Puneet Kaur
Business Development Executive: Kritika Pareek
Book Project Manager: Manisha Singh
Senior Editor: Esha Banerjee
Technical Editor: Kavyashree K S
Copy Editor: Safis Editing
Proofreader: Esha Banerjee
Indexer: Tejal Soni
Production Designer: Jyoti Kadam

First published: October 2024

Production reference: 1060924

Published by Packt Publishing Ltd.
Grosvenor House
11 St Paul's Square
Birmingham
B3 1RB, UK

ISBN 978-1-83546-634-6

www.packtpub.com

Breaking glass ceilings requires grit and determination. We do this not for ourselves, but for the generations of women to come, like Kinley Rogers and Paloma Rocke-Berrocal. We celebrate the women who made it in the male-dominated technology industry, and we thank the women before us who paved bright futures for us and for STEM badasses such as Dr. Magdalen Beiting-Parrish, Meridith Paluck (RN), Nell Watson, and Anna Benbrook (MS, CHES).

Keep fighting.

~ Lillie and Rachel

Contributors

About the authors

Lillie Beiting began her Salesforce experience in Fortune 500 companies such as General Motors, Stanley Black and Decker, and Anthem. For her expertise in Salesforce products, Beiting was recognized as a Salesforce Trailblazer and one of the *30 Marketers to Watch*. She has spoken at multiple conferences and Salesforce events, notably at Dreamforce 2018.

Beiting has contributed to the field of Data Ethics as a United Nations Delegate in Data Ethics in Sustainable Development Goals. She was also a contributing author for the first artificial intelligence ethics certification program, The Ethics Certification Program for Autonomous and Intelligent Systems (ECPAIS), from the Ethical Institute of Electrical and Electronics Engineers (IEEE).

I'd like to acknowledge the Salesforce Ohana for their assistance in the creation of this book, as well as my friends and loved ones who supported me while I worked nights and weekends to write this.

Rachel Rogers stumbled into a technology-first career when she was introduced to Salesforce. In a world driven by hyper-connectivity, she pushes to understand: what do we lose when we remove people from the equation? She has led multiple companies in the quest to curate technology with the people at its heart.

Rachel spoke at Dreamforce from 2012 to 2018. In 2013, she was honored as a Salesforce MVP and was inducted into the Salesforce MVP Hall of Fame in 2019, recognizing her expertise and commitment to the Salesforce Community. She won the Lighting Bright Ideas Award, Data Driven Business Leader Award, and was the original Lightning Champion. In 2024, she was awarded the Honored Listed as Who's Who in America 2024.

This book has been a blessing and has pushed me to hone my technical skills. I want to thank Jamie and Kinley Rogers for their support through the late nights and early mornings that made this book a reality, and my inner circle for the courage to tackle something new. Together, we will keep moving onward and upward!

About the reviewer

Since 1995, **Ryan Headley** spent nearly 30 years working in different areas of IT. Having started his career in desktop support, he moved to Chicago, US, to work in the LAN group at a large data center in the late 90s and ultimately relocated to Madison, US, where he taught himself Java and worked as a contractor and consultant. In 2013, in the course of helping a former colleague build his practice, Ryan logged into Salesforce.org for the first time. Within a couple of years he became a Salesforce MVP and wound up working for Salesforce directly in 2018 where he became an Engineering Manager. In 2023, he joined a Fortune 100 company as a Senior Director of Engineering to oversee the governance and delivery of Salesforce solutions.

Table of Contents

Part 2: Infrastructure Setup to Support and Customize Design Strategy

5

Understanding Experience Cloud Templates   77

6

When to Use Aura Components, Lightning Web Components, and Lightning Runtime Components   95

Part 3: Human-Centric Development

7

Leveraging Screen Flows versus Apex   117

8

Understanding Inputs – Emails, Chats, and Text Messages   135

9

Marketing Automation Setup   155

10

Leveraging Case Management and Knowledge Bases   175

Part 4: Site Launch

11

Security – Authentication, Data Sharing, and Encryption   201

12

Monitoring Your Site – Salesforce Native Reporting   227

13

Site Launch, Maintenance, and Moderation   249

Part 5: Certifications

14

Best Practices and Certification Test Preparation   265

Index   297

Other Books You May Enjoy   306

Preface

Empowering your target audience to easily interact with you and your product offerings is a critical aspect of business in the modern era – your users now expect easy, professional digital experiences when they engage with organizations. However, setting up engagement applications from scratch is challenging, and getting user behavior to connect with your organization's data is even harder.

Enter Salesforce Experience Cloud sites – website portals built off the Salesforce data model that cleanly connect your user data to your user experience. *Mastering Salesforce Experience Cloud* focuses on the human-centric nature of this product, beginning with a comprehensive guide on designing for your organization's desired users and ensuring that you're setting your internal teams and end users up for success. After contextualizing the real-world use of Experience Cloud and reviewing license models, it coaches its users through a beginning-to-end guide to mastering the technical backend of this product, both out-of-the-box settings and customization techniques.

You'll learn the Experience Cloud data model and options for customization, standard template and component structures, Visualforce, Aura, LWC and LWR UI used in Experience Cloud, Salesforce screen flow and custom trigger options, marketing automation, Knowledge Base, reporting, and more!

Who this book is for

If you are looking to understand the intricacies of Salesforce Experience Cloud, transform your client experience, enhance your enterprise architecture, and create a scalable, world class-customer web experience that seamlessly integrates with an existing Salesforce instance, then this book is for you. Mastering Salesforce Experience Cloud is for Business leaders, IT leaders, Salesforce Developers, Salesforce Admins, and web teams tasked with delivering and maintaining an excellent, integrated Experience Cloud portal experience.

What this book covers

Chapter 1, *Defining Your Digital Experience Strategy*, helps you determine your target audience, identify your stakeholders, and determine if Salesforce Experience Cloud is right for your organization.

Chapter 2, *Translating Your Audience and Interactions into Meaningful Technology Features*, teaches you how to organize your stakeholder feedback and connect it to Experience Cloud features.

Chapter 3, *Technology Component Identification – Which Parts of Experience Cloud Do I need?* aids you in aligning your features to technology stacks and determine your optimal technical stack.

Chapter 4, Curating Data Models, explains how to determine the data you need to create an Enterprise Relationship Diagram.

Chapter 5, Understanding Experience Cloud Templates, covers your options for basic and custom site templates in Salesforce Experience Cloud.

Chapter 6, When to Use Aura Components, Lightning Web Components, and Lightning Runtime Components, teaches the difference between the custom UI development components and when to use them.

Chapter 7, Leveraging Screen Flows versus Apex explains when to use the declarative tool, Flow instead of Apex to accomplish complex UX.

Chapter 8, Understanding Inputs – Emails, Chats, and Text Messages, talks about the digital communication offerings within Salesforce Experience Cloud.

Chapter 9, Marketing Automation Setup, explains how marketing automation works and what tools are available in Salesforce and third-party tech stacks.

Chapter 10, Leveraging Case Management and Knowledge Bases, covers how to implement scalable Salesforce Service Cloud solutions in Experience Cloud.

Chapter 11, Security – Authentication, Data Sharing, and Encryption, teaches you to define a security model and leverage common web security techniques to keep your Experience Cloud site safe.

Chapter 12, Monitoring Your Site – Salesforce Native Reporting, explains how to leverage native and third-party reports to monitor your Experience Cloud site.

Chapter 13, Site Launch, Maintenance and Moderation, helps you plan for your site launch, and create maintenance and moderation strategies to keep your site fresh.

Chapter 14, Best Practices and Certification Test Preparation, helps you put your knowledge to the test and prepare for the Salesforce Experience Cloud Certification.

To get the most out of this book

To get the most out of Salesforce Experience Cloud, it's helpful to have knowledge of the core Salesforce Clouds, specifically Sales and Service Clouds. For business users, understanding the basic functions of these core clouds will make Experience Cloud concepts clearer. For admins or developers, familiarity with the declarative order of operations and the Lightning Framework will be beneficial. Additionally, a web development background can help demystify some of the concepts in Experience Cloud.

Software/hardware covered in the book	Operating system requirements
Salesforce Experience Cloud	Windows, macOS, or Linux
Salesforce Marketing Cloud	Windows, macOS, or Linux
Salesforce Service Cloud	Windows, macOS, or Linux
Salesforce Sales Cloud	Windows, macOS, or Linux
Salesforce CMS	Windows, macOS, or Linux

If you are using the digital version of this book, we advise you to type the

A great way to test your knowledge of Salesforce Experience Cloud is to use Salesforce Trailhead and download a demo org. A demo org will be a developer sandbox of a net new Salesforce instance, allowing you to configure and test your designs.

Conventions used

The following text conventions have been used throughout this book.

Bold: Indicates a new term, an important word, or words that you see onscreen. For instance, words in menus or dialog boxes appear in **bold**. Here is an example: " Find **All Sites** and locate the **Builder** link for the site you wish to create a page on."

> **Tips or important notes**
> Appear like this.

Get in touch

Feedback from our readers is always welcome.

General feedback: If you have questions about any aspect of this book, email us at customercare@ packtpub.com and mention the book title in the subject of your message.

Errata: Although we have taken every care to ensure the accuracy of our content, mistakes do happen. If you have found a mistake in this book, we would be grateful if you would report this to us. Please visit www.packtpub.com/support/errata and fill in the form.

Piracy: If you come across any illegal copies of our works in any form on the internet, we would be grateful if you would provide us with the location address or website name. Please contact us at copyright@packtpub.com with a link to the material.

If you are interested in becoming an author: If there is a topic that you have expertise in and you are interested in either writing or contributing to a book, please visit authors.packtpub.com.

Share Your Thoughts

Once you've read *Mastering Salesforce Experience Cloud*, we'd love to hear your thoughts! Scan the QR code below to go straight to the Amazon review page for this book and share your feedback.

https://packt.link/r/1-835-46634-6

Your review is important to us and the tech community and will help us make sure we're delivering excellent quality content.

Download a free PDF copy of this book

Thanks for purchasing this book!

Do you like to read on the go but are unable to carry your print books everywhere?

Is your eBook purchase not compatible with the device of your choice?

Don't worry, now with every Packt book you get a DRM-free PDF version of that book at no cost.

Read anywhere, any place, on any device. Search, copy, and paste code from your favorite technical books directly into your application.

The perks don't stop there, you can get exclusive access to discounts, newsletters, and great free content in your inbox daily

Follow these simple steps to get the benefits:

1. Scan the QR code or visit the link below

https://packt.link/free-ebook/978-1-83546-634-6

2. Submit your proof of purchase

3. That's it! We'll send your free PDF and other benefits to your email directly

Part 1: Curating a Digital Experience Strategy

When building a digital experience strategy, there are several key components. First, you need to identify who you need to engage internally, and what type(s) of customers you are trying to attract. Then, you need to turn that information into what parts of the Salesforce technology stack you will need to leverage.

Keeping that in mind, we have curated this part to have the following chapters:

- *Chapter 1, Defining Your Digital Experience Strategy*
- *Chapter 2, Translating Your Audience and Interactions into Meaningful Technology Features*
- *Chapter 3, Technology Component Identification: Which Parts of Experience Cloud Do I need?*

1

Defining Your Digital Experience Strategy

Hi there! We are excited that you have selected *Mastering Salesforce Experience Cloud* as your guide to all things Experience Cloud. In this book, we will walk you through your journey from creating your Experience Cloud strategy to monitoring your digital site after the release. Along the way, we will introduce you to real-world examples and leverage a fictional company to teach you how you can curate the next generation of digital experiences.

Experience Cloud is a product that helps you curate a digital storefront for your end consumers/customers. You can leverage it to have interactions with third parties. It can be your central repository, with the addition of Service Cloud, for your end consumer interactions. This will empower you to understand where your end consumers are in terms of their relationship with your company. Thus, in turn, you can respond with the appropriate tone to their concerns. The possibilities are as big as you can dream, but we must start at the beginning.

This chapter focuses on setting expectations from the beginning of your Experience Cloud project, in addition to providing tips on creating successful strategy workshops, determining how to communicate with external advisory committee members, level-setting expectations of the committee, and setting up the best first engagement. The goal is to set the foundation for the project you will undertake setting up an Experience Cloud site.

Once you are done with this chapter, you can easily navigate the initial stages of setting up your Experience Cloud strategy, which will put you in the captain's chair of your Experience Cloud project! If you have already started a project, there are still a few tips you will pick up. The chapter will help you identify any gaps in the information you received and give you a jump start on product education. By understanding how the information you receive from the business translates into technology, you can produce a top-notch implementation.

Let's look at the key topics covered in this chapter:

- Introducing to Experience Cloud products
- Determining your Target Audience
- Identifying internal stakeholders
- Curating external advisory committees
- Determining success metrics

Introducing Experience Cloud products

Where to start? Well, isn't that a loaded question? But it is the most important question in any technology implementation. There are so many offerings and combinations in a technical application deployment that can lead to world-class experiences or first-class disasters, and Salesforce Experience Cloud is no different. Experience Cloud follows a very similar model to Salesforce's other product offerings. Salesforce focuses on this collection of products in its **Digital Experience Platform** (**DXP**) solutions. Within that platform, there are two different categories: *profit* and *non-profit offerings*.

For this book's purposes, we will concentrate on the profit offering. In *Chapter 14, Best Practices and Certification Test Preparation*, you will find some test pre-questions for the non-profit offerings. The profit offerings can be broken into four main categories: Self-Service, **Partner Relationship Management** (**PRM**), Salesforce Content Management, B2B Commerce, and External Apps. Each element contains edition options and license options. To give context to the offerings, here are brief descriptions of the main elements:

- **Self-Service**: This solution is a combination of assets that allows you to quickly deploy customer service in a digital fashion. It enables your customers to submit issues or leverage the curated FAQ center. Additionally, your internal users are empowered to create knowledge centers/FAQs. Ultimately, this offering facilitates collaboration between end users and the company.

- **Partner Relationship Management**: This solution is tailored to help you work with external partners; that is, people who share a part of your business process and need access to sales objects in Salesforce. For example, it could be external sales representatives, branding agencies, franchisees, customer support, and so on.

- **Salesforce Content Management**: This solution is tailored to allow you to build content once and deploy it across multiple channels. There are plenty of tools and templates to get you started that we will dive into in *Chapter 5, Understanding the Experience Site Templates and Theme Setup*.

- **B2B Commerce**: This solution provides a configurable online storefront, allowing you to quickly get your products online for sale. It also includes the ability to provide Self-Service as a feature.

- **External Apps**: This solution leverages the Salesforce platform backend but is completely configurable to your needs. Note that this module does not offer a template base like the other solutions do.

You can refer to Salesforce's website to review the features of those areas in detail. Before you reach out to your handy-dandy Salesforce account executive, you first need to figure out what your business is trying to achieve.

To identify this, we need to gather information, so let's break this information gathering into three sections:

- Determining your Target Audience
- Identifying internal stakeholders
- Curating external advisory committee

Once we have the key elements from these exercises, we will then be able to translate those findings into what technology components are necessary to execute the product vision.

Determining your Target Audience

For illustrative purposes, assume that we all work at a company named **Delivery International**. We specialize in providing a top-notch food delivery service across a variety of franchises. Our product team has decided to launch a net new consumer and franchisee digital experience. We need to empower our franchisees with the ability to open new pizza delivery locations and allow consumers to directly engage with ordering from independently owned franchises and locations.

As the head of technology delivery for this new digital experience, how do we understand what they mean when they mention those two market segments? What technology can we purchase and what stories to support these business goals do our teams need to develop? Talking through what we are trying to drive, as well as actions we expect our Target Audience to complete and where, will set the tone for your Experience Cloud design. To answer these questions, we will start at the beginning of any good strategy: with a collaborative internal workshop. In this workshop, we need to identify the needs of the different groups in our own organization and interview prospective users to uncover what will drive value for both sides.

The first step in actually setting up the session is engaging the product team to articulate the Target Audience for this new digital engagement strategy. We need to understand who they envision as the end consumer of the digital experience. For our company, they have said that there are two groups: franchisees and end consumers. We need to ask clarifying questions to determine whether these groups represent two distinct digital experiences or whether they should have a shared experience. Here are some example questions that help curate the direction:

- What are the intended functions of each population of people?
- Is there any information shared between the populations?
- Can you assume that the populations are related in any way?
- How do you plan to capture information on these two populations?

- Do you need to use their data in the future?

- In a perfect world, what would their experience look like? How would you improve it as time goes on?

Once you have those questions answered, create ideal profiles for your Target Audience These are typically one-pagers that call out key information. There are many different techniques to accomplish this. Here are some options to put together profiles:

- **Demographic-based profiles**: These profiles focus heavily on the demographic data associated with the Target Audience. Some items featured in this type are age range, gender, location of residence, education level, and socio-economic status.

- **Channel-based profiles**: In some cases, there are different target audiences based on the medium you are trying to attract them with. Some items featured in this type are preferred channels, preferred content types, and key psychographics.

- **Purchase intention**: Target Audiences based on the type of product(s) that they would potentially purchase from the vendor. These types may be heavily related to different sales cycles within your company as well. Some items featured in this type are socio-economic status, preferred channels, key psychographics, and product alignment.

For most projects, a combination profile works best. Combine the key features that you need from each type into a single profile. This will be an asset that you will distribute to your internal stakeholders for feedback in your strategy session. It will be a great pre-read to get everyone aligned on the vision. We have created our profiles on a combination of data based on our conversations with the delivery team. Here is a sample profile for our end consumer.

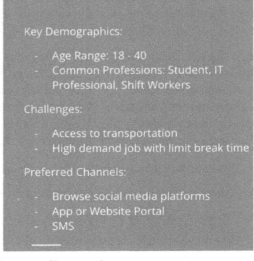

Figure 1.1: Target Audience profile example

Delivery International's target audience profile for the end consumer covers what they have deemed to be important topics to design around. Knowing that this group wants to be able to quickly access information on the go will be key to how we develop the UI/UX. Starting with a mobile-first mindset will help limit the information we add to the digital experience. Why limit information? That sounds counter-intuitive, right? Well, consider that you have limited digital real estate, so you will want to use it for information that provides the most value.

Identifying internal stakeholders

Starting with the product team is probably the easiest method by which to identify internal stakeholders. They are the ones who created the need in the first place, but where do you go next? Let's think through who else in the company is necessary to achieve this vision. Sure, we can look at anyone who directly interacts with our End Consumer; for example, our customer service department or sales associates. Or, we can look at the executive sponsor, the voice of the customer representative, or even your head of quality.

However, the people you really need at the table are your internal operations team, that is, the people who get things done behind the scenes. They are the unsung heroes of how your company can go from good to great in terms of fulfilling your customers' products and support needs.

Be bold and invite the unconventional. Why? Well, remember that your consumers don't all look and think like you. They also don't look exactly like your executive team. So, by excluding voices/ideas at the table, you are limiting the creativity and the possibility that what you create resonates with your end users. To get the best results, we want to check our own and/or the company's bias. Let's look at a few different questions to locate your unconventional attendees:

Question	Why?
Who is a good example of someone who executes the internal process as intended today?	The purpose of a good example is to have someone at the table that adheres to how the company prefers to do business in an ideal state. They will be able to articulate any challenges with the existing process based on the proposed changes.
Who is an example of someone who does the process internally in the "wrong" or the most inefficient way?	On the flip side, having someone who does things "wrong" provides a challenging viewpoint. There are reasons why they go around the process. Bringing them to the table provides you with the opportunity to incorporate their feedback into the new process, and hopefully helps them adhere to the new process since they were involved in its creation.
Who are seen as the challengers to conventional processes in the company?	Challengers are not a bad thing. Challengers help people think differently. Think beyond what is currently available/doable and what needs to happen next. They will provide process creativity.
Who would be the blocker to a process change?	Understanding where your blockers are and inviting them to the conversation will ultimately help reduce conflict during change.

Question	Why?
Who represents the company culture the best?	Culture is a key component of any successful company. If the people working there believe in the mission, then it makes it easier to delight your consumers. Having culture champions engage will ensure that the culture extends to the new venture.

Table 1.1: Unconventional audience identification questions

Do you have some people in mind? Or maybe you still have a few questions? Let's check in on who we've identified at *Delivery International* who we believe are critical to our success. While we may not reference every single one of these parties as we work through our future technical examples, it is an important exercise to identify stakeholders early in the design process.

Person	Role	Why?
Kinley	Head of Product	Her team is responsible for delivering the new product to market. She has set the initial two-line project in the team's backlog. She will be the person in charge of the project vision and ultimately agreeing to the success metrics. Kinley is responsible for reporting the success or failure of the project to the board of directors.
Anna	Head of Quality	She is responsible for ensuring that there is quality across the products and supporting experiences we curate for our consumers. Anna's team is the front line of defense for any issues reported by our franchisees or consumers.
Jack	Service Representative	He is the person who has challenges with any process. He understands the way in which we would like for items to flow; however, his adherence to making it happen is less than desirable.
Jamie	Sales Representative	Not only does he follow the process to the letter, but he is also our top producer. His input has previously guided sales processes that have produced high-grossing revenue.
Maggie	Director of Finance	She challenges today's company vision and operating standards. She is always looking for efficiency gains and how those gains translate to the next generation of consumers through our digital strategy.
Dalbert	Head of Marketing	Communication is a key factor in success, and he knows more than anyone why words matter. Dalbert is always challenging us to be tone sensitive in our journey with consumers and communicate with them in the right way, at the right time.

Table 1.2: Delivery International's Unconventional Committee Members

What information do we need to structure the initial internal conversation? You will want to work with your product team to help frame the conversation. Let's break the meeting into key information topics you would need to move the conversation forward:

- **Target audience**: Who do we want to join us in this new or modified digital experience solution? For example: all customers, prospects, partners, franchisees, and so on.

- **Value proposition**: Why do we want them to join us in a digital experience?

- **Benefit statements**: What benefit will the consumer get by participating online? What benefit will the company get from the online consumer experience?

By focusing on these elements, you can lead structured exercises. You can do this via a remote option or in-person exercise. For optimal results, we do not recommend a hybrid approach. Why? Typically, with a hybrid approach, those in the room can end up excluding those on the phone, or it is hard for the remote folks to truly speak up. We understand that in today's environment, many companies, due to travel constraints or other items, are really pushing hybrid environments. So, make sure that you have good online collaboration tools that allow you to gather feedback from people in their own words. If you are in-person, break out the sticky notes and markers. Give everyone their own stack, give objectives, and let creativity flow!

Now, let's focus on what information you need to get out of the meeting, based on the information you have received from the product team. First and foremost, you are looking to gather the high-level requirements. We have the asset we created for the target audience profiles previously, which you can use as a starting point. Next, we will focus on identifying the key processes/actions that people should be able to engage with on the portal(s). You should have something to go off based on the initial charter of the project. Let's look at *Delivery International*. Kinley's original request to us was *"We need to empower our franchisees with the ability to open our new pizza delivery locations AND allow for consumers to directly engage in ordering from our solely owned franchise locations."* This would lead us down the path of reviewing the following:

- How do our partners/franchisees engage with us via a new or existing portal?

- Are we signing up new partners/franchisees, targeting our existing base, or a mix?

- Can our consumers order directly from us online today?

- Is there anything outside of ordering that our consumers need to be able to do online?

Any materials you can send out as pre-reads so people know what processes to start thinking about will help. In addition to your target audience profile(s), you can send out a project charter, any existing processes (if applicable), or slides regarding the financial and cultural mission of the project. Make sure that you give people ample time to read the materials and understand that, for some, no matter how much time you give, they will simply not come prepared. It is a good idea to make your first agenda item asking whether everyone had an opportunity to read the material or whether they need a quick recap. Here is a sample meeting agenda to consider framing the conversation:

- **Introduction**: Who is in attendance? Why are we here?

- **Level setting**: Are there any questions about the pre-read documentation? Specifically, are there initial thoughts about the Target Audience and high-level project scope documentation?

- **Product vision**: The product team expands upon the vision of the new business venture.

- **Process review**: Identification of what process(es) need to change to support the new venture. Are there new processes that need to be created?

- **Moments that matter**: Brainstorming on what needs to be present in a digital experience to achieve the product vision and support the processes.

- **Recap**: Understanding what we accomplished and the next steps.

Make sure to clearly outline the role you will play in the meeting. You can either facilitate the meeting yourself or partner with someone else. Depending on your style, it could be very helpful to either be a participant focused on curating the new process or a facilitator who guides conversation. If you try to split your focus and do both, remember to capture everyone's ideas, not just summarize your own contributions. Whoever facilitates the meeting needs to remember that their role is to stay neutral.

Leverage tools such as having a meeting "parking lot," a place where you capture items that were brought up, but the exact way in which those items will be addressed will be saved for a later day/audience. Before the meeting adjourns, ensure that everyone is on the same page about the next steps and who owns those steps.

"Next steps" are what you should walk away from the meeting with. Identifying what artifacts you want out of the meeting will help you continuously guide your agenda toward the optimal outcomes you need. For each of the questions you are posing, here are some ideas on feedback to walk out with:

- **Target audience**: Remember that before the meeting, we sent this list out as a pre-read. We want to leave the meeting with a confirmed list of the types of people/parties who need to interact digitally.

- **Digital interaction list**: Actions/processes that the end user should be able to perform digitally. Each action should align with the target audience identified.

- **Gap list**: A place where you have put processes that have been identified as needing modification to become digital first, tagged with whoever is responsible for modifying those processes.

- **Project management cadence**: An agreed-upon way in which the team will communicate decisions and who has the authority to make the decisions. You can break authority out into categories such as process, digital experience, and target audience. If you have multiple parties, consider a RACI matrix. **RACI** stands for **Responsible, Accountable, Consulted, and Informed**. Then you can break out each group and the roles people play within them into focused conversations.

Once the session is over, take time to gather all the items into a consumable format. You want to ensure all participants have access to the decisions made and outstanding items. Pick a central place to store the information so that everyone can access it in real time, as centralizing information will increase project collaboration. Your organization may have a standard such as Confluence, a wiki space, or maybe a Microsoft team site. Take a look at your standards and make sure you consistently leverage them throughout your project.

> **Readout from Delivery International meeting**
> *Delivery International* first confirmed the Target Audiences identified in the previous section. Next, we moved into the ideal state of digital interactions that each group wanted to cover. As they were going through that list, they identified gaps in their existing offering/process that would need to be solved to further enable the desired state.

In the following table, you will see the list of gaps they identified for the new process. They started with the digital interaction they were trying to outline. As they continued conversations, they identified the gaps in executing the requested interaction based on the existing business processes.

Digital Interactions	Gap List
Report issues	What can we offer to encourage people to do this?
Sign up for new franchise opportunities	How do we communicate the value of new franchise opportunities?
Order pizza online	How can we display the franchise locations for the new delivery-only option?
Loyalty program for repeat customers	How are the new offers priced?
Franchise marketing materials	Training for service team on offerings and programs
See order status	How do the internal service teams know the status of orders?

Table 1.3: Internal target audience digital interactions gap list

You can see from the list they created that it is OK to have large unknowns coming out of the meeting. One meeting isn't meant to solve every process in the company as it relates to the new product. The goal is to call out the gaps so that they can be broken into small teams to solve those questions. These aren't necessarily technology items that they need; the gaps could be simple items in how they handle their process. It could be simple items in how they handle their process. It will be important to keep an eye on these items to see how/when they get added as requirements.

As for project governance, the team has agreed that the product roadmap is ultimately prioritized by the head of products. Process decisions go to the person responsible for the process. Now that we have process squared away, let's talk about how we engage our Target Audience through external advisory committees.

Curating external advisory committees

There is no voice better than the end consumer when it comes to building a platform you expect them to engage with. They will provide continuous feedback on features and designs for your digital experience. Keeping consistent engagement with your top critics will help ensure that you continue to hit the top marks that are impacting your audience(s) as you evolve from initial launch to established product. Engaging external actors is typically more of a business activity versus a technology-driven activity. However, the outputs of this activity are invaluable to the curators of the digital experience.

In partnership with business/technology, we need to start by identifying how many committees we may need. Reference the target audience(s) that we identified in the previous section. Then, we need to look at those audiences and see whether they are unique or whether there is a possibility to combine them. A good rule to follow is that for each unique digital experience, you should have a unique advisory committee. However, that does not have to be a "per-channel" rule. This means that if your target audience has channel preferences of email versus SMS versus portal usage, you don't necessarily have to have a committee for each one of those. You would host one more channel-agnostic meeting and focus on the outcomes/drivers similar for that group. This will help ensure that your meeting content is targeted and you can get the most value from the committee.

So, where do we find these people? If you use Salesforce CRM, you could start by running analytics to find which people even meet the criteria for your target audience. If you don't have any system data for the audience you are attempting to attract, then reach out to your sales team for references. If your organization hasn't yet set up a sales team yet, then social media research will be invaluable. You can set up searches to reach certain demographics. You could even sponsor surveys to that search and ask whether they would be willing to participate in a new offering research panel.

However you get potential Target Audience candidates, it is best to produce a list for people to react to versus asking for recommendations. If you only ask for recommendations, your committee will contain some level of bias. Whether it is a group that is shaped on the historical view of a customer segment or only high-level spenders, you may miss different levels of customers. In either case, you are repeating the historical viewpoints and practices. By presenting a list for people to react to, you are naturally introducing the demographic cross-set that your Target Audience viewpoint confirmed in the first place.

Equally as important is identifying who from within the company will be participating on this advisory committee. You will need visionary supporters to help you articulate the vision, showcase forward-looking product demos, help challenge the thought process of the group, and listen to the challenges. These people need to be open-minded and come neutral to the conversation. What you want to avoid is having internal parties that are very protective of their vision of the future. If they come with an "I know best" mentality, then they will not be open to listening. They will miss key feedback moments and create a product that may not be aligned with the feedback from the customer.

So, how do you entice people to show up and participate? Well, there is a tried-and-true method of identifying the **What's In It For Me? (WIIFM)** proposition statement. If people don't understand what they will get out of participating, they are less likely to participate – especially when you are curating an external advisory committee. They have no reason to take time out of their busy schedules to help you. This is where your product team comes in. They guide what incentives they can offer to encourage participation.

When it comes to the actual meeting sections, typically technology will be engaged to showcase prototypes or experiences that are in the **User Acceptance Stage, UAT**. Keep the demos focused on the new features and allow the committee to tell you what they believe the value or lack thereof is in what you are showcasing. To help with a smooth presentation, consider having one person speak about the features while another person controls the screen. This allows each person to have a focus on their role in the demo. Typically, your product team will be capturing feedback to summarize for technology after the session.

Let's assume that *Delivery International* has decided on a target audience list, but their session won't contain any demos. We are building new experience sites, so what we want is an audience of dreamers: people who can articulate their ideal purchasing experience.

For our WIIFM, we decided to give the consumers vouchers for free delivery for their first 10 delivery orders. For our franchisee audience, we gave them 10% off their franchise fee if they signed contracts to open stores in target markets within the next 30 days. The incentives returned a 75% participation rate of the target audience and gave us some great feedback. Here are some items that they wish to incorporate based on the vision:

End Consumer	Franchisee
Know who I am when I log in	Easily access branding materials
Set favorite orders	Easy access to location specifications
Save my payment information	Ability to order customized store package
Easily access coupons	Easily see YTD sales
Save my delivery locations	Ability to take care of subsidized offerings
Order from my phone	Easy access to support
See my order status	Ability to register a new location

Table 1.4: External Advisory Committee Feedback

At the end of the session, the committee sponsor set up a timeline of when the group should expect to be engaged again. They were informed that, next time, there will be an email readout and a future session scheduled for a demo. Now, let's jump into how we turn feedback into themes and tangible processes that need to be created or changed.

Understanding key interactions

You have been collecting a lot of feedback, but what feedback is the most important? It is best practice to make sure that you are identifying what your **Minimal Viable Product** (**MVP**) is. What takes priority on the MVP build and what may future phase activity be? Having people prioritize as a group can be very challenging but it is necessary to get the highest-value items reviewed by technology first. Look at each feedback item and answer these questions based on the information you have:

- What are the key factors from the external advisory committee? What are their priorities to build into a site that would be meaningful for them to leverage?

- What are the key company factors? What does the company want to achieve in the portal as its entryway into a digital experience site?

- Where is the intersection between the external advisory committee and company factors? This intersection will help you identify what the key elements of the MVP are as they are important to both groups.

- For those items that do not align, how do we sort them into a product roadmap?

If you aren't sure about any of the questions, reach out to the decision-maker responsible for each area for clarity. Once we have gone through the scenarios, we will then summarize the product roadmap vision to the internal and external committees to ensure that everyone has one more view before we kick off the detailed assessment of the request. In *Chapter 2, Translating Your Audience and Interactions into Meaningful Technology Features*, we will parse this information into themes and a true prioritized roadmap connected to the Experience Cloud features you will need to activate.

Determining success metrics

The last step before we move into a business translation of which components of Experience Cloud you will need is ensuring that everyone is on the same page for the vision of success. This goes beyond just what the executive sponsor or product team may set. It isn't as simple as saying, "Well, we want x logins." Logins may be a part of the process, but it shouldn't define the entire vision of success.

Understanding what the business says success looks like is a key factor for your project. You must account for enabling features in your data module, UI/UX, and general processes that are built. You will have to enable the ability to track the metrics. It is the final "checkpoint" of the experience build.

When looking at business objectives, you need to break the requested objective into the technology/process output. This will help you connect the dots to the data module. Let's look at a few examples.

Business Objective	Technology/Process Output
Increase sales by x%	Ability to track sales. Ability to either leverage existing data within the system or set a variable baseline of prior sales to measure against.
Decrease customer service time by x%	Ability to track the time it takes for a service representative to resolve an item. Ability to measure the time of resolution. Ability to either leverage existing data within the system or set a variable baseline of prior sales to measure against.
Achieve x% ROI within y time frame	Ability to store the ROI metrics and create a report to demonstrate the reality of achieving them. Typically, this is a dashboard as several factors determine ROI, not a single metric.
Delivery SLA met x% of the time	Ability to track the time it takes for a service representative to resolve an item. Ability to measure the time of resolution. Ability to set a predetermined SLA variable. Ability to report on the resolution time of an item versus the predetermined SLA.
Drive digital engagement	Ability to see community growth via a baseline versus current enrollment. Ability to measure the frequency of logins via a grouped report of how many members engage within certain time intervals. Ability to see how many Self-Service items are submitted and the correlation between the submission and current call volumes.
Reduce phone minutes by x%	Ability to track original inbound call times. Ability to measure current call time against historical call time.
Increase attachment rate of products to customers by x%	Ability to track the original ratio of how many products a customer has versus the average number of customers. Ability to measure the new product attachment ratio against the historical attachment ratio to show up-lift or downturn in attachment.

Table 1.5: Delivery International's KPI request list

These elements have started the outline for the key data fields. In *Chapter 4, Curating Data Models*, we will show how to translate this into the data structure.

Summary

Yes, this chapter had a business-heavy focus, but as we move forward, each chapter will become more and more technical. No highly successful implementation ever just started with, "Well, let's wing it!" That's what makes aligning across stakeholders from the beginning so critical. Even if these aren't elements you personally lead as a technical leader/developer/admin, they are questions that you should be asking before you start building anything.

To guide business conversations, remember that there are three key areas you need to focus on:

- **Target audience**: Who is the confirmed audience for the build?
- **Product vision**: What are you expecting to ultimately achieve with this experience?
- **Product roadmap**: What are the expectations of the releases?

Those areas of understanding will enhance your skill set and set you on the right track for the project! At this point, you should have honed the following skills:

- Learning the key inputs needed to set a strategy
- Understanding who needs to be involved in decision-making for the site
- Understanding who needs the ability to log in to the portal
- Understanding what actions users are expected to carry out via digital interactions
- Creating key success metrics for the portal's success/failure measurements

In the next chapter, we will turn our findings into features, diving further into technological design.

2

Translating Your Audience and Interactions into Meaningful Technology Features

Now that you have clearly identified who needs to engage and have a mountain of feedback, what do you do with it? In this chapter, you will learn how to translate that feedback into what features need to be enabled in your new Experience Cloud site. We will break them into sections related to which technology (Service Cloud, Experience Cloud, Sales Cloud, and so on) that you will need to partner the feature with.

Here is what you will learn as part of this chapter:

- Organizing and prioritizing feedback
- Identifying themes
- Connecting feedback to product features

Organizing and prioritizing feedback

In *Chapter 1, Defining Your Digital Experience Strategy*, you collected feedback from your internal stakeholders and external advisory committee. Here, we will organize that feedback into which Experience Cloud site(s) fit their requirements. These relationships will be based on the Target Audiences identified in the first chapter. First, let's resurface our discoveries to provide context for the next exercise. Here is the readout from *Delivery International*'s meeting:

Digital interactions

- Report issues
- Sign up for new franchise opportunities

- Order pizza online
- Loyalty program for repeat customers
- Franchise marketing materials
- See order status

Gap list

- What can we offer for loyalty?
- How do we communicate the value of new franchise opportunities?
- How can we display franchise locations for the new delivery-only option?
- How are new offers priced?
- Training for the Service Team
- How do the internal service teams know the status of orders?

Now, let's review the viewpoint of our external advisory committee and what was important to them, Starting with our End Consumer Target Audience:

- Know who I am when I log in
- I want to set favorites
- Save my payment information
- Easily access coupons
- Save my delivery locations
- Order from my phone
- See my order status

Last but certainly not least on this feedback train, here is a recap of what we heard from our Franchisee Target Audience:

- Easily access branding materials
- Easy access to location specifications
- Ability to order customized store packages
- Easily see year-to-date sales
- Ability to take care of subsidized offerings
- Easy access to support
- Ability to register a new location

So, how do we organize the two sets into a prioritized, single view? Let's start by having a conversation regarding your Target Audience as to whether they have enough unique features to mandate separate Experience Cloud sites. Answer these questions to see which way your feedback leans:

1. Are there any data elements that should not be shared between Target Audiences?

   If there are data elements that need to be separated for security reasons, you may consider putting the "ultimate wall" in place by creating two different Experience Cloud sites. If there are no data concerns, then you need to review the functional aspects of the site.

2. Do all audience members need to be able to do the same interactions/features or are any features specific to a Target Audience?

   When you pick a site theme in *Chapter 5*, *Understanding the Experience Site Templates and Theme Setup*, it applies underlying base functionality. Picking the wrong template could limit the native functionality available to you. It is important to note that you can only apply a single template to an Experience Cloud site. So, if there are different drivers of behavior, you need to consider separate sites.

3. Are they both the same focus? Meaning, are both sets of features focused on sales, service, or marketing?

   If you are looking at one set of features that are driven by sales processes and another by service processes, then you may need to consider separate sites. Depending on how you envision sales interactions, you may need the **Partner Relationship Management** (**PRM**) module of Experience Cloud versus the Service module.

If any one of those questions triggers you to say that not everything is a one-for-one match between your Target Audiences, then you need to further explore having unique experiences. As you consider building distinct sites, remember that, if for any reason things do start to align later, you can come back to this architectural decision. For now, you should identify the themes of the work and continue to develop the product roadmap as per the digital experience site.

As we look at *Delivery International*, we notice that it seems that we may need two distinct experiences. Our End Consumers are focused on the process of ordering and support for their orders, while our Franchisees need to be able to open new locations, obtain promotional materials, and check on the status of their sales. These interactions lend themselves to creating unique instances, as it looks like they need distinct user access as well. In this situation, we would have answered the aforementioned questions as follows:

1. It is possible data elements should not be shared between two audiences, but it depends on what information we need for the experiences.

2. No. There are specific features per Target Audience.

3. No. They have different focuses: end-consumer ordering and franchisee location setup/monitoring.

We concluded that we were going to need two sites based on these answers, and we will continue down the path of investigation, creating two different roadmaps as we identify our themes. *That means for our End Consumer and Franchisee, we will evaluate what their needs are separately instead of pursuing this project as a single site.* That is a large distinction as we move forward. Purchasing decisions on the type of site, type of login model, and type of security may all vary for the individual sites. The great news is that these distinctions also empower us to create distinct **return on investment (ROI)** strategies for the business.

But wait – what if you still are unclear about what you may need? The next step of identifying themes will help you solidify your answers. Plus, remember to leverage your product team to help you clarify answers as you go through the next steps. Let's dive into how we identify themes of the requirements.

Identifying themes

When we look at our feedback, we want to categorize anything we can into a theme or process. By bucketing groups, you can see all expectations are of a particular feature. This is typically a joint exercise between product and technology. The goal is to align what we heard someone say to what that means from a business perspective. For reference, you can pull the identified process(es) that will be impacted from your internal stakeholder meeting and see if there are any correlations.

Let's start by looking at our consumer feedback and putting it into themes. The left column is what we heard the End Consumer say. The column on the right is the theme we have identified that the comment relates to in terms of *Delivery International*'s new business model:

End Consumer	**Theme or Process**
Know who I am when I log in	Login
I want to set favorites	Ordering
Save my payment information	Ordering
Easily access coupons	Promotions/marketing
Save my delivery locations	Ordering
Order from my phone	Accessibility
See my order status	Delivery

Table 2.1: Delivery International's theme/process identification

As you can see from the example, most of the consumers' requests are regarding their ability to order. That information would be contained within their Account/Contact record in a traditional Salesforce model. It impacts the process of servicing or placing an order from an internal process standpoint, so you will have to account for whatever the internal process is to now incorporate inputs from external parties.

It is important to note that if there is a potential crossover between your new experience and bringing in legacy data from other customer experiences, you should clarify with your product team if historical ordering and servicing needs to be brought into view in this new digital experience. If it is not going to make the journey, plan to communicate to your users of what they can expect to be in the portal and what didn't make the journey.

These features all lend themselves to a service and/or e-commerce model of the project. From the e-commerce lens, it is a **business-to-consumer (B2C)** model, not a **business-to-business (B2B)** model.

Let's do the same thing with the list that our internal stakeholders came up with as their key features from earlier. In this table, our Target Audience represents who the internal team said the feature was for. Then, you have the digital feature and our recommended connection of the internal process, based on the request:

Target Audience	Digital Interactions	Theme or Process
Both	Report issues	Service
Franchisee	Sign up for new Franchise Opportunities	Franchise onboarding
End consumer	Order pizza online	Ordering
End consumer	Loyalty program for repeat customers	Loyalty
Franchisee	Franchise marketing materials	Franchise onboarding
End consumer	See order status	Delivery
Franchisee	Ability to take care of subsidized offerings	Ordering

Table 2.2: Delivery International's audience-to-interaction alignment

It may seem like because there are fewer items that map to a particular theme or process, that they are less important to the internal process. However, this typically means that the group was not at the same level of detail as the consumer group. For example, consumers would not be worried about the franchisee experience. So, they would have spent their time digging deeper into the processes than the internal team, who must curate both experiences at once.

We can see that for both parties, each identified ordering as a key process and experience. The service/loyalty aspects tie into the process and should be considered an aspect of co-development to ensure that the experience delivered is a holistic offering. This is where your product manager will take over to determine what is above/below the line of the initial deployment.

You may be thinking: They tie together, but we said that they were going to be two different sites, so how does that work? Well, that is where your data model will be key. Sharing information between sites is a common practice. What you are trying to do is enable the unique experiences that empower your end users to quickly execute functions with little training since they are external users.

You want a Self-Service site to be intuitive so that you get adoption. What exactly does that mean? Think of it in terms of the sites you visit. If you create a login at a company (pharmacy, banking, online orders), you don't typically get a training session before you start using it. The expectation is that the site is "simple enough" so that when you log in, you know exactly where to go to get the things you need. From service to order fulfillment to bank management, you should be able to clearly see your options and execute functions without training.

That is what brings us to our next section on product features. How do we connect what we hear to how we build this intuitive site – a site whose users needs little to no training to use it successfully? Let's dive into connecting this all to product features that we can develop against.

Connecting feedback to product features

Regardless of the role you play, paying attention to the words people use when they describe how to achieve each question is the key to uncovering the solution. Those words can help you pick up on critical phrasing you will want to incorporate into your Experience Cloud design later.

For example, consider if someone says they want a "concierge" experience for their customers versus wanting a place where someone can merely find information. Both may be valid items you incorporate into the design; however, the concierge requirement elevates expectations. A concierge doesn't simply answer your question; they anticipate your next question. You can parlay that into a readout back to the group about how AI might be a feature they need to build into the site. Here is a table that can help you identify which technology to use:

What they said…	How it translates…
Concierge service	Service Cloud: cases and/or Voice
Like articles	Knowledge base: like/dislike
"Chat"	Salesforce Chat
Anyone can contact support	Self-service login-based model
Collaborate on deals	Name-based login model
Ability to comment on your articles	Knowledge base: commenting

Table 2.3: Delivery International's key activities

As you start to connect the dots between what was said and how to translate it to specific Salesforce-focused technology features, make sure that you leverage a format that works with your technology team's existing framework for stories or work intake orders. There are a few different frameworks you can leverage. You can leverage Waterfall or Scaled Agile frameworks. The two most common methodologies for projects are Waterfall or Scaled Agile frameworks. A Waterfall project involves waiting until a project is completely developed before launching it. If you continuously released features of your product when they made sense to be available to the public, that would be an Agile type of project.

The big thing to note about them is the difference in the **time to market** (TTM). With agile methodologies, you will recognize value in the marketplace quicker than with waterfall. However, sometimes, you may find that blending the two works better for a platform launch. A blend could look something like quarterly releases to ease consumption versus the traditional agile every-sprint delivery. This is where we stop on the details of those methodologies. Note that conceptually, they are two development frameworks that you can leverage, but both require well-defined features to be successful. You can find much more information on development methodologies by looking up that topic in Packt's library or directly on the web.

The key to any structure you choose is to have clear wording on what you want someone to be able to do inside of your experience. Your technology team probably already has a format that they work with, so try to follow that. If you don't have an existing technology team, here are example features based on *Table 2.3*:

- **Concierge service**: "*We want to be able to have a concierge service that allows our* End Consumers *to quickly contact our internal team. We want to empower our internal team to answer any question presented by effectively routing the end-consumer request to the most qualified associate to answer it.*"

- **Like articles**: "*We want our franchisees and end consumers to indicate whether they like/dislike or agree/disagree with an article we have published.*"

- **Ability to comment on your articles**: "We want our franchisees and End Consumers to be able to provide feedback on the articles. This feedback should be free text comments that they can put in context with the article."

- **Chat**: "*I should be able to chat via the portal with a qualified associate based on the type of question that I have. It should recognize who I am and only ask me what I am trying to accomplish.*"

- **Anyone can contact support**: "Any end consumer *should be able to reach out for help if they are authenticated into the site/portal. We should be able to track what they are requesting and the frequency of logins.*"

- **Collaborate on deals**: "*In order to further collaborate with our franchisees, we need to be working on deals as a team. The ability to share information and see the overall status will help us increase our financial forecast accuracy.*"

Note that you may have multiple Features that you group together to talk about a complete end-to-end experience for a specific process. You don't want to have a paragraph as a Feature. Keep it specific enough for a particular part of the process. As you get further into the details, your features should also have a notion of Acceptance Criteria. That is where you detail specific actions someone should be able to take for a feature to be successfully implemented.

> **Tip**
> It may be helpful to create a visual chart of how things connect. This can empower you to identify dependencies and further define what features you need for each block in your process chart.

Here is an example of a flow chart for *Delivery International*:

End Consumer
Actions by Function

Security
✓ Site Registration
✓ Authentication
✓ Data Access

Orders
✓ Place an Order
✓ Modify an Order
✓ Cancel an Order
✓ Check Status of an Order

Self Service
✓ Report an Issue
✓ Chat with a Specialist
✓ Review FAQs
✓ Review User Guides

Figure 2.1: Delivery International's end-consumer actions by function

How exactly is *Figure 2.1* a flow chart? Well, they come in many shapes and sizes. You would read each bucket as a specific process that we want to execute. Underneath that bucket are the features in order of how the process would be executed. Those are the key callouts that a user must be able to execute inside the Experience Cloud site. You can think of them as site sections or buttons. We will design those interactions more as we head into our human-centric design series. You will find that starting in *Chapter 7, Leveraging Screen Flows versus Apex*, through to *Chapter 8, Understanding Inputs – Emails, Chats, Text Messages*.

Identifying differences between Experience Cloud offerings

In the first chapter, we introduced the different product offerings as two-line introductions. Here, we will decompose the offerings to the next level in context with how we broke our items down into themes. This should help you take the list you are developing of themes/features and start to map them to an offering. If you aren't there yet, don't worry. In *Chapter 3, Technology Component Identification – Which Parts of Experience Cloud Do I Need?*, we break down a feature-specific list and the correlating Salesforce Service/Sales Cloud products that are needed to round out the internal experience.

Remember from our last chapter that the main elements of Experience Cloud are broken into five products: Self-Service, PRM, Salesforce **Content Management System (CMS)**, B2B Commerce, and External Apps. Make sure that you read through each offering before you determine which one(s) you need to dig into further. Some have very similar features, so understanding the differences is key in your selection process.

Note that outside of the External Apps offering, all these sites will offer templates. This is the easiest way to kick off your build. It provides a declarative way to jump-start your experience. Details on these templates and why you should select one over another will be covered in *Chapter 5, Understanding Experience Cloud Templates*.

You will have a mobile site rendering included as part of each package. So, you will initially develop your page construction via the desktop view. Salesforce will automatically create a mobile version of that page. Note that these pages are not optimized for a mobile experience, meaning that if you want to have a mobile-first toolset, you will need to optimize those default pages. You should also consider when you need to create an app-based community versus relying on mobile browser pages to render the experience you desire.

The most common sites are **Self-Service** or the **CMS** offering. To test the Self-Service offering usage, the next time you interact with any support center/authenticated content, run the dev tools from your browser and see if there are any Salesforce dev extensions in there. Aren't sure how to run the dev tools from your browser? In Chrome, you can click on the three dots on the right of the URL bar, then select **More Tools**, then **Developer Tools**. That will expose the code of the site.

You may see things such as the following:

- `helpcenter/s/sfsites`
- `forceCommunityToastManager`
- `siteforce`

Some companies may not even rebrand the URL, so it may be even easier to detect if their experience is leveraging Salesforce Experience Cloud sites. If you do find the extensions in dev tools, you can also see how people are modifying the code base to create the experience that you are in. Many people overwrite the themed templates, but how they do it has a unique element to it. If you work via tickets, write yourself a research spike and take some time to dig around. You will be surprised by what you learn via publicly available sites.

In the next sections, we will also call out some companies to reference when looking at unique sites. At the time this book was published, Salesforce was identified as the underlying technology for that experience. Some of these public assets may be harder to review than others, given that you may have to be a customer to authenticate them.

Experience Cloud – Self-Service

Self-Service features empower the site's users to get answers to items they need in relation to your product and/or company. Think of this as the **Frequently Asked Questions (FAQs)** and Contact Support options you encounter in your own online purchasing/servicing journey. These sites provide the ability to attach consumer records to a consumer account, curate communities, and report stats on usage of Self-Service by account and/or by individuals. You can track those metrics by looking into your internal associates' engagements with consumers.

The Self-Service model also allows you to target specific **service-level agreements (SLAs)** by type of account. Let's say you get a consumer that is your ideal consumer and you want to ensure that they get your best service offerings. You create rules that automatically escalate any case they submit to a special group instead of that case getting mixed with the general population of work. This empowers your organization to offer a next-generation service by leveraging automation.

If you are looking to expand your offerings, there are Salesforce products that allow you to add on features, such as the following:

- **Track the sentiment of the consumer**: Requires leveraging Einstein Analytics
- **Generate personalized recommendations in a peer community**: Requires leveraging Marketing Cloud
- **Conduct real-time surveys**: Requires leveraging Salesforce Surveys

There are many flavors of Self-Service capabilities available today. You can check out Bank of America, Wells Fargo, Southwest Airlines, Hulu, and Cochlear, to name a few.

For *Delivery International*, we will be levering a Self-Service site for our end-consumer experience. There will be components of a B2C solution that we will incorporate into this existing template. For the B2C components, we will look at options for building that out. It may leverage another internal product of Salesforce's called Commerce Cloud, or it may be a custom build. The technology you choose heavily depends on the business process complexity.

Experience Cloud – PRM

PRM takes your Experience Cloud site in a direction that is focused on trusted advisor working relationships. These are the people who have signed up to do business on behalf of or in conjunction with your company. They sometimes need access to sensitive company data, need to work directly in your sales process, or may even service your clients on your behalf.

The most important thing to remember when leveraging PRM is that these are named licenses with financial implications. You treat these more like a license that you would give to an internal employee. For some people, this may change the overall benefits and costing model you pulled together. It is important that you justify this model with its future-state return of sales or potential customer loyalty.

Future state, you can expand your PRM offering outside of the basic Salesforce reporting and dashboarding by leveraging Einstein Analytics for Communities. By adding this product, you can present visual representations of your data in easy-to-consume formats. It is a simple extension to make with a license fee per user. Given Einstein Analytics' complexity, we recommend holding off on adding this as your product MVP and instead focus on enabling the core features of the platform.

Identifying who uses these sites on the web can be a little tricky given that you must have a login to see them, but IBM and Databricks are a few companies that use PRM. Several of these login sites are hosted outside of Salesforce, so the front "screen" might not tell you a whole lot about what technology the underlying site is built on.

For *Delivery International*, we will be leveraging a PRM site for our franchisee experience. We may also need to leverage parts of the B2B solution, but we will dive deeper into that discovery in *Chapter 3, Technology Component Identification – Which Parts of Experience Cloud Do I Need?*

Experience Cloud – CMS

CMS creates a way for you to create content once and deploy that content across multiple assets. The Experience Cloud CMS goes beyond just publishing in Salesforce Experience Cloud sites. You can publish this content across your other web properties as well. In this respect, it replicates more of a true marketing CMS product by keeping a single container for content and empowering your teams to be able to save time in the creative creation and distribution process. Think of content in this context as articles, newsletters, FAQs, or instruction manuals – something that is more static in nature.

For content you publish within your Experience Cloud site, you can add the content to your **Aura** and **Lightning Web Runtime** (**LWR**) site pages. We realize Aura and LWR may be new terms for you, so let us explain. An Aura page is referencing a site template. There are many different site templates you can pick from for your experience. We will be covering those in *Chapter 5, Understanding the Experience Site Templates and Theme Setup*. It can also refer to a type of custom development component created by your development team.

LWR refers to a specific type of component that a developer can put together for the site. It is known as a LWR component. Those components can be based on the original type of component known as a **Lighting Web Component** (**LWC**) component. For more information on these components, reference *Chapter 6, When to Use Aura Components, Lightning Web Components, and Lighting Runtime Components.*

One key callout – CMS is listed as an Experience Cloud product per Salesforce's website. However, the site links take you to purchasing Marketing Cloud. Marketing Cloud is a very powerful tool and is robust in its offerings. It can power any experience you like, but it will not give you a community experience. If you are looking for a community-type experience, one of the other four offerings will be better suited for your needs.

Here are a few companies that leverage the External Apps model: Toyota, NBC, RED, Greenpeace UK, and IQS University of Barcelona.

This type of experience is not currently on the list of needs for *Delivery International* based on the decomposition we have done. That does not mean that they will not need to deliver content. It simply means that this isn't the sole experience. It is still possible with one of the types that we can deliver content, just through different vehicles.

Experience Cloud – B2B Commerce

Are you in the business of selling things online to other companies? If you are or think you might want to, look no further than the B2B Commerce solution. It allows you to quickly set up a storefront for your products and get online ordering moving. The volume handling for adding hundreds of items to carts easily and modifying carts are key differentiators from a B2C experience.

You can also customize your storefronts to specific companies that you are selling to. So, if you hear your marketing/sales teams saying that they want to "co-brand" products, this may be an opportunity for B2B.

Don't worry, though – you can also set up a B2C experience inside of your existing Experience Cloud site. You don't need to leverage the B2B site if it does not make sense.

Companies that excelled in this area were McKesson and GE Renewable Energy.

Experience Cloud – External Apps

If your company is looking to build scaled applications without having to worry about the maintenance of the infrastructure, this is where the External Apps platform comes into play. Here, you can build applications that you can deploy to external users with ease, creating differentiated experiences for your customer segments without having to maintain servers.

Typically, this solution is selected when the aforementioned templates don't meet your needs. It has the same connected Salesforce data sources, allows for APIs, downloads from the AppExchange, and/or connects to other third-party apps.

Note that while this product has "Apps" in the name, it doesn't mean that it is building a mobile application. These are still browser-first-based applications. As we noted at the beginning of this chapter, Salesforce will give you default mobile renderings, but you will need to optimize these. If you are looking for a true mobile application setup, you may want to compare this offering and how you can wrap it into an app versus another Salesforce product, Heroku. They both have their strengths and weaknesses, so make sure you understand the differences.

Here are a few companies that leverage External Apps via web browsers: IBM, Toyota, and Macy's.

Identifying the "why not"

Understanding high-level differences between the products will help ensure that you can articulate the "why not" case for your organization. This empowers you to spend your time focusing on a subset of possibilities versus continuing to investigate all four in full depth. If you are studying for the certification exam, consistently keep in mind the top use cases for the product. With so many overlapping feature sets, keeping with the core case will help you reduce answer possibilities.

As we look at *Delivery International*, we can see the "why not" for the products based on our themes. Of course, we reserve the right to reverse this decision as we dig into the next chapter. However, here would be our "why not" conclusions as they currently stand:

- **CMS**: Based on our requirements, our scope for both Target Audiences goes beyond simple content delivery. Given that this product is focused solely on content delivery, it does not meet the need. That does not mean that the project itself doesn't need content delivery; simply that it isn't its sole focus.

- **B2B Commerce**: Based on our requirements, we have an element of sales related to both Target Audiences. The first Target Audience of an End Consumer is focused on a B2C ordering module. The second Target Audience of a franchisee is a B2B model; however, this falls more into the PRM module. We should review the B2B module as we get more requirements to see if there is a further fit to combine both PRM and B2B.

- **External Apps**: While this type would allow us to create any experience we could dream up, it wouldn't be the quickest TTM. The other products offer native connected solutions that would help *Delivery International* meet its business goals quicker.

Understanding the direction will help keep the conversation focused on your goals with your Salesforce Account Representative. Your goal in conversations with other technologists in your organization should also stay focused on the core offerings you wish to enable. Truly understanding why you wouldn't do something helps get others on board with the methodology/approach you are recommending. All of these tools will help set you up for some concrete technology decisions in the next chapter.

Summary

In this chapter, we have gone through digital experience concepts and feedback conversations we had in *Chapter 1, Defining Your Digital Experience Strategy*, to further define what that means in a technology feature. All of this sets the stage to connect the dots in *Chapter 3, Technology Component Identification – Which Parts of Experience Cloud Do I Need?*. Your skills are starting to increase in how to conceptually align with Salesforce's Experience Cloud product suite. Understanding the nuances of the products and subtle differences will be key in exam questions as well. There is a lot of overlap, but the right solution comes down to well-defined and prioritized business features connected to the quickest TTM solutions. At this point, you should have honed the following skills:

- Understanding how you should look at the series of data collected in stakeholder and external advisory board conversations

- Identifying what the feedback themes are

- Aligning the themes with the features needed to pull together the Experience Cloud site

We also started introducing you to some Salesforce-specific development terms: LWR components and LWC. Over the next few chapters, we will dive deeper into those concepts and how they apply to user interfaces. These are key interaction models that drive any custom development you may need to support your experience.

In the next chapter, you are going to learn how to further refine your features and connect them to product offerings. Then, with all the overlap, you'll figure out how to make the perfect combination to achieve your business goals effectively and efficiently.

3

Technology Component Identification – Which Parts of Experience Cloud Do I Need?

Now that we have the features lined out, let's map them to which technology accomplishes that feature. This is a critical step to ensure that you are recommending what's needed for purchase with Experience Cloud. There are many things that you could buy, but keeping your purchase focused will ensure that you aren't artificially inflating project costs. When you start the map, you may notice that there are multiple ways to accomplish a required feature. We will consider best practices on how to narrow down those options so that you can create the optimal feature set mapping.

This chapter focuses on enabling you to become a product expert – that person that people go to for information on technical design and platform possibilities. By completing this chapter, you'll be able to speak to the tradeoffs on decisions. This will enable you to guide conversations and match features to relevant aspects in order to add value.

Here's what you will learn as part of this chapter:

- Aligning features to technology stacks
- Narrowing down the optimal combination
- Tracking your digital experience strategy

Aligning features to technology stacks

The first thing that we need to go through is the difference between **product offerings** and **user licenses**. We know that may sound simple, but when Salesforce starts to speak about their products, they will often intertwine the two. At the simplest layer, they break product offerings into two categories based on what population the process impacts. In the following table, we're pulling together sample populations that fall into each group. Not all examples may be relevant to your organization, but Salesforce transcends industries. We're trying to cover a wide range of examples: business, but Salesforce transcends industries. We're trying to cover a wide range of examples:

Customers	Partners
Consumers	Channel sales reps
Clients	Vendors
Shoppers	Suppliers
Patients	Insurance agents
Insurance policyholder	Franchisees

Table 3.1: Sample end users of digital experiences

There are many more you could list in each category. The goal of this table is to give you an idea of what to look for. For many of these options, you will be given either a login-based or named license offering. What's the difference? Let's take a look:

- **Login-based license**: When you evaluate a login-based model, you purchase a bucket of how many logins you project to use per month. Now, Salesforce won't just "cut off" your access if you hit a spike, but there will be a bill associated with overages. So forecast accurately. Note that this counts for each time they go through any SSO process if they're switching between your company applications.

- **Named license**: This limits who can log in to your digital experience by forcing access through a named user. This means you must assign a license to a specific user so that they can access your portal. You cannot cycle these licenses, either. This means that if you deactivate a user, you can't simply reactivate them a few months later. There is typically a 12-month cycle built into the contract.

The primary difference between the two is the cost. It doesn't impact the portal selections that you make, simply the financials of the login model based on how many people you are targeting to log in monthly. Typically, you would likely select the **named license** model when you're looking at the **partner relationship management (PRM)** model, since those are long-term, frequent users.

Now that we understand how Salesforce identifies groups of users and the license offering associated with all the Experience Cloud products conceptually, let's dive into the detailed offerings of the products. Note that this feature list is a combination of Salesforce documents. You will not find this list directly on Salesforce's website. It is accurate as of publication. However, we always suggest that you contact your local Salesforce sales representative for the latest feature set.

We're going to continue to focus on the core offerings. Salesforce has recently introduced what they call *industry offerings*. These are specific solutions that sit on top of one of the core Experience Cloud solutions. There is an extra fee for these services. Their goal is to save you time to market by having pre-built processes for specific sectors, such as healthcare and life sciences, finance, government, higher education, travel and hospitality, media, retail, and others.

As we review these key features, keep in mind that there may be products Salesforce offers that accomplish a complex version of the feature. However, there may be an opportunity for you to create custom objects that better represent your desired business process. In either case, the foundation is available based on the key features. So long as you have the right data, you can execute any of the desired processes – it's just a question of how you put the data together. That's why the all-important data model construction process will be covered in the next chapter, *Chapter 4, Curating Data Models*.

Experience Cloud – Self-Service

Flipping back to *Chapter 2*, we talked about how **Self-Service features** empower the site's users to get answers to items they need concerning your product and/or company. Typically, Self-Service is going to act as your portal when you're interacting with the end-consumer population.

If you're dealing with the partner population, as defined previously, we recommend that you check out the PRM model. It has the same features as this module, with a lot of additional features. It is probably the most feature-rich Salesforce product aside from a full-blown instance of Salesforce CRM.

As for Self-Service, we're going to look at this through two lenses: *external* and *internal* interactions. It is possible to have an external portal that is mainly a knowledge base site, so it will have very few internal processes that interact with it. More than likely, though, you're going to implement something that allows a customer to interact with an employee directly. It's important to know which features sit in each container. Let's start with the external interactions:

Self-Service Key Features (External)	
Features	**Explanation**
Issue reporting	The ability to submit a request to the company via an online portal. This may/may not contain pre-filled-out information based on a customer's account.
Knowledge base	The ability to have a space on your site where there are published articles. These could be FAQs, industry articles, promotional materials, product training materials, and more.

| Self-Service Key Features (External) ||
Features	Explanation
Community connections	The ability to have users interact with other users either in the external community or inside your own company.
Crowdsourced question-and-answer	The ability for anyone in the community to post a question. You can then either select members who can respond or completely open it for anyone to answer.

Table 3.2A: Self-Service key features (external)

You need a strong internal process to power external issue reporting via an external experience, and you need to leverage Self-Service for issue reporting. This is where the Salesforce Service Cloud suite is going to pick up to curate those internal processes that drive the external experience.

In case you haven't been introduced to the Service Cloud lingo, note that anything that comes into that configuration from an external party comes in as a "case." This is a unit of work that has been reported and lives in the Case object. It can have its own classifications, fields, workflows, and more. Keep that in mind when you go through the features mentioned in the following table:

| Self-Service Key Features (Internal) ||
Features	Explanation
Case assignment workflow	The ability to have an incoming work item assigned automatically based on a set of business rules. These rules can be based on information about the submission, the user submitting, the company the user belongs to, or a combination. You will have unique groups that will be assigned the work based on the criteria created previously.
Auto-response workflow	The ability to automatically send a message to the submitter based on a predefined workflow. These messages can be unique or based on the same combination of features listed for the case assignment workflow.
Escalation management	The ability to have a unique escalation process when items have gone outside the ideal internal business path. This could be due to a case sitting in a particular part of the process too long, overall resolution SLAs being met or almost met, and so on. You define what happens when an item needs to be escalated.

Self-Service Key Features (Internal)	
Features	**Explanation**
Case management	The process of managing an inbound work item. What are the steps to resolution, what information is shared directly with the end user via the portal, and what do you send via outbound communication? These are just a few of the questions that can be asked.
Service entitlement	What level of service are you entitled to? You may have different types of customers/partners. They may have purchased an extra service package. This entitlement feature helps ensure that you live up to the service, as outlined in your contract.

Table 3.2B: Self-Service key features (internal)

There are, of course, many more features of Service Cloud. We will cover more of the practical implementation as it relates to the external experience in *Chapter 10, Leveraging Case Management and Knowledge Bases*. However, this isn't a book about Service Cloud. If, through the implementation of your Experience Cloud project, you find yourself needing more information on the internal setup of Service Cloud, there are resources on Salesforce's Trailhead education site that you can leverage. This includes reading material and a free sandbox for you to try out the practical knowledge application of Service Cloud features.

Experience Cloud – PRM

Recapping, **PRM** excels at empowering relationships with companies that have signed up to do business on behalf of or in conjunction with your company. It can facilitate many different parts of the business process. Given the vast depth and breadth of features, we're going to break features down by the process with which they are associated. There are five key areas of the product. We're going to start at the beginning of the partner relationship and cover recruitment and onboarding. All companies who embark on having partners need to be able to attract them to do business with them. Once they've reached an agreement, the partner needs to be effectively onboarded so that they can start to recognize the value of the partnership quickly. Let's dive into the key features of the PRM feature set:

PRM Key Features (Recruitment and Onboarding)	
Features	**Explanation**
Agreement management	When you sign up a partner, there are a series of items both parties must agree to. The ability to connect a unique agreement to each partner account ensures that you can consistently refer to the items in that agreement. You can also keep them with statuses or version IDs so that you know you're always looking at the most recent, active copy of the contract.
Profile management	When setting up a partner company, individuals who will have access may play different roles in the partnership. The ability of the partner to manage those items will keep the internal overhead of partner management lower.
Registration	Having someone register for an account can be as simple as setting up a user account and as complex as setting up a new partnership agreement. The registration process allows you to handle both types and tailor experiences.
Directory	Via account setup, you can create a directory for the partner account and have all their associates listed as contacts. Note that you will need them listed as contacts on the account if you intend on using a named user model.
Recruitment	The ability to have external partners or internal associates nominate a target partner list, helping direct onboarding efforts by accepting/rejecting nominations.

Table 3.3: PRM key features (recruitment and onboarding)

Now that your partner has been set up, how do you keep and maintain them? How do you keep evolving the relationship to create a deeper connection and profitable growth? That is where the *development and growth* functions come into play. To understand this better, take a look at the following table:

PRM Key Features (Development and Growth)	
Features	**Explanation**
Certification management	In some industries, certifications must be held by a partner for them to be authorized to sell certain products. The ability to maintain what certifications are active, as well as their issuing parties, will help ensure that your company stays in compliance with regulations.

PRM Key Features (Development and Growth)	
Features	**Explanation**
Programs management	From time to time, you may run targeted programs that focus on company initiatives. These drive a holistic approach to what you're asking a partner to focus on for a specific period.
Communications	Messages are typically broadcast through multiple channels to ensure that the message not only reaches the Target Audience but that it is understood. Enabling a community with Chatter allows you to broadcast information to groups and collect feedback, allowing people to ask questions and collaborate in real time. Plus, they can see other people's responses and might be able to self-serve.
Enablement	Having your partners trained consistently ensures that your message is being delivered to customers the way you intend. If you wish to have more of a formal learning management system (LMS), there is another product you may want to check out to expand this feature: MyTrailhead, a Salesforce LMS offering.

Table 3.4: PRM key features (development and growth)

Nothing says collaboration quite like putting your two company logos into a single marketing collateral. For most businesses, it isn't just as simple as swapping logos. There are typically many different business review sessions that go into ensuring that both companies are represented in the likeness and image they wish to portray.

These features focus on the collaboration to deliver joint materials in a controlled manner. It also empowers real-time communication not only between a single partner to an internal employee but across your partner ecosystem. You can set up specific groups to limit who can interact or you can open the groups to anyone with a valid login. Let's take a look at the following table to learn more about joint marketing:

PRM Key Features (Joint Marketing)	
Features	**Explanation**
Co-branded materials	Marketing materials typically have to go through a series of controls before being distributed. This process allows you to show approved content in the portal, even some specific to the logged-in account.
Lead distribution	As your marketing team collects more prospects, you can assign those prospects directly to partners to work on. You can do this via assignment rules or manual assignments.

PRM Key Features (Joint Marketing)	
Features	**Explanation**
Joint planning	The ability to create joint marketing plans/strategies in a single location. You must agree upon objectives and measure progress toward those plans.

Table 3.5: PRM key features (joint marketing)

In a lot of partnerships, the goal is to increase each other's revenue. This may be done through joint opportunities, the resale of products, and so on. In this view of Sales Management, most of these features are going to relate to the joint management of deals. The sole management of deals is possible in Salesforce Experience Cloud, but everything that is entered in the partner side of the Experience Cloud will have to be shared with the internal process.

Think of it this way: if your company's goal in a partnership is to understand the inbound revenue stream from their partners, then the robust sales management offerings will do the trick. However, if forecasting sales from outside parties isn't in your company's process, then you can enable little to none of the sales management capabilities. Let's take a moment to review the sales management features of the PRM product:

PRM Key Features (Sales Management)	
Features	**Explanation**
Joint account planning	The ability to create joint strategies for targeted prospects or existing customers in a single location. You must agree upon objectives and measure progress toward those plans.
Sales forecasting	The ability to jointly forecast the likelihood that a potential deal will become a sale for the company.
Promotions and discount management	The ability to send targeted promotions/discounts to partners. This allows partners to either pass them along to their customers directly or use them as a negotiation strategy without impacting the partner's sales margin.
Opportunity collaboration	The ability from within an opportunity (sales deal) to reach out to an internal company employee and ask questions within the context of the deal.
Deal registration	The ability for a partner to register a potential sales opportunity. This empowers your internal partner managers' insight into partner activities and ensures that you don't have multiple partners pitching to the same prospect, increasing your chances of securing the business.

Table 3.6: PRM key features (sales management)

When you look at the process of servicing a partnership, there are varying degrees of service. Some service items are with the relationship itself – for example, you may need to renew your partnership agreement. Other service items are post-sales support – for example, you may need to follow up on your customer's order. Both types can leverage similar servicing processes.

The systemic difference between the two kinds of services is the types of requests and how you direct those types of activities. In general, you will have many ways to present Self-Service to your partners via Salesforce Service Cloud cases through the PRM Experience Cloud module. Let's take a look at the following table:

PRM Key Features (Service)	
Features	**Explanation**
Service contracts management	You may have varying service levels for your different partnership levels – for example, a 48-hour response versus the same business day. This helps ensure that those contracts are honored by automatically tracking SLAs and escalating anything that may breach them. This is the same concept that service entitlement follows in the Self-Service Experience Cloud offering.
Rebate and compensation management	The ability to automatically calculate compensation based on the deals sold/revenue recognized by the partner agreement.
Performance management	Having dashboards and reports that show your partners their performance at a glance. This helps them understand their sales and level-setting expectations.
Issue reporting	The ability to submit a request to the company via an online portal. This may/may not contain pre-filled-out information based on a customer's account.

Table 3.7: PRM key features (service)

Just a few features, eh? Well, we did say it was the most robust. The opportunities can be limitless with this offering. If you're going to start with PRM, we highly recommend limiting the features you're going to implement initially. One thing to remember about partners is that the orientation and adoption of your tools need to be straightforward for them. Highlighting the most important processes first and getting those right will be your key to adoption.

Experience Cloud – content management system (CMS)

To recap, **content management** creates a way for you to create content once and then deploy that content across multiple assets. Once again, the features shown in the following table are going to tie to Marketing Cloud products. However, which Marketing Cloud product you should select depends on your overall use case. They're reusable across not just Experience Cloud products but also properties such as your outbound emails and/or website. Let's dive into the key features of the CMS toolset:

CMS Key Features	
Features	**Explanation**
Digital asset management	The ability to manage digital assets across multiple properties with clicks, not code, to update assets seamlessly.
Content delivery network (CDN)	The ability to deliver a single piece of content across multiple digital platform streams without having to duplicate the content.
Content life cycle management	The ability to control content from creation to managing that content, enabling you to keep track of engagements over a certain period to showcase the value of the content and help you target the next series of content to develop. CMS empowers single views into your 360 content.
Version control	The ability to ensure that content has set version controls. This ensures only the approved version is distributed and allows you to work on modifications without having to recreate items.
Language translation	The ability to take content that is in the creator's primary language and automatically translate it into targeted languages for your customers.

Table 3.8: CMS key features

Marketing Cloud's product suite contains many different product flavors, and it has a specific product for small businesses. No matter which product you select, content creation is included in all of them: their CMS offering is referenced as Experience Cloud Content Management.

Experience Cloud – business-to-business (B2B) commerce

This product is another one of those interesting Salesforce redirects. While it's called B2B, technically, when you go through the site, you will land on Commerce Cloud. The features mentioned in the following table focus on a combination of the Commerce Cloud offerings. This is another one of those applications that you can deploy on any of the Salesforce Experience Cloud sites:

B2B Commerce Key Features	
Features	**Explanation**
Digital storefronts	You can curate a storefront that is personalized toward your business partner or have a generic site. There are pre-defined templates that you can leverage to get you up and running quickly.
Embedded commerce apps for CRM	These pre-configured solutions allow you to bring your commerce configuration into Experience Cloud or Salesforce Sales/Service Cloud with ease.
Order management	The ability to see orders for purchase through to delivery, as well as empowering the return process.

Table 3.9: B2B commerce key features

Commerce contains many different product solutions. When evaluating features, you will see that a lot of the offerings contain "AI." Remember that you need a large volume of data for AI to provide value. That is a purchase you may look at a year after you've been running on the Salesforce platform.

Experience Cloud – External Apps

When exploring External Apps, note that it comes with a lot of the same features as the offerings mentioned previously. Think of this as a combination package offering where you get all the offerings of Self-Service and PRM. However, with that comes a pretty hefty price tag given its robust nature.

Don't let it be "all the things" that automatically drive you to the conclusion that it is the best for you. The drawback is that you still have to decide whether you wish to use login-based or per-user access. This means you could be significantly overpaying for the same experience you could have created by separating your user base into the applicable functions.

> **Recap**
>
> While the features mentioned previously may sound exhausting, we promise you that there are more you will uncover with each product. Our goal was to highlight the key callouts so that you have enough information to select the appropriate features for your project. Remember, at their base level, all of these applications can scale. If you stick with selecting the product that excels with your use case, you will be able to achieve value quickly and create a differentiated customer experience.

Let's look at our case study on *Delivery International's* business request. Based on the information we've learned, *Delivery International* has confirmed that they will curate two different Experience Cloud sites. They will leverage Self-Service for their End Consumer and the PRM module for their franchisees. They did discover more about the e-commerce solution and have that on their radar so that they can continue investigating what offerings may be leveraged there to order/deliver pizzas. So, where do we go from here? The next step is to narrow down our options and hone in on our ideal combination of products.

Narrowing down the optimal combination

Salesforce offers 60 pages worth of product variations to choose from. With so many choices within choices, how do you possibly figure out what you need? You may consider looking at their solution offerings by industry. These are packages that are even more "pre-built" to get your community use case up and running quickly. At the time we drafted this book, they recognized 15 industries. For the latest view, check out `https://www.salesforce.com/solutions/industries/`. However, industries aren't one size fits all. They don't offer an industry-specific offering for every product they offer.

Let's assume that the industry offerings aren't for you. They don't exactly fit your use case or your industry simply isn't represented. How do you pick what you need to set up based on the features that the business has provided? Let's look at the object models that support the workflow.

Service functions

Let's briefly talk about the service functions to give you context for the next chapters. Note that the full depth/breadth of their implementation is going to be covered in *Chapter 10, Leveraging Case Management and Knowledge Bases*. The service function comes down to a core object called a **case**. This is the nucleus of all things related to servicing an item that has been raised. Whether it comes in through your Experience Cloud site or even an email, the case is the master record. You have to make sure that you have set up an internal process to handle these submissions. Think of things such as the following:

- How do I know who to send the case to?
- Can anyone pick up a case or only a subset of people?
- Do some cases have to be handled differently than others?

Ensuring that you have a solid internal process will make your external process a breeze.

The largest decision you will have to make externally is what information you share. Of course, you want to ensure that users can always see what they've submitted, but with page layouts, you can have fields that show responses from your company as well.

So, what are my optional features to enable? Here are some additional things you can enable to support your Self-Service functions:

- **Knowledge**: This is what powers the knowledge base function. You can have a variety of knowledge bases all with different communities assigned to them. This product also lets you assign items such as internal authors, reviewers, and more to ensure that the editing and publishing processes are adhered to. Additional functions such as enablement or communications can leverage knowledge bases to fuel those experiences. The latter two depend on the use case for how you enable them.

- **Service-level agreements (SLAs)**: These represent the individual commitments that the company has made with an end user. They could be for a customer, partner, or otherwise. SLAs concern how quickly you get support, what support you are entitled to, and more. It's important to have these systematically applied if your company does individual agreements.

- **Entitlements and milestones**: These are the control elements that hold the individual service elements accountable for meeting the SLAs. They track the time from when the work is received by the company to the time in which it is resolved. They can provide alerts to key members before elements go outside of SLA tolerance. Think of them as the agnostic accountability committee, ensuring that you do what you say when you say you will do it.

- **Assets**: The last component of agnostic accountability is ensuring that you have assets set up for your end customers. This shows you the exact items that a person has purchased. You can also keep track of replacements or upgrades to purchased assets, empowering your teams to quickly understand what products a person may need assistance with.

- **Chat**: This component empowers Experience Cloud's and external sites' native ability for you to connect with a real person. It keeps the conversations in the context of your support team's regular workload by acting as a case. This integration also allows you to natively expose those interactions to your end users in your Self-Service functions.

- **Email to case**: You can configure any shared mailboxes to automatically forward emails to Salesforce and generate a case. You can then reply to those emails directly from the case. The responses are returned to the sender as an email, allowing you to keep all of the inbound requests attached to the appropriate contact/account in Salesforce. You can also display these types of cases to your customers via your Experience Cloud view.

Note that leveraging these items is always something you can add later. You don't have to leave the gate with everything turned on. Align these key items to the ones that were prioritized as **minimal viable product (MVP)** launch items.

In the *Delivery International* use case, we're going to leverage cases and knowledge to start. This will keep things very simple for people to report orders and access our FAQs. You might be wondering why not chat and email to case. Well, based on the business process and internal staffing modules, we've determined that those are not items we can support at this time. We're looking to drive traffic to our digital experience and not provide items around that process, but we will review the set up of these channels further in *Chapter 8: Understanding Inputs – Emails, Chats and Text Messages*.

Sales functions

The sales function centers around two objects: **Leads** and **Opportunities**. They both have their own sales processes that hopefully result in a win for your organization. A lead represents a person or company that your partner/sales team has yet to qualify as a person/company who could do business with your organization. Once that person has been qualified, then they convert into an opportunity with an account and/or contact associated with them.

You don't have to enable Leads to partners to have Opportunities. However, you may consider lead enablement as a way to grant approvals to partners so that they can pursue deals. They could go through a standard approval process to be granted the right to the deal. This will help prevent conflict between your internal sales team and partner sales team, as well as resolve conflicts across partners.

Let's dive deeper into the most common features of Opportunities. These represent the individual sales deal you're pursuing. This can be one deal per product, though you can have multiple products in a single deal. There is also the option of not specifying a product. Opportunities allow you to connect the individuals either working on the deal or involved in the deal from the customer's side. Here are some items you should consider enabling:

- **Products and price books**: Businesses can have different product lines and sell those as individual sales teams or they can have a universal product catalog that any sales rep can sell. The products themselves are the individual assets that are available to purchase through the company. The price books are the different categories of pricing available for an individual product. For example, you may have different tiers of partners, therefore you enable tiered pricing. You could have a price book for gold pricing, silver pricing, etc. The individual partner would only see the price based on the price book that is available to them.

- **Collaborative forecasting**: This feature enables the individual, leadership, or account team to update the forecast. Sales forecasting is an art and this feature empowers that art, allowing multiple overrides to occur while providing context for the override. This feature partners nicely with the Sales Reporting app in Einstein Analytics, which you may consider exploring to create a more holistic reporting experience.

- **Competitor tracking**: Most sales deals have a potential alternative from your company. Sometimes, the ability to make no decision becomes what ultimately closes the deal. Competitor tracking allows you to systematically capture who the competition is on an opportunity. This will empower you to create a win/loss ratio in the context of certain competitors, allowing your company to create competitive strategies/offerings in the context of the top competitors. It may be harder to capture this information in partner-managed deals as your partner could be representing multiple parties.

Note that if you're going with one of the e-commerce modules, additional objects will be automatically added to the sales process. These items will enable you to go from sales deals to delivering/installing the product for the End Consumers. You will get into aspects of this model for the *Delivery International* example, such as " locations." This would be the object that's used to house places where people want their pizzas delivered.

For more information on the sales functions, we recommend that you take a Trailhead course on Sales Cloud. This will help you understand how to set up a sales process in the context of your internal process. If this is your first sales model in Salesforce, then make sure you have a detailed product backlog on expectations.

Custom objects

With custom objects, if you can dream it, you can build it! If you find yourself needing to enable processes that don't seem to quite fit the items mentioned previously, custom objects may be your perfect solution. However, with great power comes even greater responsibility. You need to make sure that you aren't doing unnecessary customizations by repeating standard objects or creating things without a plan. They require you to plan your end-to-end process in detail so that you can enable the right structure. You have to think in terms of the following when starting from scratch:

- Are there multiple parties engaging in the process? If so, are they all internal, external, or a combination?

- If there's a combination of parties engaging, you need to ensure that you design for both UI/UX components. Have clear security rules regarding which party can access/edit which information.

- Are there any approval steps? Are the approvers all Salesforce users?

- Approval processes can be a simple yes/no or a multi-step process. Ensuring that you've outlined which parties play a certain role and their current familiarity with Salesforce is important. If they're already users, they may be representing other processes, so considering their existing UI/UX interactions will help with adoption.

- Do you have external inputs? Think of these as things that are already in Salesforce but part of another process. Do they need to be referenced?

- Leveraging data that already exists in Salesforce can be done via custom development or administration relationships. If the data that's needed is outside of Salesforce, make sure you explore how to appropriately store or call that data by taking a deep dive into *Chapter 4, Curating Data Models*.

- Is there two-way communication? If you need people to communicate concerning the process, you can leverage Salesforce Chatter on records. Think of it as any sort of feed or thread application you use today. Communications are kept in the context of the record in question.

Does this sound like a little too much for your first adventure in Experience Cloud? You can also check out Salesforce AppExchange to see if there are pre-built solutions that can fit your needs. Some of the applications have no cost and some have nominal fees. You will still need most of the answers to the questions we asked previously, but how that's implemented will be pre-defined for you. Plus, most of the applications come with automatic upgrades and can seamlessly integrate. Make sure that you test out whatever you decide to move forward with in a sandbox before directly installing an AppExchange product in production.

For the *Delivery International* use case, some elements lend themselves to being custom objects. We will go through an exercise in the next chapter to ensure that we have thought through all of the inputs. The decision we are contemplating is whether we need to leverage the e-commerce solution or whether our situation is unique enough to warrant a custom data model.

Tracking your digital experience strategy

Feeling a little uncertain that you've obtained the skills that were discussed in this chapter? Let's take a look at the high-level process you walked through to get to this output:

Defining Your Digital Experience Strategy

Understanding the Who & Why?	Technology Translation	What do I need?
✓ Internal Audience Definition	✓ Request Prioritization	✓ Understanding Licenses
✓ External Audience Definition	✓ Feature Definition	✓ Salesforce defined Features to Products
✓ Defined Project Objectives		✓ Feature set combinations
✓ Identified Measures of Success		✓ Curating product selection

Table 3.10: Defining your digital experience strategy

Summary

What a whirlwind! In this chapter, we covered all of the basics, from strategic vision to understanding various product offerings. From here on out, the chapters in this book will be more technical so that you can construct the actual digital site. This will involve administrator configuration to developer code so that you can pull off the best digital experience that meets your business needs.

Looking back, here are the key things that we covered in this chapter:

- Understanding the population and high-level license models
- Understanding which features are related to each Experience Cloud offering, empowering you to select the best Experience Cloud license set
- The ability to select the key features you need to enable and how to connect them back to your business-defined features
- Understanding the combinations within the offerings that can pull off optimal connection points while implementing a digital-first mindset

After the past three chapters, you have an official blueprint. Feeling energized? Let's head on over to *Chapter 4* and outline our data models and architecture.

Part 2: Infrastructure Setup to Support and Customize Design Strategy

This part will help you review your Salesforce and Enterprise Application strategy to identify the appropriate digital tool kit to work cleanly within Experience Cloud. You will learn about out-of-the-box Experience Cloud Features and their complementary development strategies.

This part has the following chapters:

- *Chapter 4, Curating Data Models*
- *Chapter 5, Understanding Experience Cloud Templates*
- *Chapter 6, When to Use Aura Components, Lightning Web Components, and Lightning Runtime Components*

4

Curating Data Models

The foundation of any technology project involves combining the data you have with the data you will collect in a meaningful way. However, you need to ensure that the data is stored/encrypted with the right protocols based on the dataset. While you do have to plan for data to share and collect with your audience, you also need to think about how that data is contained within the Salesforce ecosystem, so we need to review how to connect to internal and external systems.

Our focus is now on designing our data models and enterprise architecture. These data maps will ensure that all teams are aligned with how the information will flow, a key step to curating a user-centric design that will increase your digital engagement.

Here's what you will learn in *Chapter 4*:

- Connecting the data dots
- Identifying data sensitivity
- Curating an enterprise architecture map
- Create an **entity relationship diagram** (**ERD**)

Connecting the data dots

At our example company, *Delivery International*, our merciless head of product, Kinley, has tasked us with setting up a partner portal for our franchisees, and her goal is to make it easier for them to sell pizza on our behalf and engage with us. But Dalbert, our head of marketing, has set a requirement for an e-commerce portal for franchisee's clients, so they can order pizza directly from the franchisees, see their order history, log cases if there are issues with their deliveries, review commonly asked questions, and be placed into marketing automation journeys. Of course, Maggie in finance wants to make sure that the money resulting from these sales is making it into our accounting systems, and Anna in quality wants the experience to be safe and flawless for all of our users and our internal systems.

Both our franchisees and their End Consumers have unique user experience and data model needs, but both are going to need a significant amount of access to *Delivery International's* existing data, inside of our Salesforce-driven digital experience and in other enterprise applications. The first thing we need to do is group our data into what Salesforce would call an object. Is this your first time hearing the term object? An **object** is simply an organized data table that can stand alone, or be cross-referenced by other objects.

Let's review their overall needs and requirements before we assess the data model required to support both of our personas. We have combined the internal and external advisory committee's views into a single list. See *Table 4.1*.

End Consumer	Franchisee
Know who I am when I log in	Easily access branding materials
Set favorite orders	Easy access to location specifications
Save my payment information	Ability to order customized store package
Easily access coupons	Easily see YTD sales
Save my delivery locations	Ability to take care of subsidized offerings
Order from my phone	Easy access to support
See my order status	Ability to register a new location
Report issues	Sign up for new franchise opportunities
Loyalty program	

Table 4.1: Delivery International's combined advisory committee feedback list

Table 4.1 is a categorical overview of each of our end users' needs. By organizing their needs into broad buckets, we can more easily determine how to accomplish their goals.

As we look through each of our end-user needs, let's map out where each of these components would live either within Salesforce objects or elsewhere in *Delivery International's* ecosystem. Note that for Salesforce objects, we are only calling out standard objects at this time. This means that if there isn't a natural fit within the out-of-the-box Salesforce product offering, we will call it out as a gap.

You will also notice that we will occasionally reference going to **AppExchange**. AppExchange is essentially the Android or Apple App Store but for Salesforce applications. There are both paid-for and free apps that plug and play in Salesforce. For some highly regulated information, it may be more advantageous to buy an application that specializes in your specific vertical versus assuming the risks as an organization, a great example of which would be buying an app that handles credit card transactions.

If you are unsure where data lives in your organization, you need to engage other technical resources to help you appropriately detail data locations. If they are not mapped correctly, you may risk not being able to combine the right data in the digital experience for your end users or pull the desired business metrics. *Table 4.2* dives into the potential technical locations for each of these requirements.

Target Audience	Requirement	Objects
End Consumer	Know who I am when I log in	• Contact Record • User Record -> Historical Logins *Are there any SSO integrations? Are there any global profiles across applications required?*
	Set favorite orders	• Orders • Account *Are there any ERP integration objects required?*
	Save my payment information	*Look at third-party apps on the App Exchange for credit card handling. The security required to correctly handle this information is highly regulated.*
	Easily access coupons	*Salesforce Commerce Cloud has cartridges that can be used for coupons.*
	Save my delivery locations	• Account • Contact • Shipping Address *Commerce Cloud has options for shipping addresses, but you may need to create custom architecture for delivery addresses if you do not use Commerce Cloud.*
	Order from my phone	• Orders • Addresses (may be custom) • Payment (may be a paid app) • Products • Price Books
	See my order status	• Orders • Accounts • Contacts

Target Audience	Requirement	Objects
End Consumer	Report issues	• Accounts • Contacts • Cases
	Loyalty program	*Commerce Cloud has an offering for this, otherwise, this could be a series of custom objects. There may also be an app on the AppExchange to review, but we encourage you to work with your Salesforce AE to review your options.*
Franchisee	Easily access branding materials	• Knowledge articles • Files Libraries (objects officially known by the "Content-" prefix)
	Easy access to location specifications	Accounts – Leverage the "Type" field and make a type a location, combined with other objects that may impact access
	Ability to order customized store package	• Products • Price Books
	Easily see YTD sales	• Opportunities • Reports • Dashboards
	Ability to take care of subsidized offerings	• Rebates
	Easy access to support	• Cases • Knowledge
	Ability to register a new location	Leads. Create an approval process. Approved Leads can be converted to the Account Type of Location.
	Sign up for new franchise opportunities	• Opportunities • Activities (tasks, events calendars)

Table 4.2: Delivery International's standard object module

Clear as mud, right? The first thing to remember is that while you are grouping objects, there will be some that come out of the box with your product selections, and some you will have to build as custom objects or buy from a third-party application. Let's explore what you will get out of the box with the selections we have made versus some items we will have to build custom.

Standard objects

Object	
Account	There are two types of accounts: person accounts or business accounts. What you enable depends on if you are a B2C or B2B module. This is the master record that records relate to. Be advised you will have to contact Salesforce if you choose to enable person accounts.
Contact	These are individual people who are associated with an account.
User	There are two types of users you will encounter: internal users and portal users. For your portal users, they will start from a contact record. For internal users, you will be able to create them directly from setup.
Reporting	The ability to pull in objects and put them into a table format. There are multiple report types.
Dashboards	The ability to pull multiple reports into visual tables that can refresh on a cadence or on demand.

Table 4.3: Salesforce Experience Cloud standard objects regardless of options

Now, let's take a look at what is standard in the Self-Service options. These objects are set up to allow you to gather base information regarding what a person is requesting, what (if anything) they are entitled to, and how your internal teams will navigate the process. Several workflow automation tools are also included in this package. For now, we are going to focus on the high-level object structure.

Object	
Case	Contains all the information pertaining to inbound service requests. This includes email-to-case, web-to-case, self-service direct entry, SMS, and voice.
Service-Level Agreement (SLA)	Outlines the SLA program that is tied to the Account/Contacts Entitlement.
Entitlements	A time-based element tied to a contract/order. Part of the information in the data record is a relationship to the SLA.

Object	
Milestones	Mandatory, time-dependent criteria that must be met in your service process.
Knowledge Articles	Individual articles/attachments that you can share with specific audiences internally/externally. Contains freeform content and fields to allow for content categorization/management.

Table 4.4: Salesforce Experience Cloud Self-Service standard objects

Up next is **Partner Relationship Management**. Let's take a step back and say that in theory, if you have this module, you also have a Sales Cloud instance internally. **Salesforce Sales Cloud** is a place where your sales team and/or your partner management team work together on all potential and existing sales for the organization. If you are using the commerce solution, some of these deals may be automated for you. However, this module is intended to help the company centrally manage sales and report on the progress of those sales.

Object	
Opportunities	All the information regarding your individual sales deals. Related to products, price books, and forecasting.
Forecast	The ability to systematically predict your company's sales. There are predefined values based on the location of a deal in your sales pipeline. There is also the ability to manually override an opportunity's forecast category.
Products	The individual products that your company sells, coupled with the ability to flag products as active/inactive. Products contain public-facing descriptions and can plug into parts of Commerce Cloud.
Price Books	Associated with products are their prices, located in price books. You can drive price books by different characteristics, such as currency, preferred tiered pricing inherited by the logged-in user, or attributes of the account. Multiple price books can be active for a single product.
Activities	The Activities objects are actually a family of objects, including tasks, events, and calendars. These can be built against date fields to send reminders and help your users manage their work.

Table 4.5: Salesforce Experience Cloud Sales Cloud/PRM standard objects

Now that we have an understanding of who we need to design for and external systems that may come into play, let's review the requested KPIs to ensure we have the data we need to achieve the desired reports.

For the e-commerce portion, we will have to consider the following objects in *Table 4.6*. While there are also third-party order systems you could use, we're going to use the high-level object model from Salesforce Commerce Cloud. Salesforce Commerce Cloud is very intricate, but Trailhead has you covered with multiple **Trailmixes** [`https://trailhead.salesforce.com/users/strailhead/trailmixes/commerce-cloud-trailmix`] on Commerce Cloud. Commerce Cloud ties into the standard account and contact objects.

Object	
Orders	A post-transaction object that represents a client order.
Product	This is the same feature we are leveraging in the Sales Cloud offering, with a junction object called Order Product to indicate an order's individual products.
Product Line Item	A Product Line Item is an occurrence of a product on a specific order.
Categories	The category products from the Product object are organized in.
Campaign	The Campaign object is the backbone of all Salesforce Marketing features and represents groupings of accounts, contacts, or leads for various marketing activities.
Price Book	This is the same feature we are leveraging above in the Sales Cloud offering.

Table 4.6: Salesforce Experience Cloud Commerce Cloud standard objects

Depending on the level of reporting and granularity of reporting required from your business partners, you may also wish to account for Commerce Cloud's content model as well. You will also have to account for their content model to measure potential fall-off points in a customer journey, such as transaction or cart abandonment.

Custom objects

Have you found items that maybe just don't quite fit with the Salesforce standard object definitions? While you can extend the functionality of standard objects with custom fields, you also have the option to set up entirely new, custom objects within Salesforce. With the introduction of custom objects, you can leverage clicks, not code, to quickly set up custom data tables. You can even leverage a file import function to have a custom object automatically created for you.

But wait, there's more! You can also relate custom objects to any standard or custom object, allowing you to create data extensions, such as the address extension we flagged earlier. This flexibility allows us to think through all the dimensions that are needed to configure our optimal solution. The trick with a custom object is to avoid over-configuring it and remember that anything that is a free text field is going to be harder to report on. You need to take a view of what metrics you want to drive before you start creating a bunch of custom objects, and you should always check Salesforce documentation regarding custom field or object limitations: `https://help.salesforce.com/s/articleView?id=000386653&language=en_US&type=1#:~:text=There%20is%20a%20hard%20limit,install%20an%20additional%201%2C000%20objects`.

Designing for requested KPIs

In *Chapter 1, Defining Your Digital Strategy Chapter*, we worked with *Delivery International* to identify key metrics that would determine their success. While our stakeholders haven't set the exact numbers to hit, here is a refresher of those key metrics we need to report on:

- Increase sales by x%
- Decrease customer service time by x%
- Achieve x% ROI within y timeframe
- Delivery SLA met x% of the time
- Drive digital engagement
- Reduce phone minutes by x%
- Increase attachment rate of products to customers by x%

We need robust reporting around our sales projects and our customer service levels to monitor those KPIs. Let's tackle the sales portion first (KPIs 1, 4, and 7) to ensure that we have those objects accounted for. In *Table 4.5*, we identified that we were going to enable the following objects related to sales:

- Opportunities
- Forecast
- Products
- Price Books
- Activities

With that combination of objects for sales, we could predict how much sales will increase over time, leveraging the Forecasting object for Opportunities. We could then dissect the Forecast by product and profitability lenses, allowing us to predict where our product attachment rates will land.

However, we all know that, sometimes, sales to our End Consumers fall apart. The last mile of delivery can change the game. It can determine if an order gets canceled, or if damages and delays are leading to high volumes of exchanged orders. To truly track where we end up, we are going to need to reach into our e-commerce objects for verification. By enabling the following objects, we will have successfully accounted for all of the sales KPIs:

- Orders
- Products
- Product Line Items
- Price Books

Let's tackle our self-service metrics, KPIs 2 and 6. The goal is to have the ability to measure the time it takes to resolve customer interactions. The one assumption about these metrics is they assume you have an existing baseline for both self-service and phone minutes spent in relation to service. If you are setting up a new service/department, we would advise you to speak with your business partner to see whether they intend to go with an industry-standard baseline or plan to use the first few months of data as the baseline. Let's look at the objects we are enabling to accomplish these metrics:

- Cases
- Entitlements
- SLAs
- Milestones

That dataset will allow us to measure the time between when something was received by the company to when it was closed. Note that with these items, you will want to consider enabling business hours in the Salesforce settings. By enabling business hours, you can establish standard operating hours such as 8 A.M. to 5 P.M., Monday through Friday. If you do not enable them, your reporting will base hours on a 24-hour, 7-day-a-week clock. For most businesses, business hours are the only way to calculate realistic metrics.

Last but not least, let's roll into the digital experience metrics, identified as KPIs 3 and 5. These are the metrics that the company has identified to indicate usage and achievement of ROI. For most companies, the great news is that these are native to the Experience Cloud setup, and there aren't extra steps to track logins, the number of logins by customer, and so on. The one thing that you will need to do is put your parameters on your chart to define your ROI target. You will also need to develop reporting that defines the ROI targets: are they a combination of sales/service targets? Strictly login-based? Time in the portal? *Chapter 12, Monitoring Your Site – Salesforce Native Reporting*, and *Chapter 13, Site Launch, Maintenance, and Moderation*, will take you deeper into these metrics for digital engagement.

Identifying data sensitivity

The world of data security continually evolves. With the introduction of **artificial intelligence (AI)**, determining what is real and what is AI-generated can be challenging. The advances in security threats mean you have to constantly look at your protections. Safeguarding information is key, and frameworks such as the **General Data Protection Regulations (GDPR)** set standards on how data should be handled. We highly advise reviewing your company's policies for data handling/retention before you create your own security analysis. Those will serve as guardrails for how you should view information.

We will go into detail on this topic in *Chapter 11, Security – Authentication, Data Sharing, and Encryption*. What we will focus on here are the high level items to identify how to set up your data model and uncover any key architectural decisions. At a high level, you need to identify the following in the context of your Target Audience:

- **Personally identifiable information (PII)**: How much control do people need over their information? Is there anything we cannot allow them to edit once entered?

- Is there any information we do not want to be shared across Target Audience?

- Are we handling any **protected health information (PHI)** or any other kind of regulated data?

- Does our company have data retention policies we need to follow?

Answering these high-level questions will help set the direction for what universal protections you need. The next step will be to dig deeper as per your audience base. To demonstrate how to do that, we are going to head back to *Delivery International*, where Kinley is ready to explain her vision for information sharing between the Target Audiences.

Deep dive into Target Audience data practices

Kinley has aligned with technology teams to establish that we will be setting up two separate portals. In preparation, you are writing out the key pieces of data that you will be collecting as part of the processes each Target Audience is expected to execute. This information would have come from the process maps the varying business departments agreed upon. If you haven't gotten those yet, this is a good time to pause.

Let's say pausing isn't in your vocabulary because speed to market is the name of the game. You can always propose the base data that Salesforce objects come with as the information you expect to use for transaction purposes. Kinley is a tight deadline go-getter, but she won't sacrifice creating the ideal process. Lucky for us, we have the process maps to rely on, starting with our franchisees in our PRM. Here is what we need to know that is specific to a user group of this kind:

- Are all partners equal or is there a tiered partner model? Meaning, do some partners have access to certain products/features while others may have a different set?

- How much control do partners need? Do you want them to be channel managers? Do they need to be able to manage other users?

- Can everyone who belongs to the partner organization see all the information related to the partner organization? If not, what limitations should there be?

- Do they need to register the locations they wish to open?

- Do franchisee activities need to be tracked? Do they need to use events, tasks, or calendars?

- Do franchisees need to see End Consumers that buy from their locations? If so, what are they allowed to see about them?

- In terms of self-service, do we escalate any cases we receive regarding orders at a franchisee's location to them? Or, are all cases no matter who reports them managed by *Delivery International*?

Let's take this example of the partner relationship module and view it from the reverse side. Here are some questions we need to ask ourselves about our internal users' access to the information our franchisees share with us:

- Can all internal channel managers see all franchisee information? If not, what determines who can see what? How frequently can this change?

- Do we provide our franchisees with leads? If so, how do we decide who gets which leads? Is there a period in which leads can get reassigned if not contacted and therefore the original assignee should lose visibility to them?

- How do you anticipate inviting franchisees to join the program and/or the new digital portal? Can anyone register? Is it an invite-only or application process?

- What data can franchisees delete?

Now that we understand the basic object model and a broad picture of our data governance landscape, we have a foundational understanding of what we conceptually need to surface into Experience Cloud. Our next step is to determine what other external systems may play into our design, so we can understand our system architecture and create a true ERD for our teams to design against. To get there, we have to make some decisions around our enterprise architecture.

Curating an enterprise architecture map

We might have satisfied Kinley in production, but we're not done appeasing our other internal stakeholders just yet. Dalbert in marketing needs our Experience Cloud data to plug into his **marketing technology (MarTech)** stack, and Maggie in finance needs data from franchisee sales and end-consumer purchases to connect to our **Enterprise Resource Planning (ERP)** finance system. We also can't forget Anna in quality, who needs the user experience to cleanly connect behind the scenes to internal IT systems such as **single sign-on (SSO)**, our data lake, or any other middleware.

Let's tackle the potential tech stacks around each of our stakeholders as we begin to design our **enterprise architecture map**. Every organization is different, and this Architecture Map is intended as an example to inspire you; it is not intended to be seen as gospel or as the sole way to do it.

Marketing technologies

Marketing automation tools have become a specialty of their own over the past few years. In the era of ultra-tailored customer experiences, they all surround delivering, containing, and assessing data from the customer experience. Consequently, correctly setting up your CRM, the digital application that houses all your customers, is critical to a successful MarTech stack and ecosystem. Since Experience Cloud is now a portal by which marketing automation systems can collect data, we need to carefully consider how these interactions will be handed off.

For our purposes, we will primarily reference marketing automation solutions offered by Salesforce, such as Marketing Cloud, Marketing Cloud Account Engagement (the artist formerly known as Pardot), and Marketing Cloud Intelligence. However, other common marketing tools, such as Google Analytics or paid social media, should be considered in your enterprise architecture map. We will dive heavily into the specifics of marketing automation enablement within Experience Cloud in *Chapter 9, Marketing Automation Setup*. For now, we will focus on identifying *Delivery International's* existing tech stack.

Let's take a look at the technologies Dalbert wants us to consider:

Technology	
Email and Journey Automation	Email and journey automation systems allow marketers to trigger marketing activities such as emails, text messages, site experiences, and more, depending on behavioral criteria across digital properties. Salesforce Marketing Cloud and/or Marketing Cloud Account Engagement are Salesforce's robust offerings for both.
Social Media Automation	Social media automation allows businesses to plan, schedule, and publish social media content. This content might include organic posting or paid postings/media buys. Salesforce Marketing Cloud Social accomplishes many of these functionalities.
Data Management Platforms (DMPs) / Customer Data Platforms (CDPs)	DMPs and CDPs gather data from internal and third-party systems and can be used to enrich audience targeting and personalization.
MarTech Analytics	While a common standard is Google Analytics, you may have other marketing data systems, such as Marketing Cloud Intelligence (formerly known as "Datorama").
Content Distribution Network (CDN)/ Digital Asset Management (DAM)	A CDN and a DAM system are related to each other, but different. A DAM stores files, whereas a CDN distributes those files across different digital properties.

Technology	
Content Management System (CMS)	A CMS manages content across websites. This could be web page templates, articles, blogs, and more.
Search Engine Optimization (SEO) tools	Many SEO tools and plugins can be used to assess the SEO performance of pages and content blocks.
Website	Your Experience Cloud sites might need to be accessed from your primary website, so, ensuring that the transition from a public web presence to a potentially login-gated one is a crucial consideration in your application design.

Table 4.7: Delivery International's marketing tool request

Remember, MarTech systems can change more rapidly than more common enterprise software, so being aware of updates to these systems may impact how your Experience Cloud site needs to operate or the way your data flows. Marketing software can also have some heavy privacy and security rules around it, so it's critical to ensure that anything you are building involves active consent and follows your local laws.

Finance technologies

Delivery International is in the business of making money, and understanding where that money is coming from and how it moves is critical for the financial interests of the company and its franchisees alike. A financial ecosystem can be extremely vast and complex, and creating accounting architecture for a company with a B2B and B2C model like the one *Delivery International* operates could be a book of its own. Therefore, we're going to broadly categorize financial functions, such as accounts payable and receivables, general ledgers, and expense management, into an ERP system. We need to make sure that our opportunities and orders from both sites flow into our ERP.

At a high level, this is what Maggie has identified as the systems we need to account for to integrate into our Experience Cloud build:

Technology	
ERP	An ERP system is an elaborate piece of software designed to handle financial and administrative aspects of a company, predominantly accounting. It may also incorporate human resources, payroll, compliance, supply chain, and project billing.
Product Information Management (PIM)	A PIM system houses all information surrounding a product to ensure third-party systems can easily and consistently display product information. This may be descriptions, images, specifications, and more.

Technology	
DAM	A DAM system is very similar to a PIM, focused on the collection and dispersal of branded assets.
CDN	A CDN is a centralized system or network of systems that delivers content to websites, applications, and internet services.
Payment Processor	A payment processor is a third party used to process digital payments.
E-Commerce Solution	An e-commerce solution that powers an online transaction, such as Salesforce Commerce Cloud. Depending on your unique financial and shipping needs, you may need Commerce Cloud Cartridges for logistics and fulfillment tooling, too.

Table 4.8: Delivery International's finance integration request

It is important to note that an ERP integration with Salesforce is one of the most challenging integrations there is (especially with Oracle products), and an ERP integration project requires significant lead time, upfront planning, and testing. ERPs and their affiliated software may also be subject to legal and compliance regulations, so be sure you have engaged the proper parties to cover your legal bases before you design anything. Additionally, consult with your internal IT as mentioned in the following section if specialty integration patterns and data transmission protocols are required for your ERP.

IT systems

As for the backbone of internal and external user experience, we can't forget about non-Salesforce systems that can move data in and out of Experience Cloud and facilitate our customer experiences. Anna in quality wants to ensure that our Experience Cloud sites are leveraging existing architecture, safely connecting to other systems with our API structures, and complying with our company's enterprise data guidelines.

> **Important note**
>
> You may need to use integration middleware as part of your API strategy, which will involve very complex planning. Although we haven't included API middleware, such as Mulesoft, Boomi, or Azure, in our architecture, an in-depth API and **extract, transform, load** (ETL) architecture might be part of your strategy, and may involve several different applications we will broadly categorize as "API middleware." We also recommend that you carefully path out the flow of your data into your various storage systems, such as a database, data lake, and/or warehouse, and establish a system you define as a single source of truth in the event of a data emergency.

Additionally, *Delivery International* is planning to combine Salesforce data with data from our ERP to share information with our customers in real time. Some of this data needs to be encrypted and only available for our internal associates who are servicing the customer. Consider a few different facets at play here:

- Some of your data needs encryption, which will cause your APIs to be constructed differently due to the handling of keys.

- The visibility of data is different per audience and only intended for certain use cases. This may mean that how it is contained within objects requires different handling.

Let's assess which non-Salesforce technologies we may need to leverage to surface this data into our Experience Cloud sites:

Technology	
Single Sign on (SSO)	SSO is a tool that allows users to access all authenticated applications across your site by only having to log in once. Consider how users can self-register for SSO, in addition to the potential API call limit impacts an SSO may have.
Data Storage Lake/Warehouse	We are broadly categorizing any software designed to store data as "data storage." This may be a database, a data lake, or a data warehouse.
Analytics/Data BI tools	Data analytics tools combine data across all your various enterprise systems to serve up analytics to different users
API Middleware and Proxies	This is an extremely broad categorization of many technologies and may include ETL tools, API proxies, gateways, monitoring systems, and more.

Table 4.9: Delivery International's IT technology requests

You should keep all of your stakeholders apprised of future changes to your Experience Cloud releases, but it is especially critical to keep your IT stakeholders apprised of changes that may heavily impact systems that underpin your enterprise's technology. In turn, internal IT should keep you posted when it's making changes to any of the systems detailed previously, and you should coordinate potential downtime and system updates.

Mapping it out

At last, we've figured out what we need to connect to our Experience Cloud sites to capture the life cycles of our internal departments, franchisees, and End Consumers. As you've identified the various applications that interweave, identify the direction data would flow.

Here's a condensed version of what our enterprise architecture diagram would look like:

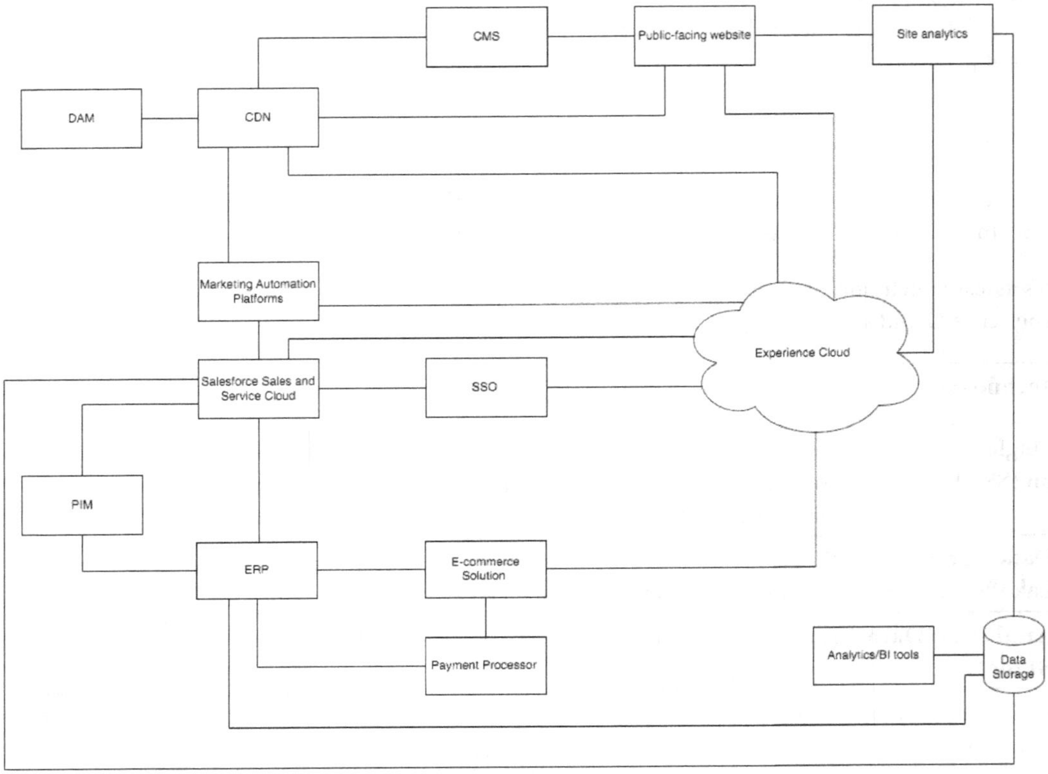

Figure 4.1: Delivery International's enterprise architecture map

While you may be tempted to commit to including all of these systems into your Experience Cloud go-live plan, kicking off an Experience Cloud launch with all of these enterprise applications already connected can be overly ambitious and potentially damaging if not done correctly. After all, if you attempt a launch with all of these included and unexpected behavior arises, isolating the location of a bug can be very challenging, even taking your user experience down until the bug is corrected. Consequently, we recommend triaging third-party applications into "MVP must-have" versus "fast follow" versus "future state" stages for your Experience Cloud launch. Some of your destination systems may need to clean their data before you connect to them, and thoroughly assessing a clean integration plan and roadmap will save you time, money, and tears down the road.

Curating an ERD

Now that we know what systems provide the data that eventually needs to make its way into our Experience Cloud sites, we're ready to work on our ERDs within Salesforce to make our Experience Cloud sites work.

Licensure considerations

Before you start spinning up custom objects in your Salesforce Sandbox environment, it is very important to speak to your Salesforce Account Executive about your licensure plan, API call limits, and storage options, as that will heavily dictate what you can do and store in Salesforce Experience Cloud.

The list of standard objects: (`https://help.salesforce.com/s/articleView?id=sf.admin_communities_license_access_retail.htm&type=5`) shared between standard Salesforce Sales/Service Cloud and Experience Cloud is very long and can change from update to update, but you should review it carefully before you design under the assumption that something can be shared with an Experience Cloud site when it cannot be. While we do review the common use cases in this book, always validate against current technical documentation. You will also need to familiarize yourself with standard Salesforce objects before building custom ones.

Additionally, your third-party applications may have API call limits or license implications that could impact how your data surfaces in Experience Cloud. So, do not neglect to cover your bases so you don't unearth nasty surprises later in your project.

Guide to reading the ERD tables

We have included *Table 4.10* for the object families involved in our ERDs to make it easier to follow along. The object families are as follows:

- Sales Cloud

- Service Cloud

- Commerce Cloud

- Custom, an AppExchange solution, or another Salesforce product not here mentioned

Note that the same object may be used in slightly different ways for each experience, such as the Case and Product objects. When you are building the objects out, the differences in usage will be indicated by tools, such as record type, or fields on the object that may indicate a different relationship. They may also have significant sharing configuration needs to properly separate the records into each experience.

We will not explore field-level security in our two ERDs, but you will want to heavily contemplate the specific information housed in each field of these objects and whether or not you want your users to see it. *Chapter 11*, *Security – Authentication, Data Sharing, and Encryption*, will dive into this topic and its security implications further.

Please note that object families, such as activities and content, can come with Service Cloud as well, but we have grouped them with Sales. Additionally, all of these objects should export into a backup database if that is part of your ecosystem, thus we did not include that as potential integration. Finally, these ERDs are high-level and do not include all the supporting objects that may be associated with each of the Salesforce products, so please consult the schema in setup or user guides for specific products for more information.

Franchisee Experience Cloud ERD

We've looked at requirements, reviewed our license needs, and thought about where all our data lives for our franchisees. Let's itemize what each of our objects is intended to do before we draw up our master plan.

Object	Object Family	Purpose	Potential External Integration
Account	Sales Cloud	Stores franchisee accounts and end-consumer contacts.	ERP, Marketing Automation, SSO
Contact	Sales Cloud	Stores both franchisee contacts and end-consumer contacts.	ERP, Marketing Automation, SSO
User	Sales Cloud	Creates login account for franchisee users.	SSO
Login Sessions	Sales Cloud	Tabulate how often a user logs in.	SSO
Campaigns	Sales Cloud	Keep track of campaigns to attract more End Consumers to buy products, allows	Marketing Automation (CDN, DAM, CMS, Marketing Analytics, Social Media)
Opportunities	Sales Cloud	Allow franchisees to log deals for new franchises.	ERP
Opportunity Contact Role	Sales Cloud	Connects people at a franchise to an opportunity, indicating their role in the deal.	ERP
Leads	Sales Cloud	Allow franchisees to track potential new franchisees or franchise locations.	Marketing Automation
Products	Sales Cloud	For both franchisee opportunities and sold-to-End Consumer products.	ERP, PIM
Price Books	Sales Cloud	Dictates pricing of products.	ERP, PIM

Object	Object Family	Purpose	Potential External Integration
Content Workspace	Sales Cloud	A library that houses documents and files uploaded into Salesforce.	Website, Marketing Automation (CDN, DAM, CMS, Marketing Analytics, Social Media)
Content Workspace Doc	Sales Cloud	Junction object between a content document and a content library.	Website, Marketing Automation (CDN, DAM, CMS, Marketing Analytics, Social Media)
Content Workspace Document	Sales Cloud	A document that has been uploaded to Salesforce.	Website, Marketing Automation (CDN, DAM, CMS, Marketing Analytics, Social Media)
Task	Sales Cloud	A business activity that can be tabulated like a to-do list.	
Event	Sales Cloud	A business activity built off a date that can be visualized on a calendar.	
Calendar	Sales Cloud	A calendar that can house Event Records	
Report	Sales Cloud	A report of data organized based on user criteria set in the interface.	
Dashboards	Sales Cloud	A visualization of reporting.	
Rebates	Custom	A B2B incentive program.	ERP, PIM
Rebate Types	Custom	Categories of Incentive programs available to franchisees.	ERP, PIM
Case	Service Cloud	Houses support tickets sent by the franchisees.	

Object	Object Family	Purpose	Potential External Integration
Case Milestone	Service Cloud	Mandatory, time-dependent criteria that must be met in your service process.	
Case Entitlements	Service Cloud	A time-based element tied to a contract/order. Part of the information in the data record is a relationship to the SLA.	ERP
SLA	Service Cloud	Outlines the SLA program that is tied to the Account/Contacts Entitlement.	ERP
Knowledge	Service Cloud	A library of articles about your organization, products, and services that you can share with specific audiences internally/externally.	
Knowledge Article	Service Cloud	An individual Knowledge article.	
Case Article	Service Cloud	A Knowledge Article that can be attached specifically to a case.	
Customer Orders	Commerce Cloud	Individual records of orders placed by End Consumers to the franchisees.	ERP, E-Commerce Solution
Customer Payments	Commerce Cloud	End-consumer payment records associated with individual orders.	ERP, Payment Processor

Table 4.10: Delivery International's franchisee objects

With that, *ta-da*! We have a high-level ERD, clearly showing how each object flows into the other:

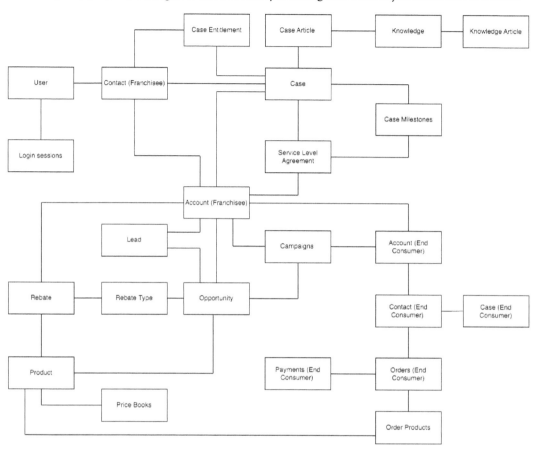

Figure 4.2: Delivery International's franchisee ERD

The *Delivery International* franchisee ERD might look complex at first, but beginning your review with core objects, such as Account, Contact, Case, and Opportunity, will help you understand how these objects interact with each other. As a reminder, the ERD is a high-level representation, and does not include all of the master/detail relationships, nor does it include sympathetic objects that may come with standard, custom, or AppExchange Salesforce architecture.

Because the Content and Activities objects are also part of the requirements but bolt onto most standard and custom objects in Salesforce, we have included them as their own diagrams. See *Figure 4.3*.

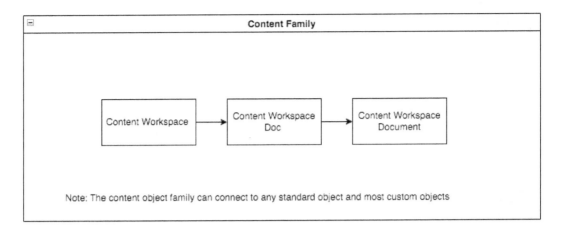

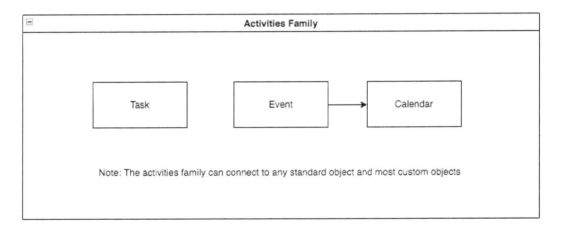

Figure 4.3: The Activities and Content families

The Activities and Content families can be extremely useful add-ons to standard and custom objects, but think through their use cases before blindly adding them to any page layouts. Also, be advised that there are field limitations on the Activities objects, so plan your customizations carefully.

End Consumer Experience Cloud ERD

We've figured out what our franchisees need to see, and now it's time to assess what our end users will be looking at. As we build our model, be mindful that you will likely want to create the most protection around information shared between your Salesforce org and End Consumers. For example, not all account and contact information will be visible to the End Consumers, and Knowledge articles designed for franchisee help should not be shared with our End Consumers.

Object	Object Family	Purpose	Potential External Integration
Account	Sales Cloud	Stores customer account information.	ERP, Marketing Automation, SSO
Contact	Sales Cloud	Stores end-consumer contact information.	ERP, Marketing Automation, SSO
User	Sales Cloud	Creates a login account for a franchisee user.	SSO
Login Sessions	Sales Cloud	Tabulates how often a user logs in.	SSO
Products	Sales Cloud	Holds products an End Consumer can buy in an order.	ERP, PIM
Price Books	Sales Cloud	Dictates pricing of products.	ERP, PIM
Content Workspace	Sales Cloud	A library that houses documents and files uploaded into Salesforce.	Website, Marketing Automation (CDN, DAM, CMS, Marketing Analytics, Social Media)
Content Workspace Doc	Sales Cloud	Junction object between a content document and a content library.	Website, Marketing Automation (CDN, DAM, CMS, Marketing Analytics, Social Media)
Content Workspace Document	Sales Cloud	A document that has been uploaded to Salesforce.	Website, Marketing Automation (CDN, DAM, CMS, Marketing Analytics, Social Media)
Report	Sales Cloud	A report of data organized based on user criteria set in the interface.	
Dashboards	Sales Cloud	A visualization of reporting.	
Case	Service Cloud	Houses support tickets sent by the franchisees.	

Object	Object Family	Purpose	Potential External Integration
Case Milestone	Service Cloud	Mandatory, time-dependent criteria that must be met in your service process.	
Case Entitlements	Service Cloud	A time-based element tied to a contract/order. Part of the information in the data record is a relationship to the SLA.	ERP
SLA	Service Cloud	Outlines the SLA program that is tied to the Account/Contacts Entitlement.	ERP
Knowledge	Service Cloud	A library of articles about your organization, products, and services that you can share with specific audiences internally/externally.	
Knowledge Article	Service Cloud	An individual Knowledge article.	
Case Article	Service Cloud	A Knowledge Article that can be attached specifically to a case.	
Orders	Commerce Cloud	Individual records of orders placed by End Consumers to the franchisees.	ERP, E-Commerce Solution
Payments	Commerce Cloud	End-consumer payment records associated with individual orders.	ERP, Payment Processor
Loyalty	Commerce Cloud	A program that measures and creates rewards for loyal End Consumers.	ERP
Shipping Address	Commerce Cloud	Individual locations and End Consumers can specify for delivery.	ERP, E-Commerce Solution
Coupons	Commerce Cloud	End users can access coupons to add to their orders.	E-Commerce Solution

Table 4.11: Delivery International's franchisee objects

Here it is, our End Consumer ERD:

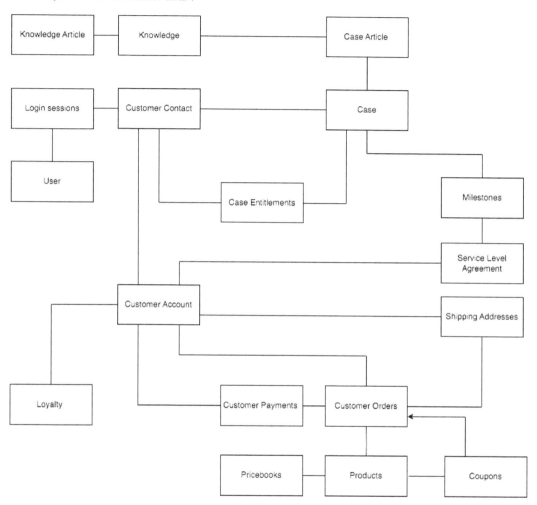

Figure 4.4: Delivery International's End Consumer ERD

As a reminder, the ERD is a high-level representation and does not include all of the sympathetic objects that may come with standard, custom, or AppExchange Salesforce architecture.

Summary

Coordinating the amount of research and resources it takes to create an ERD is no easy feat, but it is the blueprint for the rest of your design and well worth the effort. Taking the time to properly diagram your build will pay dividends in the future: it will be easier to explain your vision to your stakeholders, all while simplifying building instructions to your administrators and developers. Keep your initial ERDs as an artifact and add to them as you expand on your build work.

In this chapter, you learned the following:

- What data elements are needed to achieve our features
- Which standard objects would work with our scenarios
- When to leverage a custom object or non-Sales and Service Cloud object
- How to design against KPIs
- How to identify sensitive data and determine required security protocol based on audience
- How to account for third-party systems that may need to integrate into your Experience Cloud build and create an enterprise architecture diagram
- How to put together an ERD for two different Experience Cloud use cases that showcase your design as a data blueprint

In our next chapter, we will review the standard Experience Cloud templates, in addition to your options for customization.

5

Understanding Experience Cloud Templates

Now that we are clear on the features we need, the products we are purchasing, and how our data will be structured, we need to find the perfect starting point. Introducing: the all-important Experience Cloud template. Salesforce Experience Cloud comes with an assortment of sleek, pre-made, low-code templates that accommodate a wide variety of organizational needs and portal types, which make it a breeze to stand up professional and powerful sites.

All standard templates are configurable but can be extended into a custom experience. Setting up the right template and applying themes ensures capabilities such as global headers/footers, color schemes, and specialty fonts, all of which are focused on matching your brand standards.

In this chapter, we focus on how to identify which portal fits a customer portal versus a custom support use case and when a blend of the two is needed. We review how to make a fully custom Salesforce Experience Cloud site when your use case is unique and requires heavily specific brand standards and integrations.

We are going to break this up into the following sections:

- Preliminary setup
- Templates overview
- Customer templates
- Partner Central template
- Custom templates
- Understanding theming – declarative versus custom CSS
- Retired templates and template migrations

Preliminary setup

Now that you have made your selection of what you need to buy, you have to do some minor setup in Salesforce Settings to enable Experience Cloud. While we highly advise reviewing the templates before you even move to the setup portion of your Experience Cloud sites, there are a few levers you must pull before you can select a template within Experience Cloud.

You may be setting up a new instance of Salesforce/Experience Cloud. For general Salesforce setup, we recommend that you look for resources that enable the specific cloud you are setting up. For purposes of this guide, we are going to assume that the Salesforce portion of your setup is complete and that you are focusing solely on enabling the new Experience Cloud product you have purchased.

Enabling Digital Experiences

While **Sites** may come pre-enabled in a Salesforce org, you need to enable **Digital Experiences** to build an Experience Cloud site. Navigate to the setup menu for your Salesforce instance. From there, you are going to search in the left-hand bar for the word `digital`, and this will bring you to the **Digital Experiences** options.

You will need to select **Settings** under **Digital Experiences**. The initial page is simply verifying that you wish to enable the **Sites** feature. It will then pop up with a question regarding the domain that is being setup for the site. Don't worry; you can change this later, but refer to *Figure 5.1* to enable the setting:

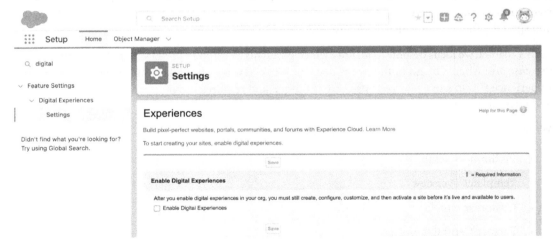

Figure 5.1: Digital Experiences Settings setup menu

To keep configuring the site, you will need to work off the **Settings** page under **Digital Experiences**. Each setting has an info box to the right of it that will explain what the setting does. We recommend starting with the basic settings so that you can expand if you need to later.

If you are going to do a custom domain, we recommend you set that up prior to going to the next setup stage of creating a site. The reason for this is that your site will be given a URL, so having your domain setup will ensure that you won't have to redo the site URL at a later stage.

If you did not set up a custom domain, then you will land on a screen where you can just start a new site. You will name it and launch straight into templates. You can skip to *Figure 5.3*.

If you did navigate away from that page for any reason, then you will have to search for **All Sites** from the feature settings menu. When you are on the master site's setup, the first thing you will be asked to do is consent to the site's terms of use. Be sure to read through this page before accepting. If you have any concerns about the language, reach out to your company's legal representative:

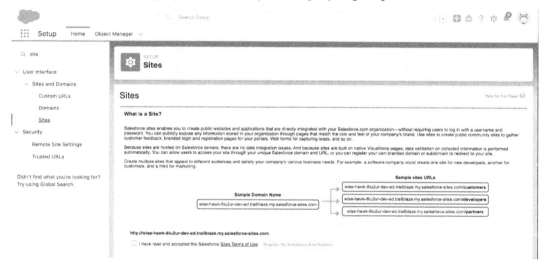

Figure 5.2: All Sites setup consent page

Assuming you consent, you will then click **New** to create a new site. Be sure to label your site and determine its proper home page. Here is a snippet of the screen you should see when you are setting up your site from inside of Salesforce **Setup**:

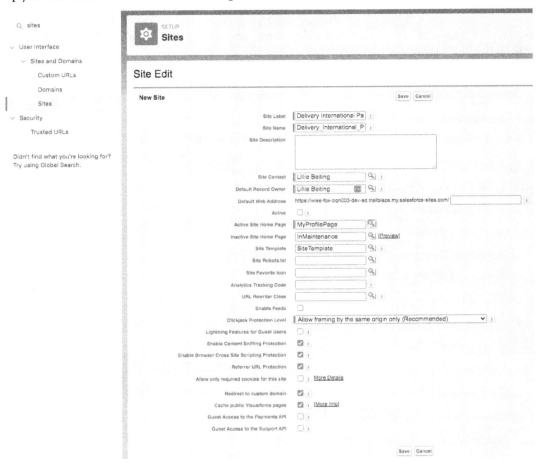

Figure 5.3: New Site setup page

You can revisit this page later to change security settings or other site settings. We recommend that you do not change the defaults on this page until you have read through all of the info boxes. There are some settings that, you cannot revert if you select them. They can also fundamentally change the data in your Salesforce org. As we get further into considerations in the later chapters, we will talk you through when it would be appropriate to enable those settings.

After saving this page, you will be redirected to the **Digital Experiences** page, where you can easily access all of your Experience Cloud sites:

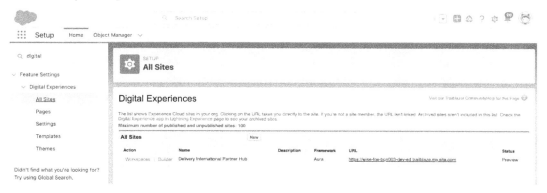

Figure 5.4: Digital Experiences site creation setup menu

When you click the **Builder** link to launch your new site, you will see that the first step in setting up that new site is to pick your template. Now that we know where to find Experience Cloud templates, let's dive into what they are and why you should/shouldn't choose them.

Templates overview

The Experience Cloud templates empower you to get your site out the door quicker than traditional custom development. Another major advantage is that they seamlessly upgrade with Salesforce's multiple releases each year. Instead of spending your time checking for compatibility during each release, you can spend time with your favorite hobby: writing fan mail to Marc Benioff. Doesn't some free time sound like a win/win?

You have to make sure you pick the right template. The great news about having so many options is that you can really tailor the appearance of your **minimum viable product** (**MVP**) based on the needs of your company. However, the drawback is that you can limit your possibilities in the future, depending on what you pick so you will need to weigh the pros and cons against your feature list and data designs. These authors know firsthand what it feels like to have to migrate a site to a new template. It is no small feat, but it is possible. So, even if you pick something now and it doesn't suit your future needs, you can do a migration down the road.

We will, of course, be continuing our overview of *Delivery International's* requirements in comparison with the templates to make the best solution. We will focus on what we know now about the vision for the digital experience and make decisions that best support that vision:

- **Customer Account Portal**

  The **Customer Account Portal** template is leveraged when you want to have customers access/update their information and interact with you digitally. This template is focused on accelerating a company's self-service vision for account information updates. This template allows users to search **frequently asked questions (FAQ)**, pay invoices (commerce connection), and/or update their general account information.

- **Customer Service**

  The **Customer Service** template is going to sound similar to the **Customer Account Portal** template. It has a focus on digital interactions but with a service-only lens. Think of it as the digital storefront for Service Cloud, allowing people who have authenticated into the site the ability to log support cases, check on the status of a case, and search for answers to general help questions.

- **Help Center**

  The **Help Center** template lets you expose your company's knowledge base externally, empowering the singular feature of Salesforce Knowledge to be embedded into your company's website via an Experience Cloud page. Help Center is the Experience Cloud site with the least amount of self-service capabilities that you could launch for your company.

- **Partner Central**

  The **Partner Central** template is leveraged when you work with a third party that sells on behalf of your organization or represents your organization. This template allows easy access to deal information and general knowledge and gets your partners up to speed on the latest offerings of your companies so that they can focus on the business of selling and/or promoting your company.

- **Build Your Own (Aura)**

  The **Build Your Own (Aura)** template comes with some predefined pages. These pages are focused on the basic functions of any digital experience site, such as creating a record, editing a record, forgetting a password, and so on. It allows you to build custom pages and components leveraging the Aura framework. What you aren't going to find here are the prebuilt pages for customers or partners that you will find in the aforementioned sections.

- **Build Your Own (LWR)**

  The **Build Your Own (LWR)** template does not come with any predefined pages. This is a true developers' platform where you will build every asset. The power of this template is that you are leveraging the scalability of the Salesforce platform and the native data connections. However, the interfaces are entirely custom.

- **Microsite (LWR)**

  Microsites are your best friend for creating quick page additions to your website. Think of them as the "pop-up shop" of the digital experience. You have the ability to archive them when they are no longer needed, helping you keep your digital asset hygiene in tip-top shape.

- **Aloha**

  This template is leveraged by Salesforce at Salesforce as an app launcher! It is a place where you can have all of your apps listed with icons in a single location and take your **single sign-on (SSO)** experience to new innovative heights. With the power of the platform, you can customize the look/feel of this template to have a brand-specific login experience for your internal users.

- **Salesforce Tabs + Visualforce**

  Kicking it old-school with Salesforce **Visualforce (VF)** is still an option. This flavor comes with tabs and leverages standard/custom objects. You can also access it through Salesforce Android, iOS, and mobile web.

Now that we understand the core competencies of each template at a high level, we are going to group them into collections in the upcoming sections within this chapter. This will help us focus on the ones with common objectives you should consider. This will also be a reference tool for you in the future in the event you have to migrate your Experience Cloud site to another template.

Customer templates

Let's take a look at the three templates that are all centered on the end consumer: **Help Center**, **Customer Account Portal**, and **Customer Service**. There are some subtle differences here that can be game-changers in the future. We are going to look at each one in terms of the overall objective/purpose of the template and how that relates to use cases:

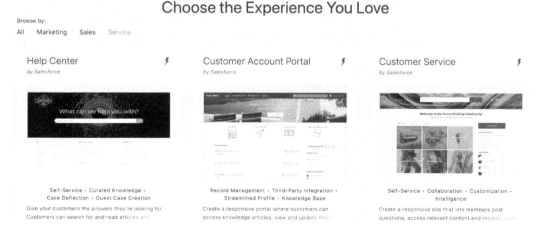

Figure 5.5: Customer template choices for Experience Cloud

Let's start by thinking of the three customer templates as levels, similar to a career path. Your entry-level template is **Help Center**, followed by your middle-ground **Customer Account Portal**, and your top level is **Customer Service**. Now, just because they are levels does not mean we are recommending starting at the bottom and migrating your way up. That would be a lot more trouble than it is worth. What we are recommending is that you consider which template will give you the longevity and scalability your business needs.

So, why pick one over the other? Let's take a look at each one in terms of use cases that would make sense for the particular template. See *Table 5.1*:

Template	Use Cases
Help Center	Need the ability to create a public knowledge base for an FAQ scenario
Customer Account Portal	Need the ability for a person to log in and update their account information, such as address, name, and so on
	Need the ability for a person to pay an invoice online
	Need the ability to see the status of the order that I placed
Customer Service	Need the ability to see my account information and ask for help
	Need the ability to allow a person to submit an item for help from a company associate
	Need the ability to display the status of a help request they submitted and any applicable next steps
	Need to create a knowledge base for people to search FAQ

Table 5.1: Customer central template use cases

Now that we have an idea of what use cases align with the mission of the template, what are the "gotchas"? Why might I want to avoid a certain template? Here are some items to consider and ask your product team questions about as you make your selection:

- **Navigation**: Templates come with a suggested navigation for the portal. If you do not have the intent of expanding your portal to include all the features offered by the template, you will have a consistent set of things you are disabling. This creates a likelihood that a feature may accidentally go dark, given the number of places where the prebuilt templates reference each other.

- **Site limitations**: This may sound self-explanatory, but if you pick the lowest module, you cannot simply add the other features to move up the maturity scale. If you want to add account management to a help center site, you will not be able to get the full features and functions. The only way to add the full feature set is to migrate from one template to the other. If you find yourself in this situation, we cover site migrations toward the end of this chapter.

- **Integration limitations**: If you need to integrate with other external services, you automatically have to pick either **Customer Account Portal** or **Customer Service**. Because it is essentially an FAQ site with Knowledge, the **Help Center** template is very basic and does not have an integration option.

Now that you have sorted through those three key items, which template makes the most sense for your organization? If you don't find what you are looking for, don't forget there are two other categories of templates we still need to cover. In terms of our *Delivery International* use case, the **Customer Service** template makes the most sense for the End Consumer portal. We still need to find out the franchisee portal option. Let's review the **Partner Central** template.

Partner Central template

When it comes to enabling partners, there is only a single template: **Partner Central**. If enabling third parties is what you are looking for, it may sound like a no-brainer to just pick this one:

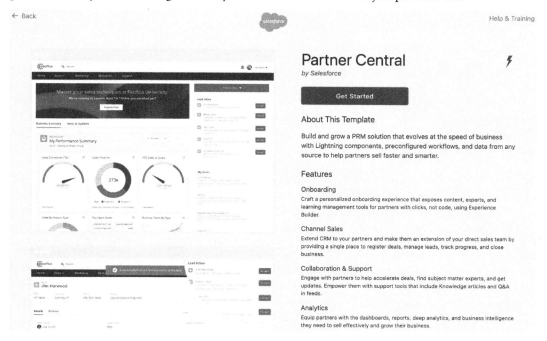

Figure 5.6: Partner Central template for Experience Cloud

The overview of the **Partner Central** template for Experience Cloud template highlights primary features that focus on tasks common for organizations empowering a partner channel. Features such as onboarding, channel sales, collaboration, and analytics insights into your partners' behavior in your portal can be a great place to begin. However, let's evaluate your options as your particular use case may actually lead you to go with a custom template instead. These items are templatized to accelerate your **time to market** (TTM), but they assume that you want to work in the standard Salesforce fashion. If you have completely customized business processes, then you may need to create a custom solution. Don't worry, though – you can use a combination of what Salesforce has **out of the box** (OOTB) plus your own customizations.

The primary use cases for **Partner Central** are the following:

- Users need access to sales objects in Salesforce, chiefly the Opportunity object
- Leads need to be distributed to users, in addition to marketing campaigns to assist them
- Files such as marketing collateral or training documents need to be shared with end users
- End users also need access to case-based support processes and knowledge base
- Partners need to be able to see advanced reporting and track pipelines
- The design needs to be customized to specific audiences and regions

Since **Partner Central** is the only standard template heavily designed around the sales process and its object families in Salesforce, its navigation and **user experience** (UX) cleanly address common sales cycles and needs. But there are still some considerations in choosing it instead of one of the totally custom options we'll get into:

- The partner license is the most expensive of all the Experience Cloud licenses. It also only comes in the named user format because of the capabilities associated with it. If you do not truly need to give your partners access to sales objects and know you will not need to in the future, consider using one of the other templates for cost savings.
- If you know how Salesforce **Lightning Web Component** (LWC) styling looks and you don't layer mountains of CSS on top of your pages, your Experience Cloud site will look like Salesforce to anyone familiar with their component design. While this is not a bad thing, your marketing and UX designers might not like the Salesforce feel instead of a custom one, especially in the Experience Cloud mobile experience.

- If you know you will have to build and custom code several pages, layering CSS on top of standard Salesforce components might not be worth it. It might not make sense to make the base of your Experience Cloud site a template *AND* have large amounts of custom pages you need to manage, as that will become very cumbersome during releases and the risk of site breakage will dramatically increase.

The drawbacks may be giving you pause given the expensive nature and limitations on easy branding, but remember: you can still theme your templates to brand standards. Talk to your product team if you believe this is the way to go to ensure they understand the increased ROI the digital experience will have to produce given the cost.

You may also consider leveraging the **Partner Central** template for a sub-digital experience site. You can fragment your partner community into two sites behind the scenes. For general education partners, you would use the **Customer Service** template, and for those that do sales functions, you would leverage the **Partner Central** template. Yes – it will be a larger deployment, but it is a cheaper long-term alternative.

Now let's recenter on *Delivery International*'s use case. For ease of use and quick turnaround, *Delivery International* is going to use the standard **Partner Central** template with a few custom pages. They were excited about potentially leveraging a combination architecture with a few franchisees going to a **Customer Service** template site and the more back-office franchisee associates leveraging the **Partner Central** template. However, their head of product, Kinley, has informed them that the franchisees in this market who leverage the digital experience site do all the training of others at their facility. There is no need to support a secondary site at this time.

Custom templates

If the robust **Partner Central** and **Customer Service** templates don't suit your needs and you have stringent design standards the standard templates can't meet, let's review other options we referenced earlier. Salesforce has five templates focused on custom development on the platform: **Build Your Own (Aura)**, **Build Your Own (LWR)**, **Microsite (LWR)**, **Salesforce Tabs + Visualforce**, and **Aloha**:

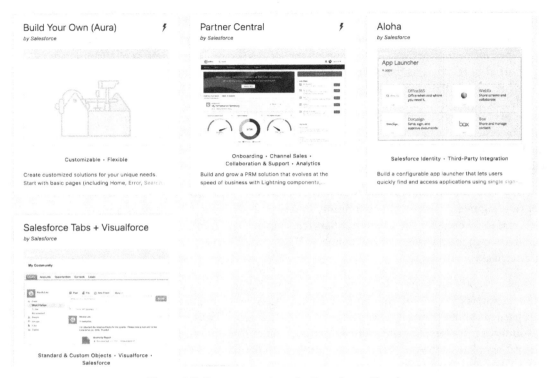

Figure 5.7: Custom templates for Experience Cloud

The primary difference between these sites with the exception of Aloha is the language you can use to customize them and call data within Salesforce and/or to APIs. While you can layer HTML and CSS on top of your code base for styling, **Build Your Own (LWR)**, **Microsite (LWR)**, **Build Your Own (Aura)**, and **Salesforce Tabs + Visualforce** each use their own language as specified in their name. To use any of these templates, your developers will need to be skilled in their respective languages:

- **Lightning Web Runtime (LWR)**: LWRs are built on top of LWC, the most current Salesforce UI standard and continuation of Aura. LWCs are built on modern web standards such as HTML, CSS, and JavaScript.

- **Aura**: An open source framework, Aura is the older version of the Lightning Component framework, with its own markup language and interactions with Apex.

- **VF**: The OG Salesforce UI language, VF is an HTML-like, server-side language with its own tag-based markup. VF is most commonly used in Salesforce Classic, before the advent of Salesforce Lightning.

> **Note**
>
> While Salesforce still supports Aura components and VF, both languages are being phased out in favor of LWCs and, therefore, LWRs. Additionally, depending on your edition of Salesforce, Salesforce Tabs + Visualforce might not be an option for a net new Experience Cloud site. As always, check with your Salesforce AE to ensure features are available to you before diving into your build.
>
> If you're going to custom code a new Experience Cloud site as of the time of this book's publication, our recommendation is to use the most current Salesforce web standard, LWRs. Whenever possible, it is advisable to use Salesforce's most current framework for net new development, even if other ones are available.

Now that we're aware of the difference between Salesforce languages Experience Cloud uses, let's dive into some use cases that may direct you to a specific custom template to enable your digital experience in *Table 5.2*:

Template	Use Cases
Build Your Own (LWR)	You need to leverage the ultra-fast LWC standard, as LWRs are built on top of LWCs
	Your Salesforce strategy already involves the use of custom LWCs that can be repurposed and leveraged by LWRs
	You want to easily leverage existing Salesforce components and Flow Builder
	You want to use the standard Salesforce Action bar
	You want your developers to use the dev console instead of the CLI they'd have to use on VF
Build Your Own (Aura)	You want a few basic Salesforce components to come with your custom build, such as the Related Record component and a home page
	You need easy access to native features such as Audience Targeting and Google Analytics
Microsite (LWR)	You need the ability to set up a temporary site to collect leads, cater to a marketing campaign, or advertise an event
	You only want to use a single page with flexibility for authentication
	You wish to leverage existing Salesforce CMS assets and search
Salesforce Tabs + Visualforce	You need a heavily customized experience based on Salesforce Classic
	Your company uses JavaScript frameworks such as Angular or React
	You wish to host static content on your site

Template	Use Cases
Aloha	You need a site that acts as a one-stop shop to easily launch all your apps that can be used behind SSO

Table 5.2: Custom template use cases

As you can see, the custom template use cases have some significant variation. The most flexible of all the templates is going to be **Build Your Own (LWR)**, although the most flexible template used to be **Build Your Own (Aura)**, and you will likely see many high-powered custom Experience Cloud sites operating off the Aura templates. Now, just because they are the most advanced custom development templates doesn't mean that they are needed for your site. Let's take a look at some of the gotchas that may give you pause in your evaluation:

Template	Gotchas
Build Your Own (LWR)	LWCs and LWRs take some practice to master because you're technically building an app instead of a page.
	Standard action overrides don't work for the Action Bar in an LWR site.
	Does not currently support referential integrity for object API names, meaning a renamed object needs to be updated in the code or the API will break.
	Many features that were available in Aura are no longer available in LWR; for example, no default navigation menu, surveys, certain template features, or certain app-level events. Check the Salesforce Developers site for the most current list of unsupported Aura features.
	Sandboxes may experience issues with the `ContentAsset` web component reference.
	Only supports up to 500 unique URLs, so be mindful of using dynamic content to avoid hitting limits.
	Does not support chatter feeds.
Build Your Own (Aura)	Aura was recently the most advanced custom Experience Cloud template, but LWRs are replacing Aura components as the design standard.
	A pleasant gotcha: Aura and LWC pages can co-exist on the same page.
Microsite (LWR)	They are not intended to run long-term. You need to ensure that your use case is truly a short-term company initiative. If it is longer than a quarter, we recommend evaluating another site template.

Template	Gotchas
Salesforce Tabs + Visualforce	This site must be built through the CLI; it cannot be accessed through the Experience Cloud builder. Therefore, this is a developer skill set only. VF is also being phased out as new programmatic approaches advance in Salesforce. A VF page is server-side, unlike Lightning, which runs client-side. This means that a VF page has to fully load for users to see any changes, and sites can be very latent. VF is a dated standard but can be useful for simple database operations.
Aloha	Aloha is not technically considered a site. It is a branded app launcher. You cannot expand it beyond your SSO launcher.

Table 5.3: Custom template gotcha considerations

Don't let these gotchas overwhelm you or dissuade you from doing a Salesforce Digital Experience. If you were to really break down even true custom development, there would likely be some very big "gotchas" there as well (for example, things that make it cost-prohibitive, inability to scale without significant planning and effort, and so on.) By calling these items out, our goal is to help you walk into your development effort with eyes wide open and help you understand what you are about to embark on.

As we head back to *Delivery International*'s use case, we see some great potential for future use cases on sites we should consider. However, at this point, nothing quite fits the bill of needing to go custom. This is a great thing, because the more you can adopt native standards, the easier and quicker your deployment will be. So, we are going to celebrate the win with our head of Sales, Jamie, as we empower a shorter lead time to enable our teams to bring in higher company revenues.

But even though *Delivery International* has decided to lean on templates, when does it make sense to go custom?

Understanding theming – declarative versus custom CSS

You might be wondering what declarative versus custom CSS means. If these terms are new to you, let's talk it through. The use of the word "declarative" in the Salesforce ecosystem refers to an activity a Salesforce Administrator can perform with little or no code. This means that there are tools such as pre-configured wizards, backend settings pages, drag/drop components, or onscreen guided rules engines that an admin can leverage to develop on Salesforce. These are activities that do not take an advanced technical skill set to complete. When we speak of custom CSS, we're referencing more of a traditional developer skill set in the Salesforce ecosystem, in addition to skill sets you would likely find in standard web development.

Now that we understand the difference in terminology, let's dive into why you would go through the hassle of doing anything with custom CSS when Experience Cloud has so many templates. While Experience Cloud's vast capabilities are enough for many businesses, your direct design needs may require more code to execute than can be accomplished with standard configuration. If you have a complex branding strategy with highly stylized components, then the custom CSS track will certainly find its way into your development practice.

While there are many occasions where it would make more sense to use custom CSS instead of one of the templates, standard navigation is probably the most commonly referenced challenge UX designers face when dealing with Experience Cloud standard templates. The standard navigation bar is very limited in terms of customization without CSS. On desktop, Experience Cloud standard navigation is at the top of the page, reading left to right in English. The standard navigation only points to specific landing pages or URLs; it doesn't allow complex nesting logic or breadcrumbing. Many UX designers want their navigation to appear as a menu on the sides of the screen instead of the top or want to create the ability for users to go back to a previous page without clicking the browser's **Back** button.

All of that being said, when possible, it is best to stick to declarative methodologies. It helps ensure that your digital experience site is "future-proofed" in terms of upcoming system upgrades. This means that you will not have to worry about compatibility as the design changes; just focus on new capabilities. Staying with a standard template means Salesforce does most of the upgrade work for you during their seasonal releases. For example, you won't have to do the heavy lifting of migrating your custom components from Aura to LWR, which owners of a **Build Your Own (Aura)** template will eventually have to perform.

For more information about the true abilities to level up your customization game with custom code, we are going to do a deep dive in *Chapter 6, When to Use Aura Components, Lightning Web Components, and Lightning Runtime Components*.

Retired templates and template migrations

From time to time, Salesforce will retire templates in Experience Cloud. That does not mean that you have to immediately migrate your template. They will still support the template for a period of time after retirement. However, you will eventually have to migrate.

Let's go through which templates are actively in the retirement phase, and then we'll talk you through the considerations you should take when looking at a migration project.

Retired templates

The two most recently retired templates are **Koa** and **Kokua**. Even though they are no longer in use, you might have inherited one and need to know what their original intended use case was. Understanding the prior use case will help you identify the appropriate replacement stack, but here's a quick primer on the difference between the two and their use cases:

Template	Use Cases
Koa	The original Salesforce Knowledge site and case user hub, with the ability to log in, search for articles, and submit cases.
Kokua	Another iteration of a self-service hub designed to search information by category and submit cases. Kokua was optimized for any device.

Table 5.4: Koa and Kokua original use cases

Of the standard templates, **Koa** and **Kokua** could be replaced by **Help Center**, **Customer Account Portal**, or the **Customer Service** template, depending on your needs and what you wish to keep. Make sure that you take into consideration not only what you have but also where your product manager's desired experience for the digital site leads you. Understanding the future will help you ensure that you aren't having to do another migration in a few months.

If you are migrating a Knowledge site to a new UX, it's always a good idea to clean up your Salesforce Knowledge Base articles and organization strategy, too. Have your business partners run metrics on usage to help with an archival strategy. Speaking of template migration, let's transition into talking about those meticulous transitions from one template to another.

Template migrations

So, you've determined you have to do a migration, now what? Well, depending on what you are migrating from/to, be prepared for it to be a tedious process. If you have invested significant effort into any custom components, there will be a lot of work that you need to refactor in order for it to work with the new site. Here are a few things to take into consideration when you are planning for a migration:

- Ensure that you allocate time to verify any custom components. In the event you are moving from Aura to LWR, note that your components will need to be refactored in order to take advantage of the LWR feature set. Additionally, refer to Salesforce's consideration guide before migration to the LWR template: `https://help.salesforce.com/s/articleView?language=en_US&id=sf.exp_cloud_migrate_lwr_considerations.htm&type=5`.

- Allocate time to clean up technical debt built over the current deployment's lifespan. If there are things you no longer use, retire them. If there are things that are not optimized, optimize them. There is no point in re-coding any technical debt to be exactly the way it was before. Take the time to fix it.

- You will need plenty of testing time. Between testing to see what needs to change to verifying that the new experience works as expected, the large majority of your project should be in testing. Expect and plan for defects/bugs to come out frequently in the initial testing stages if you have a significant amount of custom code.

- Consider a user audit prior to a migration, especially if you are changing user license types.

So, we need to refactor, clean up technical debt and dated users, and allocate probably double the time we normally would for testing. Additionally, it is vital that you have a true strategy for how you are going to manage two sites at the same time. Yes – migration is best done by setting up a new site, as it will prevent anything from accidentally going to production. However, this means that you are potentially releasing new features into production that you will ultimately have to factor in as part of the migration build. Having a clear strategy of what will/won't be allowed will keep the amount of change in the old site manageable.

Now, how do you plan the time needed for it? Your first order of business would be to get with your product team and explain what is driving the need to change. If they agree that the features driving the need are critical, then it is a question of getting your migration planned into the release calendar at the time your team estimates. Depending on the complexity of your site, you could be looking anywhere from 2 months to 6 months for a migration. Remember that there is a lot of testing time involved in those timelines. So, it may be possible to pull those timelines in if everything passes quickly.

What considerations should you advise business partners about? This question really comes down to what are you migrating to. If you are migrating to a **Build Your Own (LWR)** site template, for example, then we would recommend highlighting the use cases listed previously, any of the gotchas that would be relevant to your business partners, or any structural changes to the relevant experiences they interact with. The most important thing is getting their commitment on the retesting required. The path to success is heavily weighted on that testing strategy and commitment.

Summary

Digital experience templates do not disappoint! With so many things to choose from and a balanced view of the products, we hope you have found the perfect template for your company and now understand how to evaluate when to use a standard template and when to go custom.

We've reviewed how to move past the preliminary Experience Cloud setup pages to get to the Experience Cloud templates, in addition to the differences between the customer templates, **Partner Central** templates, and custom templates. We've also reviewed what to prepare for in the event you need to migrate a template, in addition to considering when to use custom CSS.

But Experience Cloud can be extended far beyond CSS. In the next chapter, we will dive deeper into LWCs, Aura Components, and LWRs, to help you understand how to maximize and create a fully custom Experience Cloud site.

When to Use Aura Components, Lightning Web Components, and Lightning Runtime Components

At the end of the day, a Salesforce Experience Cloud site is ultimately a website. And user-oriented websites require a **User Interface (UI)** to operate. While Salesforce has carefully curated a variety of pre-built templates for administrators and developers to use, all Salesforce Experience Cloud templates are built using UI components in Salesforce-specific languages.

Common web development styling languages such as HTML and CSS can be layered on top of these components. However, contemporary Salesforce Experience Cloud templates operate heavily on their own bespoke languages: **Aura Components**, **Lightning Web Components (LWCs)**, or **Lightning Web Runtime Components**. If you're using one of the many pre-baked templates we referenced in *Chapter 5, Understanding Experience Cloud Templates*, but adding custom components or starting with one of the truly custom templates, knowing how these work and when to use them will be critical to the creation of a truly customized, efficient experience.

Salesforce web development technology has come a long way as web standards have grown. Deciding which Salesforce-specific web component to use is critical for clean Experience Cloud implementation and maintenance. While Aura Components were the original standard for post-Salesforce Lightning Experience Cloud, Salesforce introduced the much more efficient LWCs in 2018 and encouraged many of its users to transition its Aura Components to LWCs. However, it recently introduced **Lightning Web Runtimes (LWRs)** built off the LWC framework. This chapter focuses heavily on the difference between the three components, when their usage is appropriate, when to transition to newer standards, and specific considerations and callouts when using these three languages.

We are going to break this up into the following sections:

- Why are there three component types?
- Aura Components
- Lightning Web Components
- Lightning Web Runtime Components
- Transitioning from Aura to Lightning
- How to make a page with declarative components

This is a very technical chapter that reviews an intricate tech stack, one to which Salesforce has dedicated thousands of pages of release documentation over the years. This chapter assumes a certain amount of familiarity with web development standards and Salesforce languages, and it does entail quite a bit of context switching.

Why are there three component types?

What a great question! In the interest of a quick Salesforce history lesson, you should know that **VisualForce**, an HTML-like, tag-based markup language, was the original Salesforce UI language, which is why the **Tabs and Visualforce Experience Cloud** template exists in the first place. Experience Cloud has had a few names over the years and has matured as Salesforce technology has grown.

What we now call Experience Cloud was originally the very inflexible Supportforce Portal, followed by the PartnerPortal Tool Kit, the Partner Portal, and the Customer Portal. All of these initial portals were built in Salesforce Classic and therefore based on the Salesforce Classic tech stack of Apex and Visualforce. Bonus fun fact: originally, there was even an on-premises version of the Partner Portal. That version was quickly retired. Then, in 2011, Salesforce heavily rebranded its portals into Salesforce Communities and offered a few stock templates with them that leveraged Apex and Visualforce.

It wasn't until the launch of **Salesforce Lightning** in 2014 that **Salesforce Aura** entered the chat and Salesforce rebranded Communities as **Salesforce Community Cloud**. While the Lightning Component framework also came out in 2014, Aura was the original web design framework that came with it, exclusive to Salesforce development and different from standard web development toolkits.

When Salesforce Lightning was announced in 2014, it revolutionized the UI and UX capabilities of Salesforce, allowing for a highly-tailored experience that empowered admins and developers to create slick, efficient UI with clicks, not code. Salesforce Lightning created a fast, easy, modern UI experience with a more expansive landscape for customization at the declarative level without having to leverage custom pre-built solutions. In addition, it enabled more options for those looking for complex customization. The underpinning of this was the brand new Lightning Component Aura framework, as VisualForce and HTML were never designed to support the kind of complex enterprise applications Salesforce had expanded into.

In 2018, Salesforce announced LWC, a framework that more closely matched contemporary web standards and it rebranded The Community Cloud product to **Salesforce Experience Cloud** not long after in 2020. Finally, in 2021, Salesforce released the **LWR**, the standard that most closely matches what other web developers use, making it easier for web developers trained on other applications to work on Salesforce sites.

Technically, the Lightning Component framework refers to Aura Components, LWCs, and Lightning Web Runtime Components, and it can be challenging to keep them straight. To make matters even more confusing, Aura Components were often called Lightning components prior to the release of LWCS and LWRs, and often still are referred to as such by Salesforce Administrators.

Many Salesforce **Original Gangsters (OGs)** still refer to the concept of Experience Cloud sites as portals and even we authors catch ourselves calling the product "Communities" sometimes. We think we speak for all Salesforce pros when we say we'd really like Salesforce to chill with the constant rebranding. As they are not Experience Cloud, we won't touch on the intricacies of **Site.com** and **Force.com**, both of which are still available today and can leverage these languages. However, our breakdown of Aura Components, LWCs, and Lightning runtime components in the upcoming sections should help you demystify these useful building blocks when designing and maintaining your Salesforce Experience Cloud site.

So, if you are joining us on this journey from a legacy Experience Cloud site with other component names, note that those are probably legacy code items that have not been fully transitioned. In true legacy fashion, you will have to migrate them at some point. We will cover how to transition from Aura to Lightning toward the end of this chapter. However, if you are looking to transition to other component types, we recommend that you leverage the Salesforce Trailhead resources on migration. If you are starting from scratch, we hope that you have enjoyed the brief history lesson!

In this chapter, we're only going to deep dive into the post-Salesforce Lightning component types. Additionally, we should note that all of these options come with a standard Salesforce Lightning component library, allowing you to leverage a wide variety of powerful, prebuilt components. You can learn more about which components are already available to you at `https://developer.salesforce.com/docs/component-library`.

We are here to help you future-proof your site and leveraging the new standards will keep you in a modern Salesforce Org. Let's dive into our first component type, Aura.

Aura Components

Lightning, the latest Salesforce Platform, comes with some really powerful tools such as the **Lightning App Builder** and **Experience Builder**, which are frontend UI frameworks that house Lightning components (also known as Aura Components) that can be dragged and dropped in an easy UI. These Aura Components leveraged the much more standardized Javascript framework, creating a flexible, event-driven framework that allows for encapsulating aspects of a page, leading to faster application creation and rendering time. The framework came with its own design library and several pre-build components, which were designed to accommodate code such as HTML, CSS, JavaScript, and other web-UI languages.

While they are considered an outdated standard now owing to the introduction of the LWC and LWR Component, **Experience Cloud templates**, such as **Customer Service, Partner Central**, and of course, **Build Your Own Aura**, still operate on the Aura framework. Aura Components are capable of managing both client-side and server-side operations. This allows you to enable faster processing time and dynamically change UI components, helping end users to focus on how to execute actions and get the support they need.

When we think of *Delivery International*, for example, we could have a better experience for our End Consumers if we validated the delivery address in the background instead of having to go through separate screens to do so. If we can make that process frictionless with existing components, then our sales conversion rate will be higher. As a result, we are going to get Aura on the radar for our Experience Cloud Site.

You may also notice that you can leverage an LWC component inside an Aura component in the new LWC framework. Why? Well, that's coming up in the next section reviewing which features are not currently available in LWCs.

Features in Aura not yet available in LWC or LWRs

Much like how certain Salesforce features remained available only in Salesforce Classic even well after the introduction of Salesforce Lightning, there are still some features that are only available in Aura. As of the publication date of this book, the features listed here are available for Aura only, but as always, you would need to check with your Salesforce account team and Salesforce documentation before making an architectural decision. The following table reviews Aura features that are currently unsupported by the new Lightning components:

Feature	Definition
Chatter feeds and Rich publisher	Allows you to integrate custom apps into native chatter features.
Certain API services	ConversationToolkitAPI, empApi, navigtionItemAPi, OmniToolKitAPI, quickActionAPI, utilityBarAPI, and workspaceAPI
Container	This is an iframe standard
File Card	Previews a file
FlexiPage Region Info	Documents width of region in component
Insert Image Button	Adds an image button into a rich text editor
Message Channel	The Lightning Message Service API, which lets you publish events between Aura, Visualforce, and LWC

Feature	Definition
NavigationItemAPI	Access methods for navigation in Lightning Console Apps
Notifications Library	Standard notifications in toasts or notice
Omnitoolkit	API access for omnichannel
Overlay Library	Method to display messages in modal or overlay
Path and Picklist Path	A UI element shaped like chevrons that show your progress dependent on a picklist
Quip Card	A UI component that shows Quip files, a Salesforce product we hope they haven't renamed by the time we publish this book
Unsaved changes	A component that alerts a user of unsaved changes
Utility Bar API	An API to a footer that gives people access to frequently used components or other tools
Workspace API	The API that allows you to manipulate the tabs and subtabs of a Lightning Console app

Table 6.1: Aura features not available in LWCs or LWRs

Our goal in providing you with a table is to help your high-level understanding of alternatives you may have to create. In addition, this should help in your decision-making as you are building custom components.

As we mentioned, *Table 6.1* is accurate as of the date when the book was published. For the latest information on what is not yet supported, make sure to check out `https://developer.salesforce.com/docs/platform/lwc/guide/get-started-supported-experiences.html`.

Aura feature considerations

As a best practice, you should not be coding in Salesforce using legacy Salesforce languages. Therefore, you should not be using Aura for new Experience Cloud sites as of the publication of this book. However, if you're still considering it, here are some aspects you should ponder:

- Aura was built against old web standards and components may have latency issues. When dealing with complex data calls or renderings, Aura may lag significantly.

- Aura is difficult to learn, not only because it is a dated standard but also because it is Salesforce-specific.

- Since Aura is a Salesforce-specific language, some web browsers will not support certain components. For this reason, it is always recommended to test your custom components of any kind against common browser standards.

- Controller logic can get messy. Since most of the business logic lives inside the Apex controller, debugging an Aura component can be very challenging.

- Event handling is a further concern. For some reason, Aura has its own event model that differs from the standard **Document Object Model** (**DOM**), making event handling and debugging tricky at times.

- Standard Aura UI elements cannot be coded over. In other words, you cannot add or remove code from a Standard component; you need to use them as-is.

- Build Your Own (LRW) Template cannot accommodate Aura Components.

- Aura components can contain other Aura components and LWCs, but an LWC can only contain LWCs.

Now that we have an overview of the original Lightning component, let's review its successors.

Lightning Web Components

LWCs are the best parts of Aura Components, but have been updated to modern web standards. As Google slowly took over the internet, they widely introduced the concept of a standard web component. A standard web component is essentially a framework that allows developers to create reusable, modular blocks of code that browsers can easily digest and load. While Aura shifted the focus from mere markup languages to facilitating full-blown applications, LWCs took this work to the next level by leveraging Google's Web Component standards and DOM: a logic tree data model that represents the structure of the website. Fun fact: this is why Salesforce Lightning works best in Google Chrome.

As mentioned earlier, the primary systemic difference between an Aura component and a LWC is that LWCs leverage standard Salesforce architecture, but follow common web development languages such as JavaScript, HTML, and CSS. LWCs' adherence to standard web technologies allows them to take advantage of two really critical web tools: modern JavaScript ECMAScript standards and what is often referred to as a **Shadow DOM**. ECMAScript is a standard that allows developers to develop code that works across modern web browsers without having to create individual pages or components per browser. A Shadow DOM isn't something that charges $500 an hour to help you work through your issues with your father in dim lighting, it's essentially a way to encapsulate your components' style and markup in a repeatable fashion without impacting the rest of your website's components. These attributes and many more lead to a lightweight framework that creates quicker load times and better CPU usage. Even if you're not a web developer, it's easy to see how these two key attributes can be beneficial to faster, more modular development.

However, LWCs are more than just Salesforce's answer to a modern web dev tech stack. They're also far more streamlined to make while still complimenting native Salesforce architecture. First and foremost, the LWC syntax is much simpler compared to Aura, but it cleanly handles API events. LWCs come with an **Integrated Development Environment** (**IDE**) and a **Command Line Interface** (**CLI**) familiar to standard web developers that help developers efficiently create, test, and debug code. They can also set preferential loading and filtering on your components, or create logic based on components on the same page, allowing UX designers and developers to prioritize the loading and caching of the most important information first.

But the best thing of all is that Aura Components can nest LWCs within them, making it easy to retrofit experiences and features that LWCs might still be waiting on. They also follow modern web security protocols, making them harder to hack.

Without getting even more technical than we already have, it's fair to say that LWCs homogenize Salesforce web development with external web development standards, making it much easier for developers who come from tech stacks external to Salesforce to learn and work on highly customized Salesforce projects. LWCs' component-based architecture allows for the modular reuse of LWC components to achieve a different object model output using the same UI application elements, all while pulling information from the standard Salesforce architecture you know and love.

LWC considerations

Even though LWCs are the Brad Pitt of Salesforce development, they still might not impress the Shania Twains of the corporate world much. There are a few things to consider while creating LWCs:

- Even though LWCs are the modern browser-supported standard, older browsers really struggle with LWCs. If you have a company that still heavily relies on COBOL, don't try to whip out Netscape and expect LWCs to perform.

- Only certain utilities, base components, APIs, and HTML concepts are supported by LWCs! Check developer guides before building any architecture.

- LWCs can have difficulty with **Node Package Manager** (**NPM**) dependencies, which is a framework repository for JS.

- Exception Handling can be different from Aura, so review nuances that might impact your paradigms.

- Some standard Salesforce components have really specific, inflexible use cases (for example, the case record component and the banner headline component).

- Always consider UX when laying out a page! Even though LWCs can load independently and you can set filtering on those components, overloading a page with too many LWCs can still create latency.

LWCs are the house for modern Salesforce UI development and it's clear that adherence to modern web standards isn't going away. With every seasonal release, Salesforce is adding more and more capabilities and standard components to the LWC offering and library, slowly replacing the work it produced with Aura Components. However, an LWC can coexist with an Aura Component, and even interact with it, making it a very flexible standard.

Wait! We said that there were three modern components, so how can we reach the conclusion that the LWC is the way forward if there's one more component to contemplate? Let's dig into the last component type to see where we land on our overall build.

Lightning Web Runtime Components

Remember how we said that the mingling of the terms Lightning Component, Aura Component, LWC, and Lightning runtime component can get really confusing? Perhaps the worst offender of this nomenclature jam in the modern era is the nuances between an LWR and an LWC. To be as confusing as humanly possible, an LWR is a subset of an LWC. An LWR is just an open-source component designed to place LWCs in places beyond the propriety Salesforce properties, such as Experience Cloud, Site.com, or force.com. An LWR has the capacity to host LWCs outside of a Salesforce property or standalone application, and while it's an open-source framework that is currently considered a vehicle for clean runtime, it's still part of the LWC family.

The LWR takes the LWC beyond the confines of Salesforce's licensure ecosystem as a high-performing component that's flexible in several contexts. An LWR is what's considered **headless architecture**, meaning it can operate without backend architecture. This means it's not as tied to Salesforce as the standard LWC; it's more widely aimed at web application development instead of at the Salesforce family.

However, the LWR is designed with efficiency in mind and with much more minimal CPU usage than the traditional LWC or Aura Component. An LWR is a lightweight, ultra-fast component that relies on a dynamic data layer that operates in near-real time, with the capacity to handle way more concurrent users and page hits than an otherwise unauthenticated Experience Cloud site with native Lightning Components might tolerate.

Salesforce brags that an LWR can render a page in under a second, and reiterates that the LWR doesn't have the same GitHub NPM challenges that a standard LWC does. This means that you can publish select page elements at a time with an LWR, unlike a standard LWC or Aura site, where you have to group publish everything. Additionally, an LWR offers features such as publish time freezing and HTTP caching, which allow the browser to save information and choose when it renders. Finally, LWRs can leverage the evolving Salesforce CMS workspaces, so you can share content between an LWR and the Salesforce CMS.

To put it in very simple terms: an LWR is designed for *true websites and public applications*, whereas LWCs are mostly intended for *internal Salesforce products* such as Sales and Service Cloud, which you'd access behind authentication with typical license types. Of course, there's co-mingling between the two, so let's talk through some considerations you should review before building on LWRs.

Considerations

We'll state it one more time: the chief use case of an LWR versus an LWC or Aura is its flexibility in public websites or non-Salesforce applications. However, you can still use LWRs behind authentication. Here are a few things to think about:

- For Experience Cloud templates, the Build Your Own LWC is about the most bare-bones template there is. You will need to build your own custom design for everything.

- Your developers need to be very familiar with Salesforce DX to leverage LWRs. They also need to know LWCs well, too.

- LWRs work best with true websites, portals, and microsites.

- You can nest an LWC into an Aura Component if you need to, but you can't nest an LWR.

- Since it is very new and designed for external applications, not everything works in LWR components.

- LWR sites have a symbiotic relationship with Salesforce CMS and can be extremely beneficial if you're using Salesforce CMS.

- If you want your site to look like it's designed in Salesforce by leveraging standard components, an LWR might not be an efficient choice, since you will likely have to recode elements that are already in an LWC.

Now that you know the design principles and philosophy behind LWRs, when does it make sense to migrate LWCs to an LWR on an Experience Cloud build? Let's look into that.

When to switch from LWCs to LWRs

OK, so we've seen a lot of buzzwords that make an LWR sound way better than an LWC as a concept, but we know LWRs aren't always appropriate. What should we do when we're trying to guide our developers on what to build?

Let's take our sample company, *Delivery International*, into consideration. We will think about a good time to counsel them on the use of an LWR component as they contemplate the creation of their two net new sites: their partner portal and their End Consumer Experience Cloud site. As mentioned, they've decided on using the Standard Partner and Support templates for their builds, but they're researching how to overcome the **Salesforce Lightning Design System** (**SLDS**) entirely if Dalbert in marketing comes back with an incredibly specific UX request and site rendering needs.

If you have the need for an ultra-fast site *and* you don't want to design with even a hint of Salesforce style but do want to leverage Salesforce data, an LWR is the way to go. In that instance, it's worth upgrading your LWCs to an LWR or starting with a new LWR site entirely. Additionally, if you have public websites you want to decouple from Salesforce, LWR is a good option for you.

However, *Delivery International* weighed the options between going for an LWR from the beginning instead of LWCs, and the extremely protracted dev time of creating LWRs from scratch instead of using one of the more fleshed-out templates has both Dalbert in marketing and Kinley in sales agreeing that it would take too long to get to market. They're going to stick with the pre-baked templates, knowing that they'll be easier to maintain. However, Dalbert is asking that any microsites the marketing department requests in the future be fully custom, so we'll assist him with a fully LWR site when the time comes.

Switching from LWCs to LWRs isn't the only migration strategy you need to think about when it comes to the long-term maintenance of your Experience Cloud site. You will also have to think about when to make the move from Aura to Lightning if you have existing Aura sites.

Transitioning from Aura to Lightning

Now that you know when an LWR could make more sense than an LWC, let's tackle the elephant in the room: Aura is a dated standard and if you have a highly customized Aura site, you will need to plan its life cycle.

Salesforce prides itself on its relevance within the modern tech stack, and it tries to keep abreast of current technologies and functionalities. Consequently, it is slowly abandoning the Aura standard in favor of LWCs and LWRs. While it's highly unlikely Salesforce will ever truly "shut off" Aura, especially considering it currently has sites built on it, it will slow down its support of legacy languages over time. It is therefore a best practice to transition to more modern languages where sensible. However, Tabs and Visualforce, a dated standard that was replaced over 10 years ago, is still available for use in Salesforce. So, when does it make sense to transition away from an otherwise stable component?

Our sample company, *Delivery International*, has a legacy Experience Cloud site that it inherited from an acquisition of Tiddlywinks Pizza. It's a non-authenticated Build Your Own Aura site dedicated to its non-profit: educating children in Latin America about the health benefits of pizza. This Experience Cloud site, referred to as ProxyPizza, has both Lightning and Aura Components. Our head of quality, Anna, has relayed to us that users are experiencing slow performance on the site. Anna wants to know if this is because there are Aura Components on the site and thinks we should migrate Aura Components over to a newer standard. Let's take a look at what Anna is reporting:

- Certain components on the page are loading really slowly
- Some components will load quickly but struggle to pull relevant data inside the component
- The site tends to crash or lag during high-traffic seasons
- Ever since the acquisition, few internal developers can support the Aura Components

Anna also wants us to asses whether this site might be better as a microsite instead of a custom Aura site. She is also exploring hosting the ProxyPizza site on AWS instead of Salesforce.

Now that we know what the pain points are, let's review each point and see whether it makes sense to transition the ProxyPizza site over to LWR and LWC components. One thing we will keep in mind is that sometimes, the answer is no and we need to rethink either the requirements or the way in which we architected the component to begin with. There may be more efficient methods of how to make calls. Let's walk through the decision criteria.

When to make the move

The major categories you need to review as you decide when to pull the trigger largely involve five questions you will need to ask yourself:

- Do I have high-volume performance needs or considerations?

- Will this component need to be used beyond the Salesforce Ecosystem?

- How custom do I need to make these components?

- Do I have really complex UI needs such as animations?

- Do I have license or resource limitations?

Let's review these questions in light of Anna's concerns:

- **Concern 1: Certain components on the page are loading really slowly.**

  Component latency can fall into the first four question buckets. If slow component load time is your major concern and if that concern is significant enough that you're losing clients over it, it might be time to ditch Aura. Aura is going to be slower than LWC or LWR, and it will be limited in what you can do for customization and animation.

- **Concern 2: Some components will load quickly but struggle to pull relevant data inside the component.**

  While this might seem like the same issue as Concern 1, there's nuance here because this is likely an API or data issue. You need to discern what your performance needs are for this component and see whether the issue is the component or the source data. If there's a ton of code on top of the object you're querying within Salesforce, it may be worth reviewing the automation around that before you ever touch a component, and then reviewing your query structure within the component.

  If your custom object structure is really clunky, it may be time to make significant architectural changes and migrate data so record relationships are smoother. If the component is built against an API external to Salesforce, consider transitioning from an Aura Component to an LWR, especially if that component will be public-facing at some point in the future.

- **Concern 3: The site tends to crash at high volume times.**

  Before you can properly answer any of those five questions, you need to dig into why the site is crashing. There could be many causes behind the crashes: are you having code errors? Are there DNS issues with your domain name? Are you getting malicious external attacks that purposely slow down your site? If you investigate and discover that the answer is genuine traffic spikes that you need to plan for, then you need to run an audit of all your components and see which ones could be causing the lag. You also need to consider whether it would make sense to put your site behind authentication and a license structure, so target users never experience interruption. Failing all those considerations, it may be time to move to LWCs or LWRs to prevent crashes.

- **Concern 4: Few internal developers can support the Aura Components.**

  This is a tricky one, as maintaining knowledge of a legacy code base does have its advantages in an enterprise system. However, if you're transitioning away from a code base, it would be worth collating your release notes and recording knowledge transfer handoffs so they're easy to access. This concern most clearly falls into resourcing limitations, and you may need to come up with a strategy to augment your team's knowledge to support until you are able to transition a site away from Aura and onto LWC or LWR.

- **Concern 5: Should this site be a microsite and potentially hosted on another platform?**

  If the use case doesn't involve user-specific interactions that would require attaching transactions on the site to a specific account, you don't need authentication or to buy licenses. Furthermore, if you're thinking about retiring this site as a vestige of an acquisition, it might not make sense to transition it over to a microsite or change its hosting since this site already exists and you're planning on folding it, anyway. However, in the future, consider creating sites such as this as a microsite, work with your internal IT and architecture teams to determine the most sensible place to host temporary sites, and use LWRs as your base component.

If you've run through these questions for your specific use case and you feel it's time to move to Lightning, let's talk about how to prepare.

Transition considerations and preparation

Now that you've decided that you need to turn these Aura Components into LWCs, how do you prepare?

The first thing you need to do is *review your current enterprise tech stack*. Are there APIs or significant SSO changes coming from other departments that may impact your component behavior, or that your component behavior may impact? Stay in contact with your friends in other tech teams to make sure your changes aren't inadvertently impacting other parts of your organization or could be impacted by changes to other data systems that your components call on. Note that you will most likely be unable to migrate components from a managed package, so review your needs there, too.

Now that you know the arena you're planning in, *take an inventory of all your custom components* and pull all your existing documentation on them (if you have any). You need to review their structure, especially if there are complex components with nesting in them. This won't be a line-to-line transformation, so understanding how the existing components work will be critical to your design process in LWC or LWR.

After identifying which components need to move, it's time to *design your new components*. There are multiple resources that can assist you in this design process, and we always advise users to review offerings on **appexchange.com** before creating something from scratch. Check the Salesforce Developer resources and dig through forums to see whether other people have attempted your build before as you design.

The best way to start a transition from Aura to LWC is to *practice on a component that is UI-only* and not one that is nested, or calling information from Salesforce or other APIs. Note that the most effective migrations come from component trees, which are components within components. However, also note that those are much easier to break than a single component.

We didn't touch on the specific component bundles that comprise Aura and Lightning components, but your first step will be to *migrate a bundle file*, which includes markup, the controller, a helper, a renderer, CSS, documentation, and design files. There are some substantial changes in Aura for data binding, so be sure you review the differences and plan accordingly.

Test, test and test again! Due to the linguistic differences between Aura and Lightning, transitioning a component isn't always straightforward. Different layers of testing are absolutely key in this endeavor. Make sure that your developers are documenting their unit testing and are going through code reviews. Have another party run QA under several different constraints to ensure that an extra set of eyes is looking at potential breakage, doing everything from browser testing to load testing to stress testing and end-to-end. Don't neglect **User Acceptance Testing** (UAT) either – your product specialists might catch things the tech teams have missed.

Plan and communicate your release! Even if end users might not see the difference between your old component and the new one, it is worth communicating with your users that changes that should speed up their site experience are on the way.

Push it live. Make sure you have an iron-clad rollback plan in place, and then push your new components during an off-hour for your organization. Create a plan for what you need to walk through to run a final end-to-end test to ensure that your build is doing what it needs to.

Of course, even though Salesforce is unlikely to truly kill Aura Components, subsequent releases will have less and less support for them, coupled with frequent calls for modernization. Be advised that the migration process isn't a quick one, so be sure to build an ample amount of time for discoveries and testing into your transition plan.

How to make a page with declarative components

Now that you know how and when to use the Aura, LWC, and LWR components, let's talk through how you'd create a standard page. Many of the low-code Experience Cloud templates are still built on Aura Components, and you should know how to work through the basic declarative page creation. So let's jump in!

To start, navigate to the **Digital Experiences** tab in **Setup**. Find **All Sites** and locate the **Builder** link for the site you wish to create a page on. If you don't have any Digital Experience sites, you need to set one up. Refer back to *Chapter 5, Understanding Experience Cloud Templates*. Assuming you have one ready to go, click on the **Builder** link to launch **Experience Builder**.

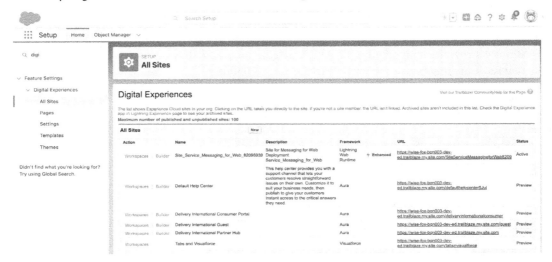

Figure 6.1: How to launch Experience Builder

Congratulations on launching **Experience Builder**! Let's build a new page. Click the **Home Page** dropdown in the top-left corner. Navigate all the way to the blue bar at the bottom that says **New Page**. There, you will find a palette with all your native and custom page types.

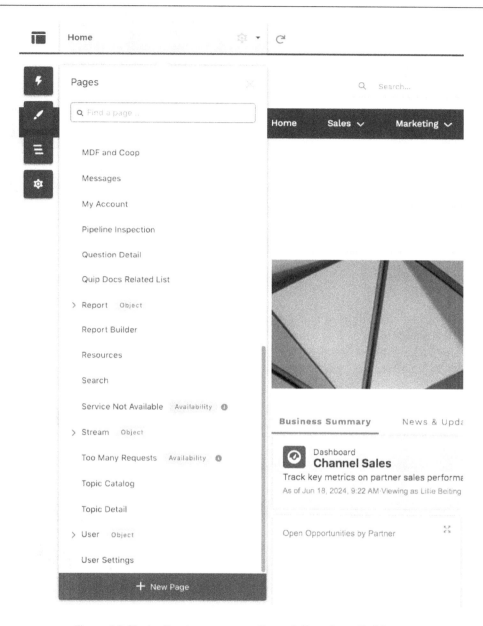

Figure 6.2: Navigating to a new page through Experience Builder

You will be given the option to create a Standard Page or an Object Page. A Standard Page follows a layout very similar to what you see in Salesforce CRM, with several flexible and predefined layouts that include sections on a page to accommodate your components. An Object Page gives you more creative freedom and exposes object layers inside of Experience Cloud. You can select your page type from the **New Page** modal in Experience Builder.

Figure 6.3: The Standard Page and Object Page options

Let's assume that you have decided that a Standard Page suits the development needs you have. You will first select **Standard Page**. This will take you to a screen where you can select a New Blank Page button. After clicking that, you will see the screen depicted in *Figure 6.4*. This screen allows you to pick a predefined layout.

Figure 6.4: Standard Page options

You can then name your page and get to work dragging components onto your template. Again, this is more of a declarative method of creating a page. With the custom components you are developing elsewhere, note that Salesforce administrators can pull those custom components into these pages. However, if you need more of a custom look or feel, let's look at Object Page design.

Speaking of the **Object Page** option, you're going to be able to pick from Salesforce objects that can be surfaced in Experience Cloud. Once you select that option, you will be guided through the process that follows:

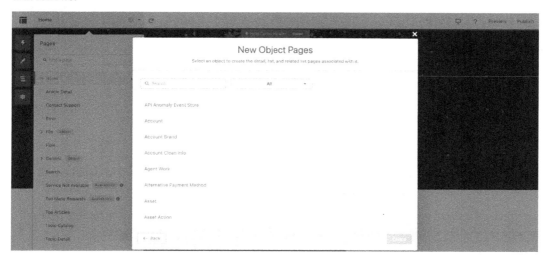

Figure 6.5: Selecting a new object for creating an Object Page

Once you have made your selections for the objects you need, Experience Builder will get to work building out your object pages.

Figure 6.6: Object Page options

You will have the option to pick a detail page that will look much like your standard detail layout in Sales or Service Cloud – a list view or a related list.

After you have created your page in either the standard or object page layouts, you will be able to select components to drag onto the page from the **Components** tab on the left-hand menu.

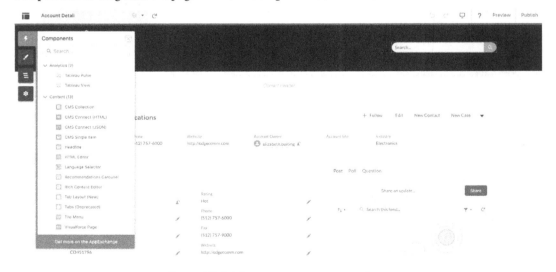

Figure 6.7: Adding components to templates

Within the components themselves, there is scope to further undertake configurations such as defining tabs or component audiences. We'll explore this further in *Chapter 9*, *Marketing Automation Setup*.

Summary

In this chapter, we reviewed the history of the site-oriented Salesforce UI and how it developed over the years. We reviewed the differences between an Aura component, a LWC, and a LWR component. We also reviewed what to consider when you're planning a migration from an Aura site to Lightning components. Finally, we gave you a quick tour of how to build a page with these components through the declarative toolset.

We know that the information in this chapter can be confusing and that there are a lot of nuances and overlap between these component standards. Deciding when to utilize one of these components instead of another can be very challenging, so we hope that this chapter has demystified this topic at a high level for those who might not have the intricate technical knowledge an architect would.

In a nutshell, the best way to think about the three contemporary web components is as follows:

- Aura was the first attempt at component architecture. It allowed visual applications to be built on top of the Salesforce CRM.

- LWC is the Salesforce component that follows modern web standards. During the transition over to LWC, LWC is allowed in Aura, but not the other way around.

- LWRs are the headless iteration of LWCs that extend Salesforce components beyond mere CRM applications.

We are aware that this may be somewhat of a gross oversimplification, but it's an easy way to think of the three component types and decide how to proceed. As always, please validate current technical standards against the Salesforce release notes or check with your Salesforce account representative, as Salesforce changes constantly.

As we conclude this chapter, we would like to remind you that this is just a chapter in a book on how to make Experience Cloud work for you, and it will never be as detailed as the developer guides and release notes that Salesforce releases. We highly encourage you to review the detailed technical documentation on the Salesforce Developer documentation site at `https://developer.salesforce.com/` or the seasonal release notes, which can be found at `https://help.salesforce.com/s/articleView?id=release-notes.salesforce_release_notes.htm&release=250&type=5`.

Now that you know how the core custom components work, you might be wondering how to automate screen experiences or custom UX through them. We will address how to make custom UX with both standard Salesforce automation and custom work in the next chapter, *Chapter 7*, *Leveraging Screen Flows versus Apex*.

Part 3: Human-Centric Development

In this part, you will define and design an Experience Cloud User Experience (UX) to incorporate the whole client journey, from guided screen input to support cases to Knowledge repositories and venturing into AI Chatbots and digital marketing. You will also learn how Experience Cloud can support your users in all aspects of their client journey.

This part has the following chapters:

- *Chapter 7, Leveraging Screen Flows versus Apex*
- *Chapter 8, Understanding Inputs – Emails, Chats, and Text Messages*
- *Chapter 9, Marketing Automation Setup*
- *Chapter 10, Leveraging Case Management and Knowledge Bases*

7

Leveraging Screen Flows versus Apex

Application design should be oriented around your users and making their lives as easy as possible so that they can engage with you. Critical to user-centric design is the idea of simplifying, streamlining, and enabling particular experiences you need your users to complete. Especially when it comes to repeated actions where you need a user to complete a formulaic series of steps, you should consider creating a digital experience tailored to make those actions as easy and as mindless as possible. After all, the essence of good design is ease of use, and the best navigation is the one a user doesn't even notice they're using.

Modern web development standards have blown the door wide open in terms of slick, guided custom experiences, and Salesforce hasn't missed the boat. From user registrations to case creation and product ordering, modern web design can package up information, pull information from databases, and dynamically change screen displays depending on data inputs. Engaging your users is integral to good UX, but the best UX is so good that it's unnoticeable. And where it makes sense, you should automate. Salesforce has a few options that can help you create and manage a guided experience for your users, but at the time of writing, the contemporary declarative mechanism is Salesforce Flow.

While we talked about the custom components and code types available in Salesforce in the previous chapter, **Salesforce Screen Flows** can dramatically enhance the UX of your Experience Cloud site by guiding users through a tailored, dynamic experience. It consists of a step-by-step UI that helps them input the information they need to accomplish tasks on your site. Salesforce released a tool known as **Lightning Flow** to declaratively create this custom screen experience, making it easy for developers or admins to configure. However, Salesforce Lightning Flow isn't appropriate for all custom step-by-step screen experiences, so it's sometimes wiser to use a custom Lightning component, CSS, and invocable Apex methods to accomplish the desired experience. This chapter reviews each technological approach, their trade-offs, and when it makes sense to go custom.

To aid in our learning journey, we're going to break our chapter into the following sections:

- Process use cases for a guided UX

- Salesforce Flow and Screen Flows

- Custom code – LWC, Apex, and CSS

- When to use custom code and Salesforce Screen Flows

- Summary and skills check

> **Note**
>
> In this chapter, we're going to review *Delivery International's* needs for custom experiences, including *Delivery International's* need to customize inputs by persona, and review. From a simple case entry that can use Salesforce Flow to an opportunity submission that uses custom code to a registration process that requires a combination of both, the many options for tailored UX within Experience Cloud will be dissected.

Process use cases for a guided UX

We cannot stress this enough: you need to define a clear process before you automate or build a guided UI for anything. Do not throw automation at a wall and see what sticks just because Salesforce makes automation easy; you will only create data holes for your end users and more work for your internal users. Whether you're digitizing a workflow that's currently manual or migrating a workflow from an existing property into Salesforce, you need to think through your process and translate it cleanly into a digital experience. You also need to be prepared to create or modify your existing architectural model, depending on what you discern from your research as you work on a process.

When you're thinking about aspects of your customer experience to automate or guide through a screen flow, focus on specific problems. Not everything should be a guided UX or backed in automation; only processes that can be easily sequenced and repeated with minimal deviations should be automated. Now, that doesn't mean that you should only create a guided UX for easy processes – if you have decision logic, you can build complex logic with both **Salesforce Flow** and **Apex**, so long as there's a finite and clear amount of options. But any user behavior that could involve a scattered experience or access to only one aspect of record creation shouldn't be thrown into guided UX. Automation and a guided UX should be selective and sequential.

Not sure where to start when it comes to automation or creating a guided UX? There are a couple of places you can look for inspiration. First, talk to your internal stakeholders. Dalbert in marketing has a set amount of information he needs when users sign up so that he can market to them. Over in product, Kinley has some pain points regarding her team managing franchisee opportunities. When we checked in with quality, Anna noticed data gaps in common case entry workflows.

As we work with our three stakeholders, let's map out their respective processes. *Don't forget about data that may already exist in Salesforce or systems connected to it that could empower your design as you respond to the requirements.*

When consumers sign up to order pizza with *Delivery International* through their Experience Cloud portal, Dalbert wants to capture a few relevant pieces of information. He wants the following aspects:

- Users to enter their email so it can be checked against the rest of the database to ensure another record doesn't exist for them.

- Users to enter their zip code first to ensure they're in a market we can deliver to. If they aren't, Dalbert wants to stop them from registering and add them to a marketing list to let them know when franchises open near them.

- Basic demographic information (name, preferred name, gender, ethnicity, and birthday).

- Communication preferences.

- A place to create a password.

- A place to store their favorite credit card.

Let's review what a sample process flow for Dalbert's requirements would look like:

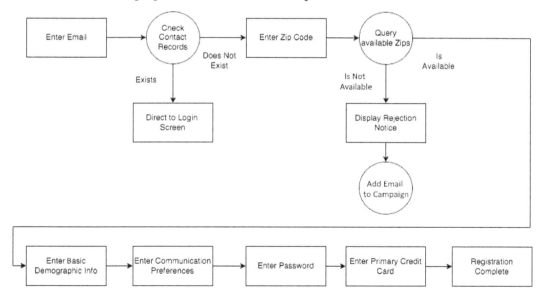

Figure 7.1: Sample process flow – consumer signup

OK, so we know what Dalbert wants for our End Consumers. Now, let's review what Kinley needs over in product. She needs certain information pre-populated in an opportunity for franchisees as they enter information for new locations, in addition to a custom visual in her opportunities. Kinley wants the following:

- The franchisee number to appear on the opportunity automatically

- Different product types to populate, depending on the geolocation of the prospective franchisee

- A custom visual of the Opportunity Stage to be dynamically generated based on the number of franchise stores already open and their billing amounts

Let's review a sample process flow for Kinley's requirements:

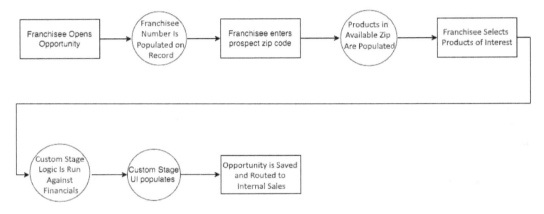

Figure 7.2: Sample process flow – franchisee's sales needs

Now that we know where we could build a guided UI for our franchisees, let's turn our attention to Anna. Anna keeps seeing cases regarding problematic deliveries come in without clear descriptions of what happened, leading to unnecessary escalations for support. To address this, she wants the following aspects:

- Users to verify that the information on their contact record is the best information to reach them at

- Users to select one or more issues from a picklist and a custom set of fields to display for each use picklist value

- A survey to appear after a case is entered

Let's review a sample process flow for Anna's requirements:

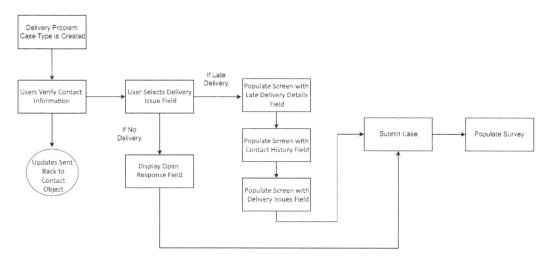

Figure 7.3: Sample process flow – service needs

Even though we know what each of our stakeholders is looking for, don't forget to support your decision to automate with data! Leverage reporting and tools such as Google Analytics to determine where users are getting stuck in your digital experiences, and look at critical information such as API calls and cross-object logic for areas you could simplify or improve. Remember, you will likely have to update your architecture beyond just UI to accommodate the process you're trying to automate. So, ensure you call out any data gaps you may have to address after you've nailed down your process.

> **Note**
>
> Salesforce also has a native feature known as **In-App Guidance** that allows you to create guided popups over a Salesforce UX. These can be used to guide new users through your app or to show off new features to your existing users. While we highly recommend considering In-App Guidance if you have an Experience Cloud site with a steady stream of new users, this chapter isn't referencing that specific feature. When we talk about automation and guided UX, we're talking more about more concrete inputs and outcomes powered by Flow, Components, and Apex instead of training tours.

Salesforce Flow is now the modern standard for declarative automation. Before now, Salesforce's point-and-click automation options were **Workflow Rules** or **Process Builder**. This means you would have to convert or retire any Process Builders or Workflow Rules you had operating in your system to accommodate your new processes, whether they're Flow or Apex. Let's take a look at Salesforce Flows and automation in Salesforce.

Salesforce Flow and Screen Flows

Salesforce Flow is Salesforce's modern *point-and-click automation tool*, but native automation tools in Salesforce have come a long way. Because Salesforce is a managed software that has always marketed itself on its ability to use clicks before code, Salesforce has had a few tools over the years that allow users to extend their software. Long before there was Salesforce Flow, there were Workflow Rules. Workflow Rules were introduced in 2001, two years after the creation of Salesforce itself. Workflow Rules allowed administrators to set automations on simple criteria such as field changes, or to complete actions such as sending emails at a scheduled time. While this kind of automation may sound primitive now, it was revolutionary for its time.

Following the release of Workflow Rules, Salesforce opened up Apex to its clients in 2006. Released alongside Apex was its original UI language of VisualForce. Both of these languages allowed admins and developers to extend the Salesforce platform with code and create new automations beyond what Workflow Rules could offer. In 2009, Salesforce released the first version of Salesforce Flow, which was called Visual Workflow. Visual Workflow was the first truly visual point-and-click tool Salesforce released, and it allowed administrators to create screens on top of business processes through a graphical UI using decision points, loops, and if/then logic. When Salesforce Lightning was released, Process Builder came with it. Process Builder was a souped-up version of Workflow Rules with a Lightning interface. Process Builder allowed for more complex process automation without having to resort to coding in Apex, although it offered very little in the way of UI automation.

Finally, in 2019, Salesforce released Lightning Flow, a much more advanced version of Visual Workflow. Lightning Flow included **Flow Builder** and **Flow Orchestrator**, drag-and-drop tools that allowed administrators to set up custom UIs that could interplay with processes built within Flow, in addition to processes built elsewhere in Process Builder and Apex. Lightning Flow allowed for far more complexity than Process Builder and Visual Workflow itself. In 2021, Salesforce rebranded Lightning Flow to Salesforce Flow, dramatically enhanced what it could do, and announced that it was the path forward for all point-and-click UI and process automation.

The reason we've provided a history lesson here is that you might have inherited an organization with some of these legacy builds still within it. The odds of a legacy organization coming with zero historical processes are pretty low, but it's not a complete unicorn. It's important to know how these solutions evolved so that you can translate them into the most efficient, sustainable technology as your organization matures. We should also note that Salesforce has heavily invested in another tool known as Omnistudio, which is a rebranding of software previously known as Vlocity. While Omnistudio is somewhere between a Flow and custom code and can be used for dynamic UI, it is not yet fully integrated into Salesforce at the time of writing. Therefore, let's talk about what kinds of Flows are available for use and when to use them.

Salesforce Flow can now handle everything from simple processes to complex logic to invocable Apex to Screen Flows to APIs. Flows are built in a drag-and-drop interface where elements such as decisions, screens, API calls, and record updates can be incorporated into an automation. Let's take a look at a sample Flow:

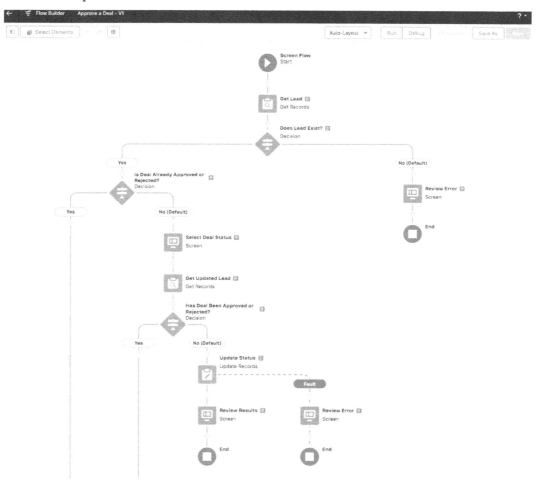

Figure 7.4: Flow Builder palate example of a lead approval process

While this example includes Screen Flows, not all flows are Screen Flows – they can be automations running in the background at a specific time interval, or from record-based criteria.

Flows fall into several categories and can be accessed from **Flow Builder** in Salesforce's settings. See *Figure 7.5*:

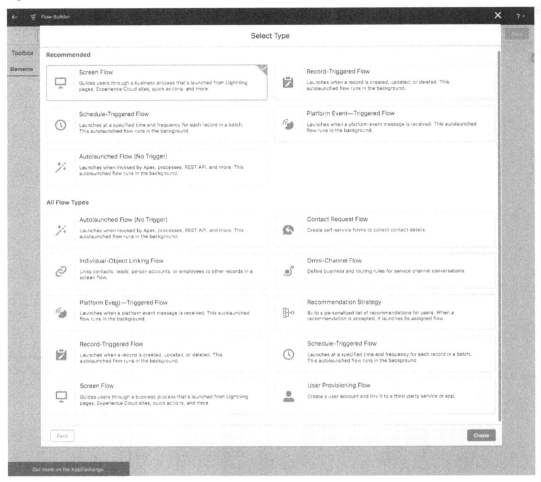

Figure 7.5: Launching Flow Builder

The Flow Builder palette in *Figure 7.5* shows all the various Flow types available, but conceptually, all Flow options roll up into six kinds of Flows. Let's take a look at what each of them does and how they can relate to UI.

Screen Flows

The most relevant to this chapter, **Screen Flows** are designed to create an interactive UI that prompts your users to enter information. While Screen Flows can reference Flow automations underneath them and even Apex and API calls, at their simplest, they allow admins to create guided user input across multiple screens. With the native ability to navigate backward and forward from screen to screen, they are great for data entry, surveys and questionnaires, onboarding, or any guided experience you want your users to undergo.

Screen Flows can be used to collect net-new information, and they can even reference existing record information from Salesforce or an API. Screen Flows have native styling options, but custom solutions such as CSS can be used in tandem with a Screen Flow so that you can style them to your needs. Let's look at a pre-baked Screen Flow:

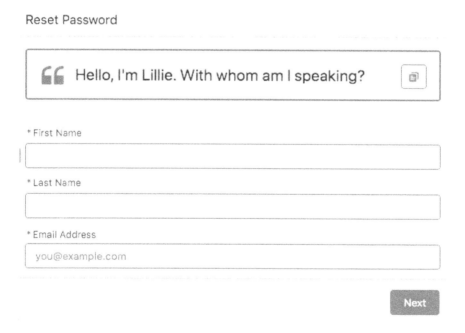

Figure 7.6: Example of a Screen Flow

Note that there are many pre-baked Screen Flows available in Salesforce that are designed to help with common tasks, such as the one shown in the preceding figure for a password reset.

Record-Triggered Flows

A **Record Triggered Flow** is going to feel most similar to Process Builder or Workflow Rules if you're familiar with those tools. A Record-Triggered Flow runs when a record is deleted, updated, or created, and it can do things such as send notifications, create business logic, update multiple records, or validate data. Record Trigger Flows can be used in conjunction with other Flows, in addition to Apex and APIs. These kinds of Flows can be executed before and after saving a record, although each kind has its benefits, depending on your use case. Record-Triggered Flows are often the powerhouse of automation working behind the scenes in Salesforce as they can alleviate the burden of repeated tasks by automating data entry in the background. They can also handle before and after events and process data immediately or asynchronously. This can be handy when you have complex UI needs that require external API calls or data validation across other objects.

Schedule-Trigger Flows

A **Schedule-Trigger Flow** runs at specific intervals and times and can be used for recurring processes. If there's a bulk data update you need, or you have time-oriented notifications that you need to go out based on criteria, a Schedule-Trigger Flow might be a better option than custom code. A great use case for a Schedule-Trigger Flow would be to send a notification regarding a standard maintenance window.

Platform Event-Triggered Flows

A **Salesforce Platform Event** is a mechanism within Salesforce that allows Salesforce to change data in real time within itself and with external platforms. This is somewhat of a gross oversimplification, but a Platform Event is essentially a message within Salesforce that creates integration patterns and capabilities, and you're most likely to hear about it in terms of APIs. A Platform Event-Triggered Flow is an automation that runs in response to an event to update data in real time or run complex updates asynchronously. These kinds of Flows can do a moderate amount of data transformation from an API event and are especially useful for standing up APIs quickly or feeding the payload from an API to a UI.

Platform events are not to be confused with salesforce Events and their subsequent actions, a feature available for `site.com` that does allow for some animation and dynamism in the `site.com` UI. You also shouldn't mistake this for Salesforce events such as Dreamforce. Once again, we wish Salesforce would think about the way it names things to make it easier on us mere groundlings who grovel at the base of the Salesforce Tower.

Autolaunched Flows

An **Autolaunched Flow** runs automatically based on certain conditions, and it lurks quietly in the background until it's called by another Flow, API, or code. Autolaunched Flows are similar to Record-Triggered Flows in terms of their ability to handle complex processes, but the primary difference between the two is that Autolaunched Flows are designed for automation that isn't tied to a specific record. Autolaunched Flows do not have a UI component and do not support screens, but they can be kicked off by UI elements such as buttons.

Subflows

A **Subflow** is a Flow within a Flow and can be an Autolaunched Flow, a Record-triggered Flow, or a Screen Flow referenced by a parent Flow. Subflows can be modular, allowing administrators to build a Flow behavior once but use it across other Flows. Subflows are especially great for dealing with failure behavior in a Flow logic. For example, if you build a Screen Flow that allows users to cancel their request at any point (and you want the records they were filling out to be deleted, not saved), you can reuse the same Subflow at any point to delete the set of records.

Even though Screen Flow is the only true UI tool within Flow, it's worth knowing about other Flow mechanisms because they can connect to code and Screen Flows to power a custom UI. Flows can also accommodate advanced error handling and interplay with native and custom Lightning or Aura components. Flows can get intricate and are extremely powerful automation tools if they're wielded properly. We suggest checking out the Trailhead or Salesforce Developer documentation if you'd like a more in-depth understanding of Salesforce Flow.

Let's think back to *Delivery International* and Anna's requirement for both franchisee and End Consumers to verify their contact information, custom fields to be displayed after each picklist value, and a survey to appear after submitting a case. Anna's process requires fairly simple query logic to native Salesforce objects such as Case and Contact, in addition to the use of native Salesforce surveys. Consequently, her requested UX is easily answered by a Screen Flow that calls a Record-Triggered Subflow to kick off surveys after the case-oriented information.

Now that we know the basics of Salesforce Flow, we're ready to explore our other automation options.

Custom code – LWC, Apex, and CSS

Salesforce Flow isn't the only way to extend a dynamic UI and create complex automations in Salesforce; you can also go the custom code route. Perhaps Dalbert in marketing has given you really strict design instructions that require your site to look the least like Salesforce as possible, or Maggie in finance needs you to make complex calls to the ERP and update several financial records inside Salesforce based on user behavior. Maybe you have animations, or you need to make part of your page read-only.

While Salesforce Flow can accommodate some of these requests up to a certain point, Salesforce Apex is designed to handle significant complexity that requires advanced coding techniques. If using Flow doesn't make sense for your guided UI, you can also look to LWC, Apex, and **Cascading Style Sheets** (**CSS**) to get the job done. When you go the custom route, you'll likely need to use a combination of all three. Let's break them down and explain their use cases.

LWC

Since we heavily reviewed LWC in *Chapter 6*, we're only calling out LWC here because of its integral role in custom UI in Salesforce. Simply put, an LWC is going to be the housing mechanism for custom automation and visuals, so you will have to build a custom UI automation with one or more LWCs in mind. While we're more focused on Apex in this section, note that LWCs can also integrate with Flows.

Many standard LWCs do not allow for much dynamism, but some allow developers a little freedom to customize and tailor. Here's a quick overview of a few native LWCs that you can make interactive:

LWC Name	Description
lightning-record-form	A form-style component that allows users to create and update records.
lightning-carousel	Allows you to rotate images. It can be used for an image gallery.
lightning-slider	Allows you to slide a button across a range.
lightning-file-upload	A file uploader component.
lightning-tree	Displays data in a hierarchy or tree-like structure.
lightning-input	Allows for input from primitive Salesforce data types, such as email, phone number, and date.
lightning-datatable	Creates a table display that can leverage features such as searching, inline editing, and sorting.

Table 7.1: Examples of standard LWCs with dynamism

The standard components listed in *Table 7.1* are by no means a comprehensive list, but we always recommend checking whether a native component will work for one of your requirements before creating a custom one. If you're considering a use case you believe to be standard across many business applications, you may also want to check out AppExchange and see what they have available. You should also consider AppExchange before you begin coding Apex.

Apex

Salesforce is powered by the language of Apex, which is a Java derivative. **Apex** empowers developers to extend functionality in a completely customizable way, allowing them to write complex business logic that might not be natively available in a declarative Salesforce tool.

Since this is not a guide to writing Apex triggers or invocable methods, we're going to review the high-level features and functionalities of Apex rather than dig into specific code. For more information on how to write Apex, visit Trailhead's and Salesforce's developer resources.

Here are a couple of key features and benefits of Apex regarding UIs and automation:

Feature	Description
Complex logic	Can handle advanced calculations and intricate conditional logic that Flow cannot review.
Bulk processing	Can optimize transactions against large volumes of records and complex object models efficiently, ensuring CPU and governor limits aren't hit
Speed and performance	Can allow you to select how your code executes under certain conditions, which can execute more quickly than declarative options.
Development via an **integrated development environment** (IDE)	Can be created as code from a **command-line interface** (CLI).
Git repository compatibility	Can allow you to easily check code into a git repository, such as GitHub. Flows can also be checked into a git repository.
Granular controls	Can enforce cleaner error handling or record rollbacks if not all conditions are met.

Table 7.2: Benefits of Apex

The benefits of Apex are numerous, but they can be broadly categorized into the ability to custom-tailor how your code behaves and executes. As a reminder, Apex is a nuanced, niche language that can take even experienced Java developers some time to get used to. Apex best practices are very involved, so be sure to research your approach before committing to it. If you know you require complex UI work in Sales, Service, or Experience Cloud, ensure you have the right skill sets to hand. A standard web developer may struggle with Apex triggers and methods without sufficient training.

CSS

CSS can be used in conjunction with Apex and custom LWCs, and it will be your main tool for some of the more visually astounding elements of a dynamic UI. CSS is a common web development language that's used for UIs, and the vast majority of modern web applications employ CSS to create interactive, beautiful experiences.

CSS is a must for creating a truly custom visual or dynamic experience in Salesforce Experience Cloud, and you will need to use it with LWCs and Aura if you want to create a more sophisticated, dynamic experience.

Here are a few capabilities for tailored, stylized dynamism that CSS can offer you:

Dynamic Behavior	Description
Animations and transitions	Animates or creates visual engagement with components on the page
Hover effects	Changes style or behavior if a cursor hovers over a button
Modals/popups	Screens within the application that allow for custom behavior, depending on navigation or input
Sticky elements	Components that can stick to the top or side of a screen as a user scrolls
Tooltips	A mechanism for displaying more information as a user hovers

Table 7.3: Examples of CSS customization

CSS customization is endless and *Table 7.2* barely scratches the surface of design possibility. Because CSS is a web standard, there are many resources for learning, researching, and debugging CSS. Check out Packt's book, *Mastering CSS*, or consider their HTML and CSS course if you'd like to learn more about what CSS can do for your web applications.

Now that we know what our options are for custom development, let's think about Kinley's request for our franchisee site. She wants a franchisee number to appear on the Opportunity record automatically, different product types to populate depending on the geolocation of the prospect franchise, and a custom visual of the Opportunity Stage to be generated dynamically based on the number of franchise stores already open and their billing amounts.

Since Kinley's first requirement likely involves a simple Salesforce formula from an Account record to an Opportunity record, it may feel tempting to choose a Flow and call it a day. However, Kinley needs a custom visual different from the Salesforce Path Lightning component to house the Opportunity Stage when it changes, in addition to some complex logic to generate a stage change. Because of this requirement alone, we know we need to create a custom LWC and Apex logic.

Furthermore, *Delivery International* stores product information in an ERP, in addition to its financial data. While some of this information is referenced inside their Salesforce instance, *Delivery International* has corporations as clients who own a few hundred *Delivery International* franchises. Because there is an excessive amount of Account records that the system will have to query to pull financial information from within Salesforce to match against data retrieved from an API call, and because product information also lives in an ERP, you will likely hit CPU limits if you don't package your calls and your logic properly. Therefore, you will need to take advantage of custom Apex and LWC.

As a reminder, any time you go custom, you will be introducing more complexity into your organization and your enterprise architecture. It may be worth meeting with Kinley to see if the standard Path component would meet her needs instead of the fully custom one she is requiring, but you will have to use Apex to handle the complex product and financial logic she requires.

> **Tip**
> Complexity isn't a bad thing and it shouldn't dissuade you from customizing where necessary, but remember that any custom code in your instance will be one more thing you have to regression test against and account for during new releases. Save your future self and developers' tears and hours of work and don't forget to document your customization!

With our custom callouts in hand, let's look at what automation tool you should choose.

When to use custom code and Salesforce Screen Flows

Now that you know the fundamental differences between Salesforce Flow and LWC, Salesforce Apex, and CSS, when is an appropriate time to use them? And when is an appropriate time to use a combination of both?

The general rule of thumb in Salesforce is to exhaust declarative methods before moving over to code. Salesforce has an incredible array of native options that solve most common business issues, and it's highly possible they already have a setting, a Lightning layout, or a declarative solution that solves the business issue you're facing. Before you go custom, do your research to prevent inadvertently introducing unintended redundancy into your system with code that could have been point-and-click. Therefore, you should use Salesforce Flow whenever feasible or advisable. However, as we mentioned earlier, Flow does have its limitations. We'll walk down the path of these limitations with caution in this section.

When to use custom code instead of Salesforce Flow

Salesforce Flow has grown in terms of its capabilities over the years, and Salesforce will no doubt add to them with every release as technology improves. However, there will always be a place for custom code in the Salesforce ecosystem, because Flow isn't the right answer for every use case.

So, when should you use custom Apex instead of Flow for UI?

Here are a few scenarios where custom development is advisable:

- You have incredibly complicated business logic with several steps, conditions, or loops
- Speed and performance are critical and you need to optimize the order of your automation processes
- You're handling large volumes of data, or bulk operations on that data
- You have a heavily custom Salesforce instance that's already very code-heavy
- You have complex error handling, logging, and notification needs
- Your visual needs exceed the simple screen-to-screen functionality of Salesforce Flow

> **Tip**
> Note that there are Apex character code limits inside Salesforce and that you cannot endlessly code on top of your Salesforce organization. While you might be able to ask Salesforce to increase your Apex character limits, perform an audit of your organization before adding large amounts of code.

Remember Kinley's requirements for her franchisees? Even though her requirement for a custom component mandated a custom LWC instead of a Screen Flow, the system behavior she needed was extremely complex and hit the bounds of what Flows could do. The complexity of query logic to pull information from multi-tier accounts and their child records could easily cause your system to hit CPU governor limits if the loop logic takes too long or if the query has to travel across too many objects and records. There are mechanisms within Apex such as bulk processing (applying the same logic to multiple records) and optimized execution (deciding which automation goes before another) that can overcome huge query limitations, in addition to speeding up the time to return data.

Broadly speaking, if you're dealing with overly complex UI requirements and intricate query logic, it most likely makes sense to go custom instead of Flow. But, it sometimes makes sense to use a combination of both.

When to use a combination of custom code and Salesforce Flow

We've mentioned before that Flows can call custom code, and that custom code can kick off Flows. Since both can exist together, when does it make sense to create a combination of both?

If you're an organization that heavily relies on Flows already for automation, then it might make sense to simply have your Flow invoke Apex for certain use cases. Additionally, if you have a combination of Salesforce administrators and developers who work on your instance, you may wish to empower your workforce to build Flows first that call custom code.

Since Dalbert's demands are usually quite elaborate, let's think about his automation request. He would like the following on the End Consumer Experience-Cloud-guided UX:

- Users to enter their email so it can be checked against the rest of the database to ensure another record doesn't exist for them.
- Users enter their zip code first to ensure they're in a market we can deliver to. If they aren't, Dalbert wants to stop them from registering and add them to a marketing list to let them know when franchises open near them.
- Basic demographic information (name, preferred name, gender, and ethnicity birthday).
- Communication preferences.
- A place to create a password.
- A place to store their favorite credit card.

Dalbert has a great use case for a combination of Flows and Apex. Because he's interested in speed to market, he's willing to let us stylize the standard Salesforce Screen Flow so that we can build the guided UI within Flow Builder. While we can reference standard Sales and Service Cloud architecture with the request to check an email against other Contact records, enter demographic information, and store a password, we have to reference Marketing Cloud to create communication preferences and add users to a marketing list if they aren't in an existing area. Sending data to Marketing Cloud can also be done with a Record-Triggered Flow called by the Screen Flow. But in *Delivery International's* case, their payment processor is a third party that requires an API and an Apex method to transform and transport the encrypted data safely.

If you're going with a combination of Flow and Apex, make sure you aren't duplicating logic or creating code collisions. Be sure you're rigorously testing your Flow and your Apex to ensure no unexpected behavior or race conditions emerge. Always keep your governor limits in mind, and try to keep your code and flows modular and easy to manage.

It can be challenging to decide between custom development, Salesforce Flow, or a combination of both, but take the time to weigh the pros and cons. If it's a light enough lift, consider building a proof of concept you can stress test. As always, review your architectural requirements internally before moving forward with any designs.

Summary

Automation is one of the most complex aspects of the Salesforce ecosystem, but it can also be the difference between an incredible UX and a complete waste of development resources. Understanding where your users' pain points are and creating easier avenues of data collection and validation will make life easier for all your system users, both internal and external. If you've carefully identified your automation and UX logic, the payoff is worth it if you've created your logic thoughtfully and easily. Rigorous system regression testing and user acceptance testing will be critical to ensuring your guided UI and its underlying automation are behaving as intended.

As it always feels to be the case in Salesforce, there can be many ways to accomplish the same task, and automation is no exception. From the legacy tools of Workflow Rules and Process Builder to the modern standard of Flows and Apex, there are a variety of ways to build a beautiful, efficient UX for your users.

In this chapter, we reviewed the following aspects:

- How and when to automate
- The functionalities and uses of Salesforce Screen Flow
- Options for custom code in Salesforce Experience Cloud
- When to use Screen Flow, custom code, and a combination of the two

Your automation journey never ends after going live! As your organization grows in sophistication, you will likely need to expand your existing UX automations, or even add new ones. As your organization grows in maturity, continue to revisit your automation and UI options, and make sure you're leveraging the newest best practices where it makes sense.

In the next chapter, we'll explore other avenues of automation and integration: when to integrate emails, chats, texts, and other messaging inputs.

8

Understanding Inputs – Emails, Chats, and Text Messages

In today's interconnected world, customers expect to be able to do anything from anywhere. Long gone are the days of only being able to send a physical letter. Customers are now accustomed to instantaneous, excellent service from the device of their choice.

If you are moving to a true mobile-first environment, you are going to have to accept inputs into your work streams that could be from many different kinds of communication models. You will have to empower your service agents to be knowledge workers who can answer anything within seconds, not minutes or hours. On average, the human attention span has decreased from minutes to only seconds, owing to the instantaneous streams of information they can get at their fingertips. Consequently, they now expect multi-device customer service options as a default experience.

In this chapter, we will focus on the common lines of communication you would want to contain in a digital experience: emails, chats, and text messages. These aren't always out-of-the-box options, so we will also explore connections and/or products you will need to facilitate the interactions in your digital-first community. Finally, we will review some of the interconnected Service Cloud and Marketing Cloud configurations that will be needed to power your digital-first experience. To aid our learning journey, we are going to break things into the following sections:

- Communication leveraging Experience Cloud
- Implementing Salesforce Chat or third-party chat
- Implementing and managing Experience Cloud emails
- Implementing and managing text messaging

With so much to learn and so many decisions to make, we are going to kick start this party by talking through how we can communicate leveraging Experience Cloud.

Communication leveraging Experience Cloud

There are many approaches to communication that organizations can implement. No matter what grand strategy you have, you can boil a communication strategy down to having a push or pull methodology. With a **push methodology**, you are expecting people to log in to your application in order to receive information. With this methodology, you may have guessed it, you are pushing messages to people to give them a reason to log in or engage. Or maybe they don't even need to log in at all – maybe the message that was pushed out accomplishes your goal. With a **pull methodology**, users are volunteering to be communicated with by completing activities such as submitting their information into a lead form to acquire an e-book. However, the most common architecture in an organization is a combination of the two methods. This ensures that information is available to your end users when they log in, while simultaneously driving traffic to the application for a login.

Think of your favorite online store. The first time you visited, you were probably told that if you gave them your email address, you'd be rewarded with a coupon. These days, there may even be two steps to get that infamous 10% off. The second step involves giving them your cell number to opt into text messaging. Then, all of a sudden, you start receiving notifications of new products or sales aimed at driving traffic to the site in hopes that you will ultimately make repeat purchases. If that scenario of an email send and a text message follow-up sounds like requirements you've received, it's because it's a very common multi-channel communication experience.

The good news is, Experience Cloud can make the logged-in user a happy customer when it's partnered with Service Cloud. Enabling Self-Service features native to Service Cloud will provide customers with the critical ability to file items such as cases. From the Case object family, you can create records to track conversations across all mediums. In Experience Cloud, it is a necessity to leverage Salesforce's native self-help features if you want to enable multiple input channels.

In addition to the world of Case objects, you can also showcase custom objects or components. Let's say you want a message to appear to only a subset of people who log in. You can curate a home page that has a custom component on it that only displays when certain criteria are met, such as geolocation or client segment. Then, after the criteria are met, you can leverage a standard page component to display an image. That image can be any branded message. Let's show you step by step how you could build the display of a custom message to a subset of users.

The first thing we need to do is create our content! You can go two ways here:

- **Option 1 – Business Controlled Dynamic Content**: This route would require you to build a custom object. Once you have that custom object, you can create a field to function as an active flag on a record. So when a business partner creates content and flips the active flag, that content would be displayed to users. If they uncheck the box, it will no longer display. This won't be as visually appealing as graphic-based content.

- **Option 2 – Graphic Inlay Dynamic Content**: This route involves static content that would require a Salesforce Administrator to swap out in the Experience Builder. However, Graphic Inlay Dynamic Content will be more visually appealing to the customer.

For purposes of *Delivery International*, we are going to go with option 2. We don't expect the message to change that often, and visually, we want people to engage. When we get further down our roadmap, we may create something a little more advanced and customized.

The first step is to create whatever graphic you want to display. Now, let's assume Dalbert's devilishly clever marketing minds have created the perfect graphic. Let's head over to our digital site and drop that graphic onto the page. Once you have navigated to the page you want to put the component on, go to **Components** and search for `Rich Content Editor`. See *Figure 8.1*.

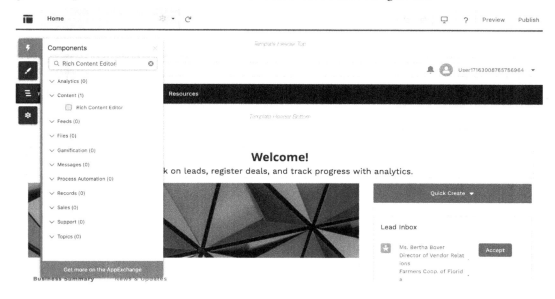

Figure 8.1: Rich Content Editor Component search

Now that you have your component, drag it over to the appropriate spot on the page. Once you drag it, you will get the option to edit the component. See *Figure 8.2*.

Figure 8.2: Rich Content Editor

For purposes of making the communication visual on the **Home** page, we are going to upload an image. Our image is the one we display frequently to let our franchisees know when we are hosting a webinar. Select the image item from the edit ribbon on the **Rich Content Editor** Component. You will then see the option to either select an image from your Salesforce library or upload an image. We will be uploading an image.

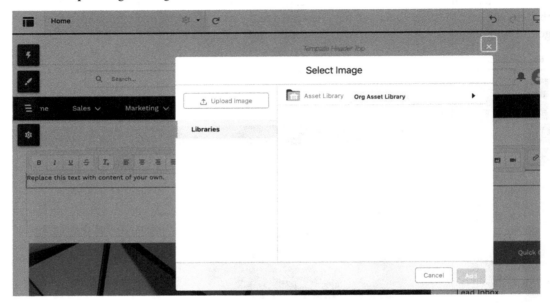

Figure 8.3: Rich Content Editor – image selector

There are different strategies your company can explore to organize your graphic library. If this is the first time your company is venturing into Salesforce, take some time to walk through your ideal asset library organization structure. Note that by virtue of placing images in your Experience Cloud site, you would be automatically creating an asset library. So, you will need a folder and file organization strategy. If you just start uploading without a strategy in place, it will appear unorganized for those maintaining your digital properties. It can lead to confusion on when and where to use images on pages.

Once you have selected your image, you will now see the placement of your image (*Figure 8.4*). You will only be able to make the image as large as the component. Why do we call that out? Well, margins are standard practice on Salesforce pages. So your image, depending on screen size, will not be the entire screen. If you want a more dynamic experience, a developer can explore the CMS-based components or build your own. CMS Connect (HTML) and CMS Connect (JSON) are available out of the box.

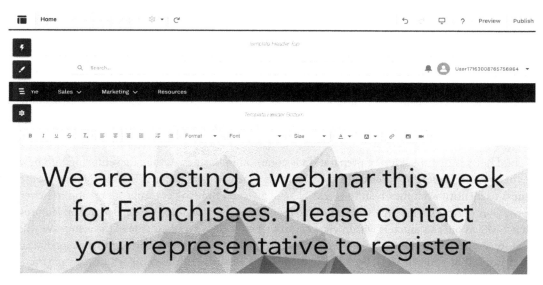

Figure 8.4: Rich Content Editor image display

Once you have your graphic the way you like it, click **Publish** and you are done! Now, you can move on to the rest of your communication strategy.

To build your communication strategy, start by working with your business partners to understand how they want to communicate and the key communication vehicles that they want to use. We recommend that you start with channels you already run, and layer in other communications channels as your offerings become more advanced.

> **Tip**
>
> The key to communication is having someone dedicated to answering the inbound messages; otherwise, the experience you are curating for customers will fail. People don't like to submit things and not get responses back in what they deem to be a timely manner. Be realistic about what you are going to take on and don't unnecessarily frustrate your clients.

For *Delivery International*, we want to implement chat, emails, and texts into its Experience Cloud site in the long term, but are not sure which use case makes sense to go live with first. We will review four scenarios:

- General messaging to customers upon login (communication center)
- Facilitating communication between users on Experience Cloud (email)
- A client needing quick answers to troubleshoot a minor issue (chat)
- An on-the-go consultation of a more significant user need (SMS)

We have agreed that our internal associates are not currently prepared to successfully manage instantaneous, multithread communication. Because of the lead time to train them, it's unlikely chat and SMS will be part of our MVP release. However, we may consider starting with a push SMS strategy to offer service notifications to our customers, instead of a two-way communication. Jack, our designated Service Representative, has requested that we keep an open mind regarding the direction, but Maggie in Finance wants us to watch our overhead costs to empower that channel. Anna, our Head of Quality, is going to start with a survey of existing employee skill sets in service so that the business can review the practicality of implementing features.

The good news is that this kind of preparation is common in businesses that are venturing into new types of communication. We aren't all experts at every type of digital activity. Taking the time for the business to identify what they believe is feasible will give you time to get things set up and to better support your partners. This time will be needed if you venture into more vendor-dependent features such as SMS, as only so much is within your control when it comes to their side of the setup. We will talk more about that in the *Implementing and managing text messaging* section of this chapter. The great thing is that you can work behind the scenes and be ahead of the game when your partners decide that they have everyone trained and are ready to implement.

We are going to move forward with the communication component we created earlier in this chapter, setting up email communication, and procuring a push SMS line for service as a first step. Let's dive into the next venture where we decide we are ready for chat. But what chat should we use? Should we build our own? Should we leverage Service Cloud Chat?

Implementing Salesforce Chat or third-party chat

Deciding when to chat leveraging native Chat capabilities instead of third-party solutions is going to need some consideration. It may seem intuitive to say "Use the free one," but not so fast. It really comes down to what you are trying to accomplish and what your plans are to integrate with AI tools and third-party analysis tools. The world of AI can be complex and hard to navigate, especially when it can communicate directly with your customers. It can be daunting to think about how to train AI to sound like your brand while being factual and helpful.

Let's start with the basics of **Salesforce Chat**. The biggest draw is that you have very little work to do to integrate it into your website or your Experience Cloud site. It integrates with Service Cloud cases seamlessly, and it acts as a centralized intake engine for your service team's workflow. In addition, you will be able to leverage the omni-routing studio to throttle inbound work and assign it to the most appropriate person, which helps you delight customers by providing relevant, high-quality service in a timely manner.

For the native Salesforce Chat, there are also preconfigured pop-up options for your external sites. More than likely, your organization will want to customize the look/feel to better align with your brand standards. To do this inside the Experience Cloud site, search for the **Embedded Messaging** component. See *Figure 8.5*.

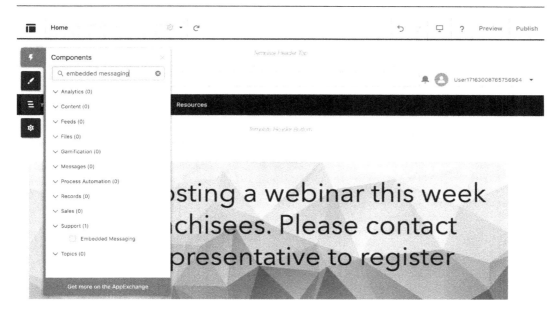

Figure 8.5: Embedded Messaging component

You will then be asked to connect Embedded Messaging to your existing configuration of Chat inside of Service Cloud. Please note that you have to set up **Messaging for Web** inside of Service Cloud before you get to these steps. If you have not done so, go to `https://help.salesforce.com/s/` for the steps on how to configure Chat inside of Service Cloud. We will touch on some of this configuration in *Chapter 10, Leveraging Case Management and Knowledge Bases*.

If you decide not to leverage Service Cloud Chat, you would then need to go with a third party, which may present some challenges for you. It's generally a good idea to avoid introducing needless complexity into your Salesforce ecosystem where you can, but sometimes, complexity makes sense.

Let's assume you went native, so we can show you what information it is going to ask you for. You are going to need your **Embedded Web Deployment** and **Site Endpoint** values and then state the chat button visibility.

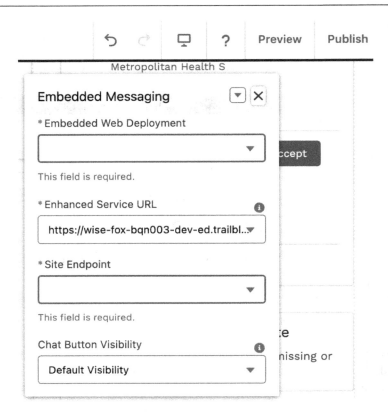

Figure 8.6: Embedded Messaging component – initial configuration

The information requested in the preceding **Embedded Messaging** widget should all be found via your previously configured version of the provided Salesforce Chat. Once you have it configured, you still need to decide how or whether you will show historical chats to your consumers via the digital experience. If you are leveraging Salesforce Chat, you can do this via the Case object. Plus, if you have set up a Salesforce Service, you can show the inbound emails, SMS, phone calls, and chats all in one easy location. We will dive into this setup detail in *Chapter 10, Leveraging Case Management and Knowledge Bases*.

Let's switch gears and start talking through some of the custom options. Imagine a world where customers schedule meetings via chat with you, using chatbots that intelligently speak to your clients. Your use case may be more sales-focused than ultimately service-focused, and you might want to answer a host of product questions or offer incentives to buy. These requirements may lead you into the world of third-party chats.

You can find alternative chat platforms listed on the Salesforce AppExchange that are made by a qualified Salesforce partner. Anything listed on the AppExchange is required to meet the Salesforce standards, and in theory, should be easier to implement. This is a shaky theory because not all AppExchange products are created equally. It is important that you test the application in a lower environment to see whether it will meet your standards. We encourage people to do a **Proof of Concept** (**POC**) to determine whether a third party is right for your organization. Several companies facilitate this. In fact, the last time these authors searched on AppExchange, there were over 270 solutions that would pop up when you typed in "chat."

If you are trying to go a route other than service, there are several options out there that have a variety of features. However, if service is the name of your game, we do recommend sticking with the native Salesforce Chat. In the long run, it will empower your service digital experience to new heights and allow your service agents to handle multiple types of inbound communication in a single platform.

What about split use cases? One thing to consider is that it isn't easy handing off a chat from one platform to another chat platform. It can create a clunky experience and, more than likely, the history of the chat will not transfer over. Salesforce does innovate on its product suite, but this particular product hasn't kept pace with some of the companies focused solely on chat. So what's the magic decision point? The reality is that it comes down to your use case and preferences. Make sure you outline the decision points and business value, then follow the data to the most logical architectural and pricing choice for your company.

Implementing and managing Experience Cloud emails

When you leverage Experience Cloud for communications, you will have some outbound communications that will come from the site and others that will come from your Service configuration. The big thing to consider is that you are now managing external users in your support strategy. This might be a new venture for your Salesforce instance, or maybe you are integrating into an existing process and extending it to Salesforce. There are a few templates that come with Salesforce that you can modify. A few of the templates include the following:

- Site Welcome Email
- Personal Information Change: Old Email Address Change Verification, New Email Address Change Verification, Device Activation Verification
- Password Related: Forgot Password, Change Password, Case Comment, User Lockout, One-Time Password, One-Time Password For Headless Forgot Password Flow

The first thing you need to do is configure where these emails are going to be sent from. You will likely want a generic company email address instead of leveraging your personal user's email address. You could also set this email address up to route replies back through Salesforce Service Cloud.

Let's take a look at how to configure this inside of the **Workspaces** portion of your Experience Cloud site. Not sure how to navigate to your Workspace? In the **Setup** portion of Salesforce, navigate to **Digital Experiences | All Sites**. Then, next to the site you want to edit, click **Workspaces**.

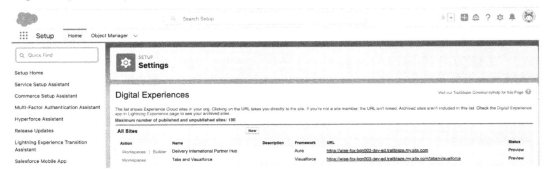

Figure 8.7: Digital Experiences – selecting Workspaces

Now that you have launched the **Workspace** portion of your digital site, we need to click into **Administration**. Here, we will be able to navigate to **Emails** on the left-hand side. This will launch the email configuration.

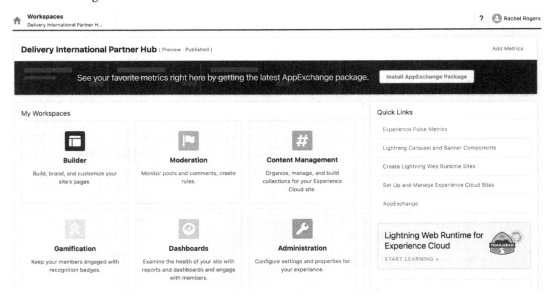

Figure 8.8: Workspaces – navigating to Administration

You are now in your one-stop shop for changing the sender, branding, and aligning email templates to its automated use case. Be aware that you will not be creating email templates on this screen. The curation of email templates happens inside of the Salesforce configuration and not within the Digital Experience setup. Don't worry, we will cover that in a few steps. Let's assume you are comfortable with the defaults.

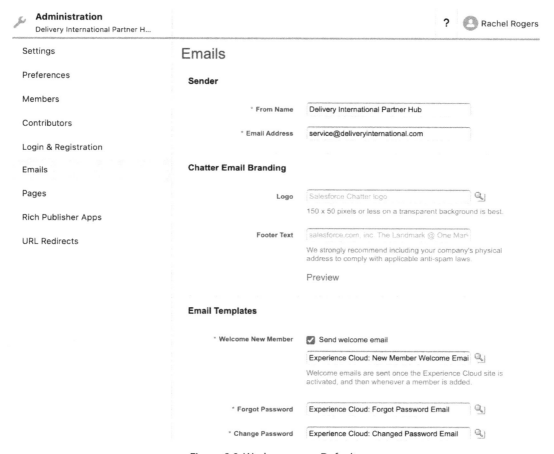

Figure 8.9: Workspaces – nDefaults

As you navigate down the page (*Figure 8.9*), you will see all the preconfigured workflows that you can leverage with email templates. Here, you will make your selections for how you want to map email templates to processes.

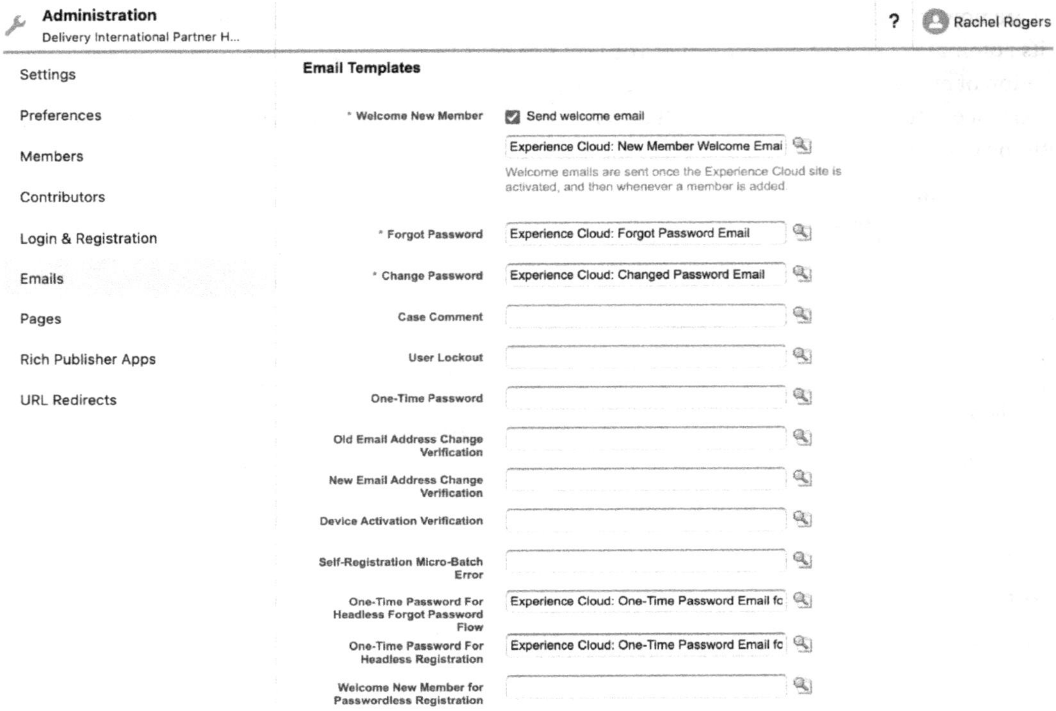

Figure 8.10: Workspaces: Email Templates

If you have everything you need, you can click **Save** at the bottom of the page to commit your email selections. Curious about what these preconfigured workflows are? The details on how these work and when they are sent are maintained by Salesforce in the Salesforce Help Center. Here is the link to where you can find the latest documentation regarding the scenarios that will trigger emails: `https://help.salesforce.com/s/articleView?id=sf.networks_customize_email.htm&type=5`.

Let's say, though, that your marketing team requests to update the branding or language in the future. How do you go about changing an email template? You have to start by going back to Salesforce **Setup**. Once you are there, search for `email`.

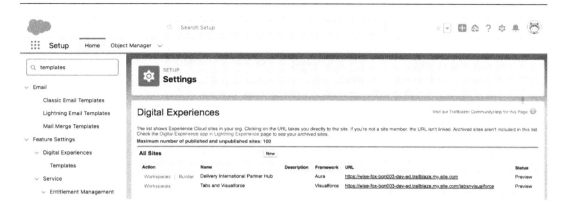

Figure 8.11: Salesforce Setup – Email Templates

You will notice that under the **Email** section, there are three types: **Classic Email Templates**, **Lightning Email Templates**, and **Mail Merge Templates**. You are going to be looking at **Classic Email Templates** for your initial configuration.

If you are working with an established Salesforce org, you may have **Lightning Email Templates** turned on. Lightning is the future, so curate your items there when the configuration allows.

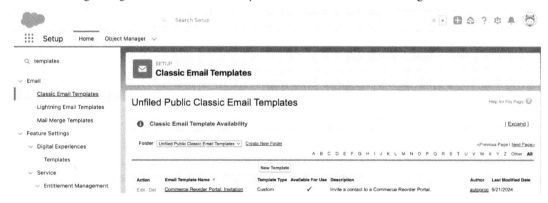

Figure 8.12: Salesforce Setup – Classic Email Templates

Now that you have navigated to your email templates, you will see everything that has been preconfigured for you. Here is your opportunity to edit existing templates or curate your own template. Remember that templates aren't emails. They are the building blocks for automated processes to automatically fill in information based on pre-designated sections of the template.

You may be thinking, so I just click the **Edit** button next to the name of the one I would like to change, right? Not exactly. If you click **Edit** from the list view, you will get to a screen to edit the template information. This will not allow you to edit the body of the email. Let's take a look at the top-line editor in *Figure 8.13*.

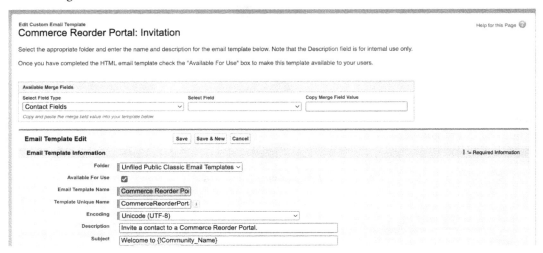

Figure 8.13: Classic Email Templates list view edit

While it is useful to edit the top-line items, let's get to the main topic of the body editor. To do that, you would click on **Email Template Name** in the list view. This will open the template and allow you to select the ability to edit the HTML version or the text version. You can copy the wording from the HTML to the text version to speed up the process of text editing. You can also send a test email so you can verify that your emails are functioning optimally for you before you start sending them to your customers. Look at our example here in *Figure 8.14*.

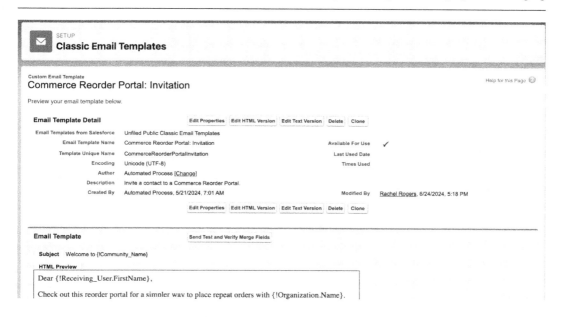

Figure 8.14: Classic Email Templates main link edit options

Once you have completed the edits in this main link edit options page, you can send test emails and verify the merge fields. This will show you exactly how the email will look when you send it out. It is a great opportunity for you to edit your content before making the email available for use. Note that once you mark something **Available For Use**, it is then open to all internal users who have access to that email template folder. Be advised that you may need to disable your **Email Deliverability** settings when you test, as you will not want to accidentally send out test emails to real users.

Those are the key points of email channel setup. The big thing will be figuring out how you want to, if you want to, and when you want to update messaging. If you are also integrating with another authentication tool, you probably won't need the password-related emails/workflows. You can just leave things you don't think you need blank for now. We will go through more of these in the security-related chapter, *Chapter 11, Security – Authentication, Data Sharing, and Encryption*. For now, let's continue to assess the ways we are leveraging communication and review the world of text messaging (SMS).

Implementing and managing text messaging

So, you want to text your customers? Well, welcome to a very complicated process. But have no fear, we can accomplish all necessary steps through Marc Benioff. Please note that if you are exploring text messaging, you will need to leverage a marketing platform technology. Salesforce of course has two products in that arena that you can choose from: **Marketing Cloud** (B2B) and **Pardot/Marketing Cloud Engagement** (B2C). Text messaging from Salesforce is exclusively sold through Marketing Cloud, but some SMS providers can be connected to Pardot for basic functions. If you do not have a marketing solution in your environment, you will want to do an evaluation of that first. For the purposes of this chapter, we are going to assume that you have Marketing Cloud and are ready to venture into SMS. Here is a high-level view of the overall process for text messaging:

- **Initial decision**: Push text messaging or two-way messaging
- **Purchasing**: One-time activation charge and message bundles
- **Setup**: Implementation partner required and carrier filings
- **Unified experience**: How you will/won't unify via Service Cloud

A key strategy we recommend is to purchase multiple SMS numbers. This enables each SMS number to have a singular use. Think of this in terms of an SMS number for each channel/department that wishes to push messages to consumers. For example, Sales, Advice, Service, Marketing, and so on. Why? You are required to submit a Carrier Filing to open a line. Don't worry, we will talk you through it. This filing requires you to specifically call out the number's business purpose and how opting out from communications from it will work.

If you have multiple SMS numbers, then you can treat them differently. This means that opt-outs would happen per number, not just a singular opt-out. Why does that matter? The goal of a communication strategy is to ensure that you are getting the right message to the right people at the right time. So separating items out by number ensures that you are targeting messaging better with your consumers. It would be the same strategy if you had different email opt-ins.

Now that you have a strategy identifying how many SMS numbers you will need, the next step is understanding the desired experience for your customers via text messaging. Confused by that statement? Our own consumer experiences vary, and if you sign up for sales discounts, you probably try to opt out before you try to contact the vendor via text. However, if you tried to text those numbers back, you may or may not get a response. That is because not all text packages are created equally. The good news is that there is a single decision to make in terms of the "type" of text messaging you wish to incorporate in your strategy. Let's look at *Table 8.1* on the types of text messages that are available for use, with purchase, of course.

Text message type	What does that mean?
Push text messaging	Ability to push messaging to your consumers where you do not intend to reply. These could be links for them to view their cases, refill orders, order status, and so on. Any replies that a consumer sends here will result in a message that the number is not monitored.
Two-way messaging	Ability to message back/forth with a consumer via text messages. This allows the consumer or the company to start the message.

Table 8.1: Types of Text Messages (SMS)

Note that you can pick a different type of SMS per line. This means that you can have your service line be a two-way messaging line and your sales line be a push text messaging line, giving you greater flexibility in your setup. It is important to remember that once you introduce the line, you can't go backward from two-way to downgrade to push text messaging. Make sure that you have your teams ready and a solid SMS management strategy.

Once you have decided which type of messaging you would like, the next step is to contact your Marketing Cloud Sales Representative from Salesforce. You will need to explain to them what you intend to use the number for, the volume of customers you wish to interact with, the frequency with which you plan to text, and so on. All of these inputs are key to the recommendations they are going to make for how many messaging bundles you will need. What you will typically get back in a quote are the following line items:

- Private SMS/MMS code lease (per the country of origin)
- Mobile message bundles
- Success plan
- Recommendation for an SMS implementation partner

Wait, why do you need an implementation partner? Welcome to the world of SMS! In order to truly activate your line(s), you have to file with all of the telephony carriers. In order to do a filing, you have to use one of the selected partners. Unfortunately, not all Salesforce Partners are qualified in the text messaging arena. Make sure you ask your Marketing Cloud representative about your options for partners. Take the time to interview the ones you are presented with to find which one will work best with your team. Additionally, consider that not all of these partners can help you with the configuration of two-way messaging in relation to Service Cloud. If you are working on two-way messaging and wish to have it come through as a case so that your service team can answer the questions, be specific about that requirement to your Marketing Cloud representative.

Let's talk about the carrier filing! This is a legal filing that you have to do with all of the cell phone companies. You have to submit paperwork to each carrier that explains your intent before you can be issued an activated number. This part of the process will be where your business partner will have to do a fair amount of articulation. There are pages of questions you have to answer, from business use to providing your company's *Terms and Conditions* for SMS. As the development team, you will have to provide screen mock-ups of the opt-out/opt-in notices, the language on the website, the locations of your SMS policy documents, and so on. Your implementation partner will instruct you on the verbiage that is required for your designs to be approved. Your implementation partner should also have samples that you can review for design inspiration. You can also search many public websites for their SMS policies and how they display their opt-in/opt-out notices.

To keep a unified experience on email opt-ins/opt-outs, you will want to put your SMS text in the same area. Make sure that you are designing a version that is compatible with your Experience Cloud site. We recommend looking at embedding Marketing Cloud into an Experience Cloud site page for the authenticated user experience. You will need another copy of the page that does not require a user to be authenticated. A standard Marketing Cloud page will work that can be branded into your website.

Once you get through the carrier filing process, your line(s) will be ready to operate! But that doesn't mean you will be ready to go just yet. If you have selected a two-way communication line, have you identified how your associates will be responding to those communications? Have you decided how or whether they will be displayed on the Experience Cloud site for your customers to reference later?

The first part of your decision should reflect how you intend to handle these messages internally. Who is responsible for responding to them? Where does that group's workload currently live? The big thing you are trying to avoid is any friction in the internal process of responding. So, if you are having sales representatives answer accounts they work on, then integrating your text message function on the Accounts page layout would be the place to put your texting experience within Salesforce. On the flip side, if this is a service function, placing this inside of Service Cloud Cases would be more appropriate since their workload is sent via case.

The second part of your decision is whether you intend to display any text message conversations on the digital site to your End Consumers. Some companies like to leverage the digital site as a place where consumers can reference any historical conversations with the company, irrespective of the channel in which they started. If this is your intent, then this lends itself better to the Service Cloud Case module.

The good news is that you have options that suit a wide variety of decisions. There are several options on the Salesforce AppExchange that will allow you to embed text messaging into different areas of Salesforce. Be advised that some of these apps may have specifics about which text message package you can purchase. So, if you intend on leveraging a third-party app to bring SMS to life internally, make sure you evaluate that app prior to purchasing an SMS package.

Not looking for that type of headache and addition to your overall implementation timeline? Another option is to have your implementation partner quote you on building a solution that suits your specific needs instead of having to pay for another app via the AppExchange. They will need the same information you pulled together for yourself regarding who will be responding and what type of transparency you wish for your consumers. Even if you ultimately choose to put text messaging into Service Cloud Cases, there is still a level of development work required to make that happen. Unfortunately, there aren't just some magic buttons you click in configuration land to enable SMS.

The good news is that this is a product that you will have a ton of help with if you choose to implement it, no matter whether you go with Marketing Cloud or a third-party connector with Pardot. You will have some level of implementation partner to lean on during this journey. If these terms sound foreign to you, we will dive more into marketing in *Chapter 9, Marketing Automation Setup*. This will be in terms of the Experience Cloud setup, so if you are a marketing enthusiast who wants to dive deep, make sure to pick up a book on Marketing Cloud! It would be great to have some familiarity before you engage a partner so that you aren't simultaneously trying to get up to speed on Marketing Cloud while instructing a partner on your vision for a complicated technology implementation. If you are a Marketing Cloud pro, then welcome to the world of integrated communications!

Summary

The world of communication can be challenging to orchestrate. It is something that we do on a daily basis, but we never think about all the intricacies of how that communication is set up to make it successful, actionable, and easy to reference. Whether you are pushing or pulling information, there are multiple ways to configure your site for optimal communication with your audience.

To review, these are your key learning opportunities in this chapter:

- Which communication channel to use in Experience Cloud depending on your user's needs.

- How to decide on Service Cloud Chat or third-party chat. Plus, a basic tutorial on how to embed Service Cloud Chat into your Experience Cloud site.

- How to set up email capabilities in Experience Cloud and what workflows come preconfigured for those templates.

- The steps of setting up SMS and how to think through the process of who will respond and how they will respond.

Now, let's grab a beverage and head on over to the world of marketing automation setup. It will dive deeper into the world of Marketing Cloud with an occasional reference to Pardot/Marketing Cloud Account Engagement. We will show you how to leverage pre-made marketing solutions found on the AppExchange, and most importantly, explain how tailored marketing automation can empower your digital experience to new innovative heights. See you there!

9

Marketing Automation Setup

We've said it before and we'll say it again: the modern era has conditioned users to expect an easy, tailored experience when they engage with your organization. Central to this is sending the right message to the right person at the right time. This expectation of timely, personalized communication extends far beyond good customer support queues and merely logging into your Salesforce Experience Cloud sites. Users also expect tailored experiences from you when they leave your properties. Users expect engagement from multiple channels now, whether it's relevant personalized emails, promotional texts, or Google Display ads.

Modern websites are now equipped with many tracking mechanisms to collect and analyze user behavior, with the end goal of ensuring that they can communicate with users wherever they go. From cookies to APIs calling different **Customer Data Platforms** (**CDPs**) and **Data Management Platforms** (**DMPs**), data is being used to create audiences. These supporting marketing automation systems that work behind the scenes are to thank for a killer digital experience.

Fortunately, there are a variety of levels of marketing automation that will support your Experience Cloud site in delivering relevant messaging to specific audiences. While the primary topic explored here will be the connection of Salesforce Marketing Cloud to Experience Cloud, there are multiple third-party apps and analytics tools that can be used to glean information from your Experience Cloud Site. A new entrant you will likely hear much about is Salesforce Data Cloud, but there are several other audience and marketing-oriented Salesforce products that can be layered with your Experience Cloud. In this chapter, we're primarily going to focus on Marketing Cloud and a Salesforce CMS, but we do caution that other Salesforce Marketing products might factor into your design work with Experience Cloud.

When it comes to digital marketing, Dalbert at *Delivery International* is making demands again. He knows that his department has to market to franchisees and End Consumers alike, so he wants to define his users and create audiences based on them for his digital marketing across platforms, such as email, Facebook, Google Ads, and more. He also wants to create a customized messaging experience within Experience Cloud by using Salesforce Marketing Cloud. Finally, he wants to leverage third-party web analytics tools such as Google Analytics to learn more about his site performance.

In this chapter, we'll walk through how Marketing Automation works on Experience Cloud to help you pick the best digital marketing software mix for your organization.

This chapter includes the following topics:

- Marketing Automation capabilities 101
- Salesforce CMS and dynamic content
- Salesforce Marketing Cloud and Data Cloud integration
- SEO setup
- AppExchange and third-party marketing tools

In case you're new to the intricate world of Marketing Automation, let's familiarize ourselves with the field of Marketing Automation before reviewing its setup in Experience Cloud. Note that a pre-existing understanding of Salesforce Marketing Cloud will help with the technical aspects of this chapter.

Marketing Automation capabilities 101

Marketing Automation is essentially the act of leveraging multiple sources of technology to create a marketing experience. Even though people often use the phrases "marketing automation" and "digital marketing" interchangeably, they are different things. Digital Marketing refers to digital channels that can be marketed on, whereas Marketing Automation refers to the systems and processes powering ultra-tailored, largely automated marketing experiences in both digital and analog media forms.

Even if you're not familiar with the specifics of Marketing Automation or the kinds of technology that power it, often called **MarTech**, you've almost definitely experienced it as a consumer. Anytime you've received a really relevant email about a sale going on at your favorite store with some of your favorite products listed inside the email, seen an ad for a product you researched following you from site to site or opened a letter in the mail advertising consolidated debt consolidation rates after you put $30,000 worth of Salesforce Astro plushies on your American Express card, you've had an experience powered by Marketing Automation.

The act of saving your user information, enriching your user information with data from tracked behavior or demographic information, and then targeting communications to you is what Marketing Automation is all about. There are many different ways to do it and many different avenues that can be configured based on use case, audience, and legal parameters.

Even though you can connect to analog media channels such as direct mail, along with **Out of Home (OOH)** ads such as billboards and television ads within Marketing Automation tools, Marketing Automation is most easily set up against digital platforms. Let's look at some different types of digital marketing channels that can be powered by Marketing Automation before we talk about the tooling that powers Marketing Automation.

Digital Marketing channel	Definition
Pay Per Click (PPC) advertising	These are paid ads on digital platforms, usually paid by the click or by a CMP model (cost per thousand impressions). Common forms of PPC advertising are Google or Facebook ads.
Search Engine Optimization (SEO)	Configuring your website and digital properties to appear higher on search engines such as Google, YouTube, or other applications counts as SEO.
SMS Marketing	Marketing to your clients with relevant text message communications using complex logic or sequencing is called SMS marketing.
Email Marketing	This is marketing to your clients via emails with complex logic or sequencing.
Website Marketing	This involves using your own website to market to your consumers.
Content Marketing	This focuses on creating or sponsoring marketing content across different channels that isn't a direct sales pitch.
GIS data/location Marketing	This refers to serving up marketing content based on geo-coordinates.
Affiliate Marketing	Partnering with other organizations to promote your product or brand, usually by giving them a percentage of sales, is called Affiliate Marketing. While Influencer Marketing is arguably its own category, marketing using an influencer's platform can be considered a subset of affiliate marketing.

Table 9.1: Example of Digital Marketing channels that can be powered by Marketing Automation

Now that we have a good idea of which digital channels we could leverage with Marketing Automation to create really custom experiences, we can look into what kinds of tools we have at our disposal. Let's take a look at some options in *Table 9.2*.

Marketing Automation tools	Definition
CRM system	A CRM such as Salesforce is the center of any Marketing Automation ecosystem. You need to have a central repository for the people you market to, in addition to the data you're querying to build audiences from them.

Marketing Automation tools	Definition
Marketing Automation platforms	These are the engines that power Marketing Automation and connect to all the systems that follow. Some may have more features than others, but for the purposes of this chapter, we will focus on Salesforce's Marketing Cloud, even though one of the authors likes Salesforce's Pardot so much more. These tools do have the ability to use or connect to other technologies in this table.
Content Management Systems (CMSs)	A content repository designed to help users create, publish, and manage different kinds of content across different websites and applications is called a CMS.
Social media tools	You can use social media for posting or targeting people within a social media audience or lookalike audience. Social media tools may also include social media scheduling automation, or social listening that monitors mentions of your name so you can protect your brand when people are talking spicy.
Analytics tools	These are tools you can apply across apps, websites, emails, and digital properties to measure user behavior. They may be cookie-based and/or tracking codes, but the most common one used in digital marketing is Google Analytics.
Ad buying platforms	This describes platforms such as Google Ads, LinkedIn Ads, or any software aggregates that allow the placement of multiple ad buys.
DMPs	These are data repositories that combine consumer data across different platforms to create audience profiles and segmentation opportunities.
Heat mapping and UX monitoring tools	Related to analytics tools, these measure UX behavior such as hovers, clicks, and timeouts.
Surveys and forms	These are direct data collection tools that allow users to submit qualitative and quantitative information on a site or application.

Table 9.2: Examples of Marketing Automation tools

The Marketing Automation tools in *Table 9.2* are a sampling of the kind of MarTech available in the market now, but new tools are always emerging as technology evolves. Many of these tools are now beginning to incorporate AI or leverage novel data sources, so you should stay abreast of what's on the market and what's legal for you to use.

The ultimate goal of all these tools is to deliver a clean, timely message to the users. While individual recipients are the goal, the mechanism by which these messages are tailored is through the creation of audiences. An audience in the marketing sense is a group of people defined by certain criteria, and audiences can be classified based on qualities or behaviors.

At *Delivery International*, Dalbert has two primary audiences: **franchisees** and **End Consumers**. He knows that he wants custom experiences for each of them on Experience Cloud, so how would we go about building assets for both of those? Let's look at the first mechanism by which to create custom content that can be sliced on behavior and audience: the CMS.

Salesforce CMS and dynamic content

CMSs have come a long way since the early days of the internet, allowing for the same piece of content to be customized, repackaged, and implemented in many different ways. Whether it's a blog post, a video, or an image, a CMS hosts content in one place for usage across different properties. While there are many different CMS tools on the market, we will focus on Salesforce CMS, Salesforce's unified tool designed to work across its properties and outside channels. Salesforce CMS works especially well with Experience Cloud, and Salesforce organizations with Experience Cloud licenses can use all the features of Salesforce CMS.

Salesforce CMS is a hybridized, centralized repository that allows for the storing, creation, and tagging of content by category and audience. By using Salesforce CMS, users can easily push content across different channels without using code, while leveraging data from the Salesforce CRM. Salesforce CMS is designed to work with both Salesforce-based and external products to generate content for marketing emails, portals, e-commerce sites, and other digital experiences. Here's how to get started with Salesforce CMS.

Setting up Salesforce CMS

Salesforce CMS is very easy to use, but it does require some setup, as well as an organization management strategy. Let's take a look at the steps you will need to go through in order to have a CMS up and running with a few easy steps. Be mindful that some of the Salesforce CMS setup features in Salesforce Settings requires admin permissions to access, and other parts are available within the Salesforce CMS application itself.

First, you have to enable the *Digital Experiences App*. You have to enable the profile that needs access to the *Digital Experiences App*. Note that this clickpath might be different if you have the **Enhanced Profiles User Interface** set up. Navigate to **Profiles** in **Setup** and look for the relevant profile. Click **Edit**.

On the **Profile Setup** page itself, you have to address two areas: **Custom App Settings** and **Tab Settings**. See *Figure 9.1*.

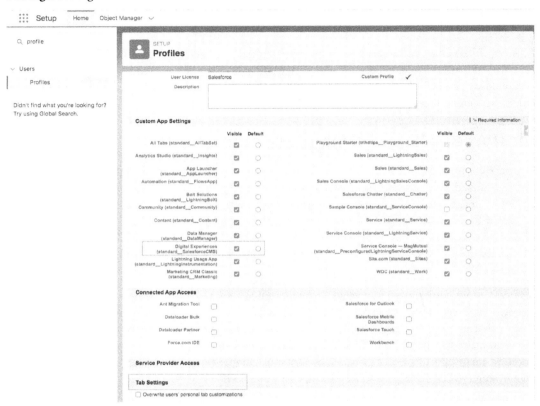

Figure 9.1: Profile settings

Within **Custom App Settings**, make sure that **Digital Experiences** is set to **Enabled**. Within **Tabs**, set **Digital Experiences Home, CMS channels, CMS Workspaces**, and **All Sites** to **Default On**. Save your work. You should now be able to navigate to the *Digital Experiences App* in the app launcher.

When you first log into the *Digital Experiences App*, you will be presented with in-app guidance, which we definitely recommend if you're new. Note that your view might be different if you already have several sites created. For now, let's look at the home page of Digital Experiences:

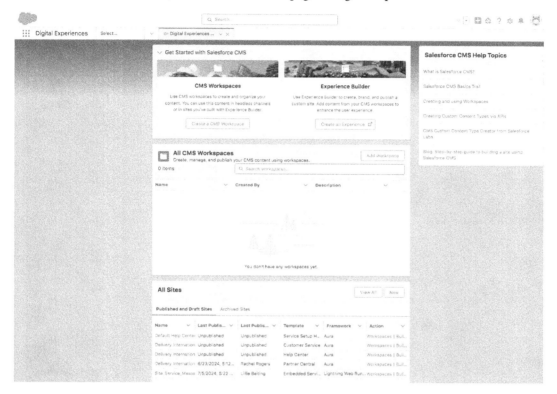

Figure 9.2: The Digital Experiences home page

On the home page, you will see five major sections: your Workspaces' guided setup, Experience Builder, All CMS workspaces, All sites, and CMS Knowledge Base help topics.

Next, let's create our first workspace by clicking **Create a CMS workspace**. Workspaces are your primary organization mechanism and can be categorized by categories such as product, geography, or audience. Note that there is a specialty setting for an Enhanced CMS Workspace for a **Lightning Web Runtime (LWR)** site, as illustrated in *Figure 9.3*.

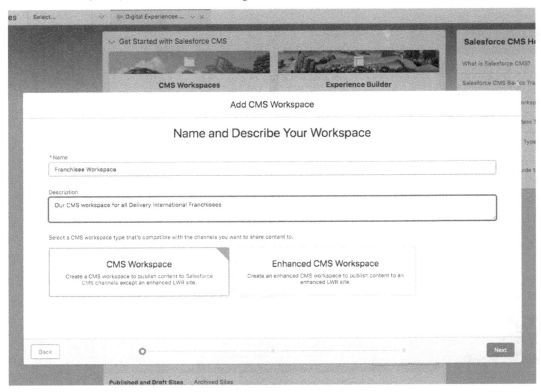

Figure 9.3: Setting up a workspace

As shown in *Figure 9.3*, we're going to select **CMS Workspace**, given that we are working on a partner portal built on Aura. On the next page of the Flow, we need to decide which channels we may have identified in *Table 9.1* that we are going to add. We can also create channels from here if necessary, as illustrated in *Figure 9.4*.

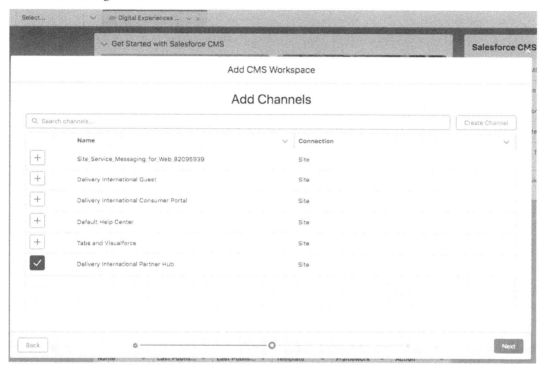

Figure 9.4: Adding channels to CMS

After picking our *Delivery International* partner site from the **Add Channels** screen, we will navigate to our next screen to select which language we want the CMS to be in and hit **Save**. As shown in *Figure 9.5*, this will then take us to our brand-new content workspace.

Figure 9.5: The content workspace interface

Within a content workspace, you can do so much more than just upload images or documentation. You can specify your contributors and their security levels, add new channels, update your language, manage a publication calendar, and more! Note that the content workspace is very different from the **Knowledge Base** setup, which we will explore in *Chapter 10, Leveraging Case Management and Knowledge Bases*. We highly recommend that you read through that chapter before you start curating a bunch of content workspaces. It is important to understand the differences in how the content is used in the sites.

Now that we know the basics of setting up Salesforce CMS and workspaces within it, we should review a few best practices to help you get the most out of Salesforce CMS.

Salesforce CMS best practices

Salesforce CMS can be powerful content tools, but they can spin out of control pretty quickly if they're not competently managed. Here are a few best practices when it comes to Salesforce CMS:

- Come up with an organizational structure for your workspaces! *Do not* just start creating workspaces because you have a few ideas about your organization and audience structures. If you need to host workshops to get a solid strategy, do it. We cannot stress this enough.

- Do not forget to create a standard structure for your folders within your workspace or it will become disorganized technical debt.

- *Be mindful of Sandbox refreshes!* CMS data is considered data and not metadata, so you will have to come up with a data backup plan during your environment refresh mapping. There are third-party tools on the AppExchange that can help with this. We suggest reviewing them.

- Salesforce CMS only works with full-copy sandboxes.

- Be mindful of language concerns if you have a multilingual marketing structure.

- CMS has specialty requirements for LWR Experience Cloud sites. Select an Enhanced CMS workspace for LWR if you have an LWR site to maintain.

With the basics of content creation covered, we're ready to move on to using it in other Salesforce properties, such as Salesforce Marketing Cloud.

Salesforce Marketing Cloud and Data Cloud integration

Salesforce Marketing Cloud and Data Cloud integrations can propel your Salesforce instance and Experience Cloud to new heights. To preface: we do not recommend taking on Marketing Cloud, Data Cloud, Experience Cloud, and Service Cloud all at once. That would be a ton of new capabilities to bring to market at once and could become painful to troubleshoot if something goes wrong. That being said, all of these products are designed to work together. Salesforce Marketing Cloud was originally Exact Target, a third-party application that was acquired into the Salesforce portfolio. Salesforce is continually retooling it to better fit into the Salesforce suite of products. The latest product roadmap shows that Marketing Cloud will even be put 100% onto the native Salesforce platform.

The great thing is that Marketing Automation can really help ensure that your consumers are engaging at a consistent rate, and that they are receiving information that is relevant and driving them to act on your call to action. When you purchase a Marketing Cloud instance, it is going to come with a separate login setup. You can, of course, leverage a **Single Sign-On** (**SSO**) service to bridge the sign-on process between the two. However, it being a separate tool to manage does have some advantages, chiefly that it limits your overall risk of an accidental email going out to consumers. So, the integration of information where it makes sense will help you limit your overall security risk.

There are a few things to note about Marketing Cloud that are going to make it different from your traditional Salesforce setup. Let's take a look at some of the key differences.

Marketing cloud term	Definition
Business Unit	This is a workspace in which a team can collaborate on outbound messages. Think of this in business terms: you may have a business unit for marketing and a different business unit for Human Resources (HR). This would be because the Target Audience is different.
Super Messages	This refers to how many targeted messages you wish to send out per month.
Journey Builder	This is the master orchestration layer of Marketing Cloud. By leveraging Journey Builder, you can do a variety of tasks, ranging from sending an email to automating Service Cloud tasks for a consultant, to reaching out to the Consumer based on certain behavior, to text messaging.
Marketing Cloud Personalization	This product allows you to modify the content on your website based on who is viewing it.
Marketing Cloud Intelligence	This is a way to connect all of your data sources for marketing into a holistic reporting platform.
Loyalty Management	This enables you to build loyalty platforms at scale to engage your consumers with clicks, not code.

Table 9.3: Marketing Cloud product offerings

Selecting the right mix of Marketing Cloud products from *Table 9.3* can be tricky and the products do change, so we can't guarantee that these will still be the exact names post-publication or that there won't be even more offerings resulting from quarterly Salesforce product innovation. We recommend that you get in touch with your business partners to determine which features they could be ready to implement and which they believe they can wait on. You will need a strong business case as these features can be pretty pricey. However, the consumer loyalty they can generate when implemented correctly can be worth the cost.

The most relevant features in Marketing Cloud for Dalbert's two audiences will be Journey Builder and Marketing Cloud Personalization. Since Dalbert wants different assets and styling to appear in the Franchisee portal than the end user portal, he will need to use both Salesforce CMS and Marketing Cloud Personalization to store content for his audience types, and then set conditions that detail when he needs content to appear. Additionally, he wants to ensure that subsequent marketing actions are also tailored to each of his audiences. To send out relevant messaging to his audiences, he will have to use Marketing Cloud Journey Builder.

To learn more about Marketing Cloud, we recommend that you pick up a Packt book. Try *Automating Salesforce Marketing Cloud*. Also, head on over to Trailhead. They will give you detailed implementation guides just like this one here in our Experience Cloud book. However, to see how we can leverage complex data to make Marketing Cloud operate like the fine-tuned machine it is, we have to talk about Data Cloud.

Data Cloud

While Salesforce is designed to be an excellent data repository, it won't ever be the sole data source for your entire organization. Don't even try to make it that way; that would be computationally crazy. In a multi-application world, data comes from multiple different sources, such as your website, phone tracking, ad buying platforms, social media analytics, ERPs, and more. While the temptation can be great to try to port all this data into custom objects on Sales Cloud, the storage and API call aspect of such architecture makes it prohibitively hard, which is why Salesforce Data Cloud was introduced.

Salesforce Data Cloud is designed to unify all of your company's data into one place. It is a one-stop shop to give you a holistic view of your customers across all the data streams they might touch. By combining all of your data into one view that's easily associated with end users or combinable into audience groups, Data Cloud empowers products such as Experience Cloud and Marketing Cloud to leverage data from different parts of the user experience.

Setting up Data Cloud

If you'd like to capture more specifics about user interaction behavior on your Experience Cloud site to build robust audience suggestions, detailed profile maps, or AI models that can suggest more ideas for personalization, consider setting up Data Cloud with your Experience Cloud.

You will have to work with your Salesforce AE to purchase Data Cloud, and Salesforce will ultimately have to enable it in your account after the contract has been signed. Once Data Cloud is enabled, you will have a *Data Cloud App* in the app launcher that you can access. As shown in *Figure 9.6*, to connect Experience Cloud to your Data Cloud, go to **Setup**, enter `Digital Experiences`, and select **Settings**.

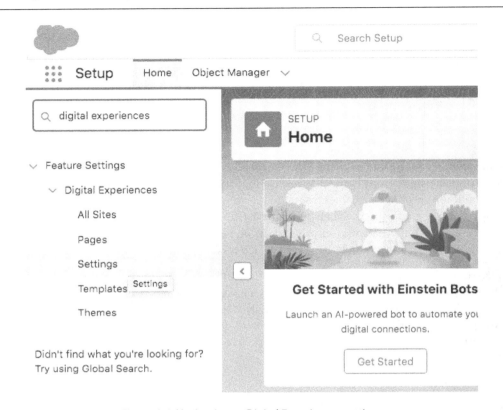

Figure 9.6: Navigating to Digital Experiences settings

From the settings page, select **Integrations**. Locate the **Data Cloud** image and select **Add To site**. Then click **Share site data with Data Cloud**.

Note that Data Cloud currently only works declaratively for LWR sites.

On the topic of collecting and aggregating data, we should switch gears and review another data-heavy facet of Marketing Automation: SEO.

Setting up SEO

The dominance of Google in the modern digital space cannot be underestimated, and it's non-negotiable that you need to set up your site to respond to the reality that people find information through search engines. Google isn't the only search engine in town, but it is the primary standard by which the web is set as of the publication of this book. While you may have tracking code and configuration for search engines such as Bing or Yahoo, we're going to focus on SEO techniques and implementation largely used for Google.

A word of caution

You need to ensure that your website is set up for Google to easily consume and then rank against other potential competitor websites. Note that you should only do this for public-facing Experience Cloud sites. There is no point in SEO optimizing an authenticated portal experience since that content is intentionally behind a login.

If you are used to setting up SEO on non-salesforce websites, the good news is that you can leverage many of the same mechanisms within Experience Cloud. Let's walk through some of the fundamentals and how you'd implement them within Experience Cloud.

Robots.txt files, sitemaps, and indexing

When you first create a site and hope that Google will recognize it for the informative work of art it is, there are a few preliminary things you need to create to install. You need to work through a few steps and submit your information to Google so it can index your site and decide whether your site is relevant to what someone is searching for.

Here's a quick table overview of what Google needs you to do so it can more easily find your site:

Action	What it does
Identify a preferred domain and a root site	This is the version of the domain you want to be public. You may have other domains that you don't want indexed, and that's OK.
Install a `Robots.txt` file	This is a crawler file that contains instructions for search engines on how to index and move through the site.
Submit an XML sitemap to the Google Search Console	XML is a file type, but this XML sitemap is a file that contains all the website's pages and subpages.
Select pages for indexing	This tells Google which pages you would like to rank in search results.

Table 9.3: Basic setup actions for Google SEO

Here is some good news; all of the preceding tasks are very easy things to do in Experience Cloud. However, you will want to give yourself some lead time to do things such as set up Google Search Console and tailor an XML sitemap. You'll also want to give Google some time to crawl your site. Thankfully, Salesforce has a setting for these if your Experience Cloud site is public in the **SEO** section of the **Settings** menu. Please ensure that the **Guest users can see and interact with the site without logging in** setting is enabled to see the **SEO** tab. See *Figure 9.6*.

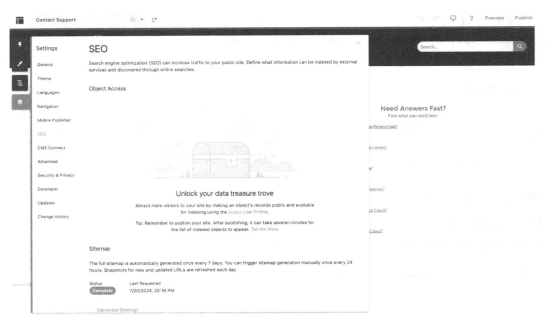

Figure 9.7: The SEO tab in Builder

Please note that correctly configuring the URL to be your root domain will handle the Robots. txt page implementation automatically, although you may have to make a custom Visualforce page for a custom .txt file if you have custom pages that you wish to suppress from Google crawlers. In addition to setting up object access here, which we will cover in the next section, you can also set up your preferred domains in the **General Settings** tab.

As you build your site and add more pages to it, you will have to send an updated sitemap to Google Search Console. Google will sometimes index your site on its own, but it's generally a best practice to send new sitemaps to force the Google robots to crawl your page faster. If you wish to automate this process instead of exporting the sitemap XML and uploading it into the Google Search Console, you will have to create a scheduled Apex job to push these to.

Since we're talking about mechanisms to show data to Google, how would we go about exposing Salesforce Object data?

Exposing Salesforce objects

By default, objects are private and won't be indexed by Google unless you enable a setting to make the object and its relevant fields public. If there's data within objects that you need to expose, review your **Field-level security** very carefully before changing this setting.

For standard and custom objects, you will have to change the visibility by going to the guest user profile. To do this, navigate to the **SEO** tab in the experience builder shown in *Figure 9.6* and click on the **Guest User Profile** hyperlink. If you want this option to appear, your site needs to be published first.

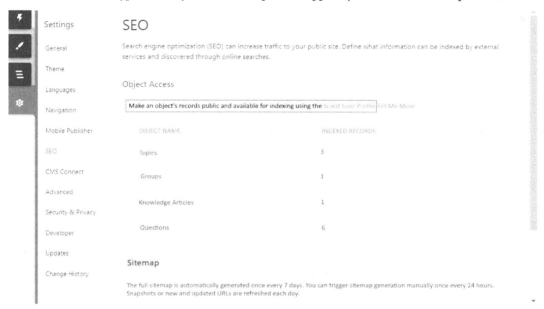

Figure 9.8: Making objects public

This image was taken directly from a Salesforce Automation blog called Automation Champion, `https://automationchampion.com/2020/05/05/salesforce-summer20-release-quick/`. You will have to select the object in setup to give at least read access, and then review the appropriate field-level security. After saving your changes, you will have to assign sharing rules to your guest user profile. You can also set your objects to provide a content snapshot to update search engines every 24 hours here. Note that records and objects can take as long as 24 hours to sync.

For topics, questions, and feed items, you merely need to navigate to the **Preferences** page under your **Experience Builder Administration** tab.

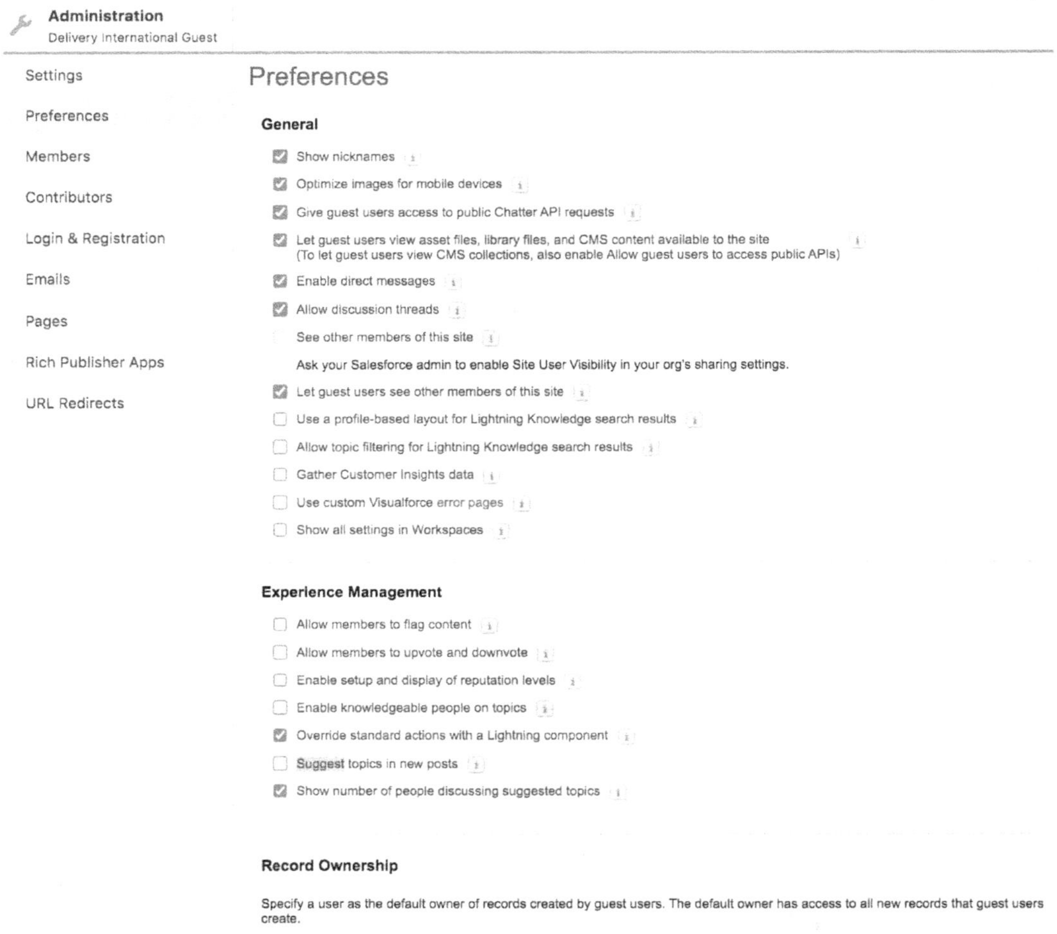

Figure 9.9: The Preferences tab in Experience Cloud Administration

Select the **Give access to public API requests on Chatter Requests** and **Let guest users see other members of this site** options on the **Preferences** page. If you would like users to access files within topics, questions, and feed items, enable **Let guest users view asset files, library files and CMS content available to the site**.

We strongly caution you to think very carefully about which Salesforce objects you want to expose to be crawlable by search engines. While you can request that a search engine de-index your page, it's not an easy task. There are many indexing mechanisms you may not have control over. If it's on the internet once, it's on the internet forever, so be sure to really take the time to think through what you expose. Therefore, it's additionally important to think about what you want to hide. This general rule of thumb includes your website pages, which we will review next.

SEO page properties

The **SEO Page Property** feature in Experience Cloud allows you to customize Experience Cloud pages themselves for specific SEO outcomes, as you would on any other website builder or CMS. Here, you can create and update the title, description, and header tag properties, in addition to setting more advanced features, such as dynamic canonical tags.

To edit a page's SEO properties in Experience Builder, open the **Pages** menu and click the ellipsis by it:

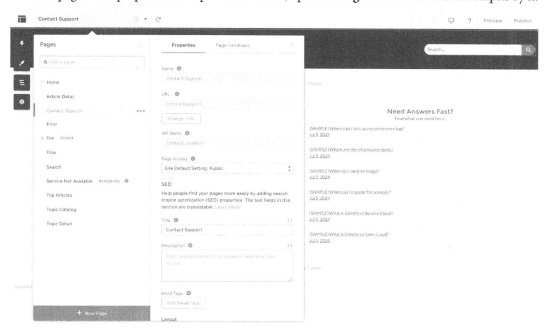

Figure 9.10: The Properties page

From there, you will be able to edit the title, tags, description, and more. Additionally, if you want to hide pages from Google through the user interface, you can do so by adding a `noindex` tag to the header.

We've nailed the basics of how to get started with SEO, but what if we want to extend our Experience Cloud site's marketing capabilities beyond Marketing Cloud, organic search, and dynamic content?

AppExchange and third-party marketing tools

After setting up custom CMS spaces and content for our franchisees and end-consumer audiences, optimizing them for their best Marketing Cloud journeys, and designing our sites to work with search engines in mind, what do we do when we want to add other marketing functions to our site? What if we want to implement features we often see on web experiences outside of the Salesforce family, such as the ability to embed scheduling, highly trackable video players, document signature capture, or even more advanced reporting?

Before you go for the completely custom route and decide to build yourself complex APIs, custom LWCs, or intricate architecture, check out the Salesforce AppExchange to see whether they have any tools you could download and embed. For common needs, such as scheduling automation, video embeds, or document generation, several third parties have already made solutions easily accessible on the AppExchange. Do your research when you're looking for custom capabilities, and do not forget to inquire about the licensing implications of these products.

Finally, the most common third-party marketing tool that we haven't touched on much in this chapter is an analytics engine for web applications that comes from our friends at Google, known as Google Analytics. We will review how to implement and leverage Google Analytics in *Chapter 12, Monitoring Your Site – Salesforce Native Reporting*, but know that setting up Google Tag Manager and Google Analytics can open up a world of possibilities and integration for your Marketing Automation tech stack.

Summary

Building a public-facing site Marketing Automation is its own discipline, and can be so complex that many organizations have entire teams of people doing nothing but Marketing Automation management. While many aspects of Marketing Automation are truly automated, it still takes human input to create content, ensure it makes sense for the associated audiences, set up content for dynamism and reusability, and assess metrics gauging what comes out of those marketing efforts.

Marketing Automation can take on a lot of shapes and sizes, and you should always assess your communication landscape to determine which tools will work for you and your clients. Depending on your needs, there are plenty of pre-baked solutions that can get you started. We always recommend starting with basic journeys and analytics collection, and as your organization scales and accumulates more data, you can expand how you collect and experiment with your marketing.

In this chapter, we reviewed the following:

- A primer on Digital Marketing and Marketing Automation, as well as their capabilities
- How to use Salesforce CMS and dynamic content to tailor content for audiences
- Features in Marketing Cloud and Data Cloud that can be used to extend Experience Cloud
- Basic SEO and object privacy setup
- When to use App Exchange and third-party tools for Experience Cloud marketing automation

Since we now know how to prepare our site for Marketing Automation and design for personalization and audiences, we're ready to review another aspect of putting your clients first: case management and knowledge base setup. We'll discuss these topics in detail in the next chapter.

Leveraging Case Management and Knowledge Bases

As we discussed in *Chapter 8*, your consumers expect to get what they want quickly and efficiently. Whether they need help or are looking for information, your site needs to provide information to them via the method they choose. Your consumer is in charge, so you need to curate your Experience Cloud site to be the concierge of information. Gone are the days of *not knowing* how to solve a consumer's request; you need to adapt to your consumer's needs, think through each design, and curate screens that resonate across devices. Your company also needs to be able to accept information outside of your desired application.

To accomplish a concierge customer support experience within Experience Cloud, you will have to invoke native features of Service Cloud. Setting up Service Cloud is required before you try to add service assets into Experience Cloud. If you have another service system, you may wish to reconsider using an external service system and migrate your experience to Service Cloud to partner seamlessly with your digital experience site. Not only is Experience Cloud explicitly designed to work with Service Cloud, but transitioning to Service Cloud will reduce your overhead cost, eliminate costly integrations, and simplify your internal workflow.

To help you get started, we will take you through a quick setup guide for case management and Knowledge bases in Service Cloud. From there, we will showcase how to set up the customer side of both assets. Please note that it is not the intent of this book to be a full-Service Cloud setup guide. Service Cloud is a complex product, and we highly recommend that you seek a resource for that setup specifically. Our goal is to provide the basics in order to get your digital experience up and running.

To aid in our learning journey, we are going to break things into the following sections:

- Service Cloud – Case management
- Enabling service assets in Experience Cloud
- Service Cloud – Knowledge setup
- Enabling Knowledge in Experience Cloud

Let's dive into the foundation of Service Cloud: the Case object.

Service Cloud – Case management

The Case object is the powerhouse of Salesforce Service Cloud, and it is the first item you will need to set up. Think of this object as a container for all types of inbound inquiries that your team will need to process. You can direct multiple channels such as email and phone calls to cases via native Salesforce connectors. This creates a seamless experience for both your consumers and your internal service agents, allowing both parties to have a single location to access information related to inquiries.

If you are evaluating whether Service Cloud is the right product for you, let's dive into the structure to showcase the platform's power. We've put together a high-level diagram that showcases the high-level function of inputs to make cases that direct to the correct person within your organization to assist the consumer:

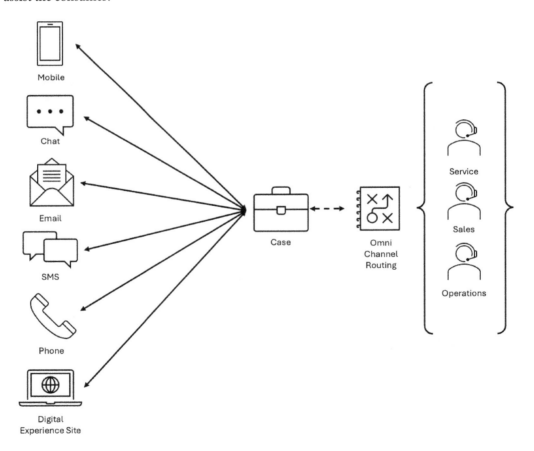

Figure 10.1: Case inputs to assignments overview

As you can see, any inbound communication can be recorded as a case. Then, we leverage an item called Omni-Channel Routing. This is a routing system that will pick up any type of inbound work and compare it to an existing associate's workload and skill set. Then, routing logic determines who the most appropriate person is to assist the consumer. You can also add custom routing rules regarding a variety of factors such as inbound language, who the consumer is, or the type of request. Sounds like a great experience for external and internal consumers, right? Let's jump into what you should consider before you start flipping switches. Here are a few key items to review with your internal team who will be leveraging Service Cloud to solve inbound consumer inquiries:

Topic	Why does it matter?
What are your business hours?	Both of these questions set the basis for when consumers should have the expectation that they will be able to reach someone in order to solve their inquiry. They also set up the foundation for your **service-level agreement** (**SLA**) enablement, should your organization choose to implement that.
Do you have any business holidays?	
What are the types of inbound inquiries?	Consider how you would categorize all of your inbound requests.
What inbound channels (email, SMS, chat, and so on) does your team have the skill set to manage when you launch the service?	As we discussed in *Chapter 8*, *Understanding Inputs – Emails, Chats, and Text Messages*, your organization may not be equipped to handle all the channels that consumers wish to use in order to interact with you. Identify what your organization has the current skill set to handle and where you would like to go in the future.
Are all inbound inquiries handled by a single group or are there multiple teams?	Understanding who is needed to solve a case ensures that you have your complete internal user base defined. It will also illuminate any gaps you may have in the user base if some teams' workflow is not currently a Salesforce process.
Are all inquiries a one-to-one relationship or are there teams that are needed to handle inquiries?	Salesforce can natively handle either single case ownership or you can enable case teams to work on a case. This is connected directly to the security module that you set up for Service Cloud and your digital experience site.

Table 10.1: Service Cloud fundamental setup questions

Those questions will start you on your way to setting up the base object of cases. This empowers you to capture the information you will need to not only process the information internally but, more importantly, to display it back to the consumer to show the status of their inquiry. Now that we understand the landscape of our case setup, it's time to jump into the base Service Cloud setup so that we can showcase how to expose this experience through your digital experience site.

From inside your Salesforce development environment, you will need to navigate to **Setup**. Then, on your left-hand setup navigation, select **Service Setup Assistant**:

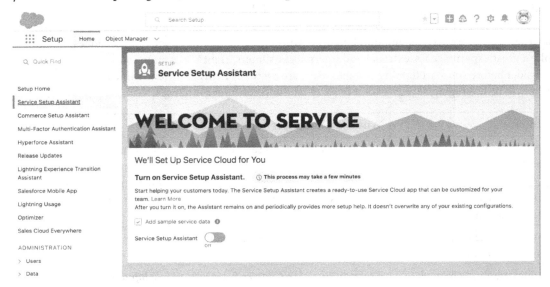

Figure 10.2: Service Setup Assistant

This assistant is an onscreen tutorial that guides you through how to set up Service Cloud. If you have questions throughout this guide, we recommend that you pick up a book on Service Cloud specifically or reach out on the *Trailblazer Community* site. It is important that you understand the settings you are enabling.

> **Note**
> You need to have the appropriate amount of time to complete the process versus attempting to navigate away and come back, so do not start this process if you do not plan to finish it in one sitting.

There is an important checkbox there, named **Add sample service data**. If you select this option, it will load sample data to better understand how the system will operate based on your selections. However, there is no simple undo functionality on this option, so you will have to delete the data later. If you are doing this in a development sandbox, per our recommendation, then adding the sample data will empower you to make quick choices. If you are doing this setup in production, we caution you if your instance is currently handling other inbound items.

Once you flip the switch on setting up Service Cloud, you will see the status of the setup onscreen. If you have chosen to load data, this may take slightly longer than if you did not:

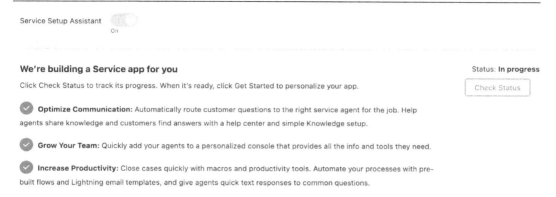

Figure 10.3: Service setup wizard status

When it is ready, the **Check Status** button turns into a **Get Started** button for you to continue your Service Cloud setup. From there, you will follow the onscreen guidance of the information you will need:

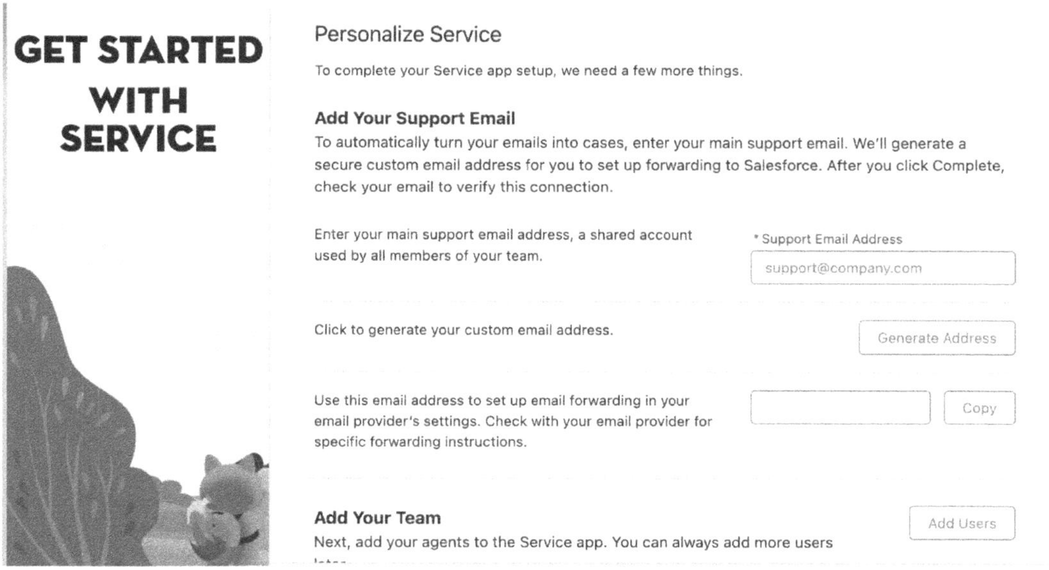

Figure 10.4: Service setup introduction screen

On the introduction screen, you will enter your company's support email that a consumer would use in order to send you an email. This will then generate your custom email address that connects your inbound email from your company's server directly into Salesforce as a case. If you need to add multiple emails, don't worry–you will be able to after you get through the initial setup.

> **Note**
> Please note that we do not recommend turning on forwarding of live inbound channels until your team is ready to launch Service Cloud. If you turn it on prematurely, you may abandon actual inbound requests, thereby creating a negative consumer experience. For testing, we recommend curating special testing email inboxes.

You will then set up your first set of users that will need Service Cloud. If you are doing this in a lower environment, you may want to start with a few test users versus immediately loading all your service personnel. It will make for a much easier setup. You can, of course, expand these once you get closer to the **User Acceptance Testing** (**UAT**) stage of your project. After you have added the users, you will click **Complete** on the introduction screen. This will lead you back into the **Service Setup Assistant** main page:

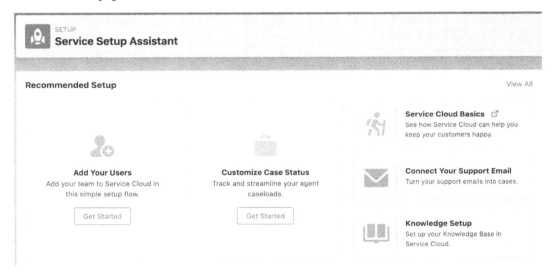

Figure 10.5: Service Setup Assistant main page

We recommend that you take the **Service Cloud Basics** course listed on the **Service Setup Assistant** main page. This will provide you with greater detail on all terms and configuration options with Service Cloud.

Now that we know how to enable the basics of Service Cloud, we are ready to dive into how to configure these assets in your Experience Cloud site.

Enabling service assets in Experience Cloud

Your ability to quickly enable service assets is going to be directly related to the template selection you made earlier in this book. Remember back in *Chapter 5, Understanding Experience Cloud Templates*, when we gave you all the trade-offs of the templates? Well, if you selected the **Customer Service** or **Help Center** templates, you are going to be in a much better position than if you selected the **Build Your Own** template. There is nothing wrong with **Build Your Own**, but it will take a little longer to enable Service Cloud assets against it. For the purposes of this chapter, we will go through a few scenarios based on service template selections.

Partner Central template – native service option

First, we are going to start with our **Partner Central** template that we started building out the communication experience for during *Chapter 8, Understanding Inputs – Emails, Chats, and Text Messages*. From inside Builder, you can change the page you are viewing by clicking on the top left where it says **Home**. Next, click the **Contact Support** option:

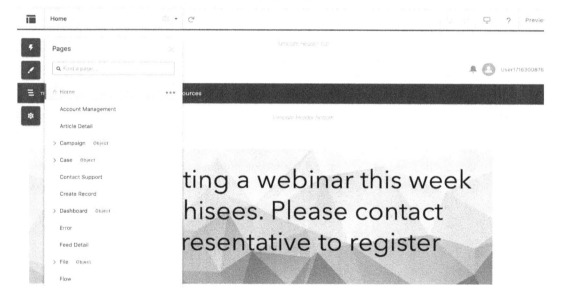

Figure 10.6: Navigating to Contact Support

Now, you will land on the default **Contact Support** page based on the template you selected in the setup. Let's review which components you are getting natively:

Figure 10.7: Partner Central – default Contact Support page

The default is for you to have two sections: **Contact Customer Support** and **Need Answers Fast?**. **Contact Customer Support** is going to create a case for the partner and route this case based on your Service Cloud configuration. **Need Answers Fast?** is leveraging the **Knowledge** feature set in Service Cloud. If you click on the **Contact Customer Support** component, you will get a series of settings:

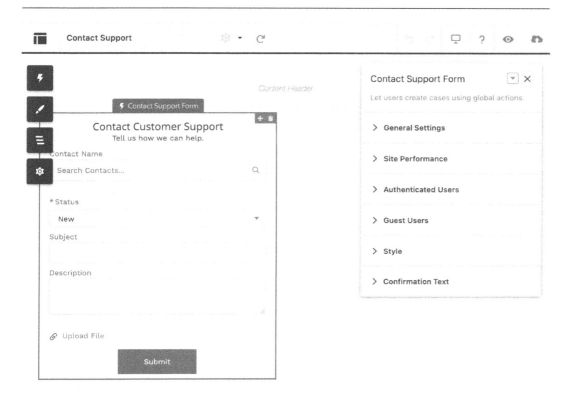

Figure 10.8: Partner Central – Contact Support Form

Inside the settings, you will be able to change several elements of the component natively, such as updating global actions or editing what verbiage is used on the different screens. By leveraging this form, you have a seamlessly integrated UI connected to your Service Cloud architecture. You will still need to curate a page that shows individuals their cases after they have submitted items, but you can create that natively. Let's take a look at how you might set that up.

The first step is to create a new page. Go to the **Pages** section at the top left, then select + **New Page**. That will lead you to a setup wizard for you to decide what type of page you would like. We are trying to showcase cases, so we want an Object page. Follow the onscreen wizard:

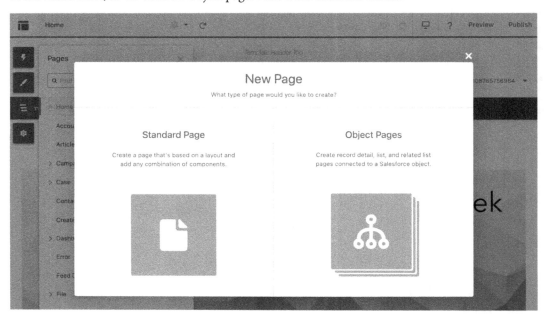

Figure 10.9: Partner Central – creating a case review page

Note that we are only showing the first page of the wizard as these are periodically updated by Salesforce. Once you have selected your Object page, you will have to select the **Cases** object to get the results we are going to talk about in the next step. Congratulations on setting up a page! Your new blank pages enable you to curate a new experience of reviewing cases that your partner has created. Yes, we said pages! With that selection, you are going to get a Detail page, a List page, and a Related List page. On any of these pages, you can add pre-configured components or custom components developers have made just for your organization, so the possibilities are endless.

Let's start by adding a preconfigured component from the left-hand side of the screen. In *Figure 10.10*, we select the lightning bolt icon and then search for **Record List**. Drag the component into the **Content** section of the page:

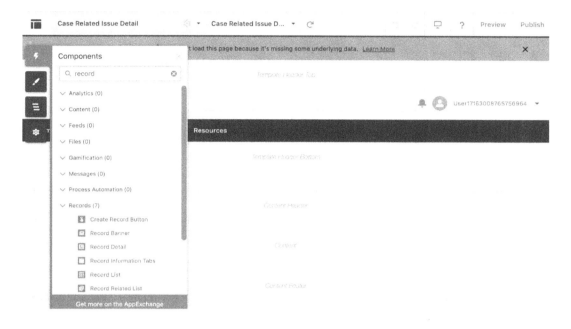

Figure 10.10: Partner Central – adding Record List component

Once you drag the component onto the page, note that it may take a minute to visually load the component onto the page. When it loads, it will default to **Accounts** as the record it is displaying. You will need to update the component to showcase **Cases**. The first thing you need to do is click on the top-right part of the component to put it in **Configuration** mode. In *Figure 10.11*, we show you what the configuration panel looks like in expanded form for the component:

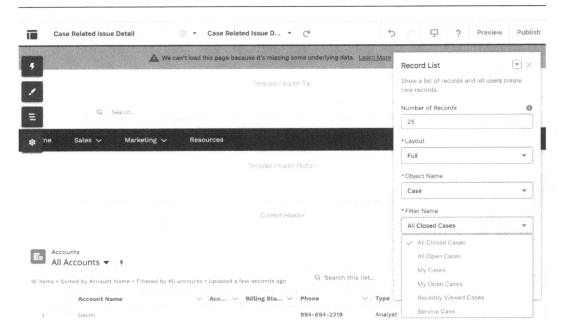

Figure 10.11: Partner Central – configuring Record List component

As you can see in *Figure 10.11*, you can control many aspects of the list through configuration, not code. You have several predefined filters that you can apply to showcase what data default displays in the table. Note that the filters your company makes internally for list views can be displayed externally. Therefore, you need to ensure you have your security updated to hide views that you would not want consumers to be able to select via the digital site.

How you build out the rest of the page is up to you! The one thing to remember is that you do not want to overcrowd or overcomplicate a page. Most of the people coming to your site will need to be able to use it without needing any training. How much you get to communicate with people before they start attempting actions on your site may be limited. Ensure that you clearly label items, keep pages with a single focus, and provide relevant information as they search for information or enter cases with you.

You may want to look at experiences you have with companies that you have an online login. Whether it is your grocery delivery service or the warranty for your computer, what are support experiences in your life that are easy to use? What are items that you wish someone would fix? Put those designs together for feedback from others. Consider giving limited instructions to users during your UAT. That will give you a true view into how easy/hard your site is to use. If your testers have lots of questions, you may want to reconsider your design.

Customer Service template – native service option

Moving away from the partner portal, let's view how the native components are leveraged for the **Customer Service** template. What makes this template offering different for the connect service experience starts at the **Home** page. It is focused on connecting consumers with other consumers and getting help for people quickly. Let's take a look at that **Home** page in *Figure 10.12*:

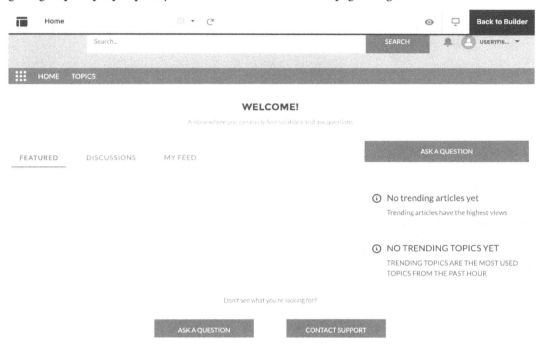

Figure 10.12: Customer Service template – Home page

We have loaded the default configuration of the page, which assumes you are using Salesforce Chatter as a communication vehicle. Therefore, this page is geared toward what is happening in your feed. Think of it in terms of a social media feed. Additionally, you can also see how Knowledge articles have been incorporated into this **Home** page. Since we don't have data loaded there yet, we are seeing error messages, as shown in *Figure 10.12*. Have no fear; we are almost at that setup in this chapter.

There are multiple options to ask questions and contact support. Providing consumers with options to take action in relation to where they are on the screen can improve usability. The experience that occurs when you click these standard buttons is a replication of the experience you saw before in the **Partner Central** template. Let's take a look at what the screen looks like once you click **Contact Support** in *Figure 10.13*:

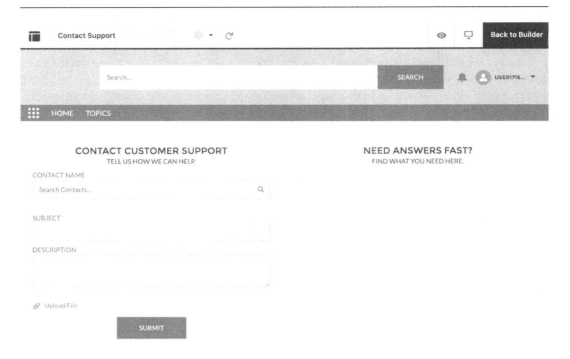

Figure 10.13: Customer Service template – Contact Support

The only notable difference in *Figure 10.13* is the default navigation. This leads you back to creating a custom page to display open cases or whatever else you may want to include. As we dig further into Knowledge setup, case deflection is indicated on the right in the **NEED ANSWERS FAST?** section. Case deflection is a native feature in Salesforce that allows you to present options to people based on what they are attempting to report, to see if you can solve the item prior to them reporting it. Having self-service options such as these is a great avenue for common questions and will lower the volume of queries your internal service agents receive.

Help Center template – native service option

Last but certainly not least, let's run through the native configuration of the **Help Center** template in relation to exposing Service Cloud through your digital experience site. When setting up the Help Center template, you will have to perform some basic Knowledge setup: initial topics, authors, and initial fields. Why? The **Help Center** template is built first and foremost as a way for people to search for information. It refers to our topic of case deflection, referred to in the previous section. Let's look at the home screen in *Figure 10.14*:

Figure 10.14: Help Center template – home page

As you can see, the prominent fixture on the page is search. That search feature is tied directly to the Knowledge articles you have set up. The two gray boxes at the bottom are also Knowledge topics. Think of those topics as a collection of articles.

The intended navigation is for a user to navigate to a topic/article collection to contact support. This contrasts with the **Customer Service** template, which offers a reach-out to support straight from the **Home** page. Let's click on one of the default topics you created to see what the page looks like in *Figure 10.15*:

Figure 10.15: Help Center template – topic collection page

In *Figure 10.15*, we clicked on the topic of **Delivery Issues** to get to a page where articles on that topic would be displayed. We are now presented with a **Contact Support** option. Clicking on the **Contact Support** option will launch a very familiar page for your Salesforce Administrators if they are looking at multiple templates. When you click on **Contact Support**, you should navigate to the page seen in *Figure 10.16*:

Figure 10.16: Help Center template – Contact Support

In *Figure 10.16*, you can see how the page looks very similar to the other two templates' **Contact Support** page. The difference is the styling that has been applied based on the overall **Help Center** template. You can still change how you style it and curate any subpages. The big thing to remember about leveraging the **Help Center** template is that it is a Knowledge-first site, and you will need to have a Salesforce Knowledge management strategy set up before you use this template. With that in mind, let's jump into our deep dive on Knowledge setup!

Service Cloud – Knowledge setup

The joys and mysteries of Knowledge will be a trail on your path to success unlike any you have experienced to date. Because the structure of Salesforce Knowledge is intrinsically based on content, it is an item that needs a lot of pre-planning before you jump into setup. This typically means working with the brilliantly creative minds of marketing, service, and even technical writing to understand the unified vision of categorizing content for your consumers. While this isn't a Service Cloud-first book, we have put together a few items you should talk through as an organization for your Knowledge strategy conversation since it will impact your Experience Cloud users:

Consideration	Why does it matter?
Article visibility	What you expose to whom will be part of your overall security considerations. You need to ensure that the information you are putting out there is only for the population of users you intend. As you grow your content, the chance for accidental exposure increases if you do not have a strong security model. For *Delivery International,* we would not want our End Consumers to receive articles intended for our franchisees, for example.
Topics	Think of these as high-level buckets people will interact with to get to a collection of articles. Visually, having a bunch for people to scroll through will tend to get you fewer clicks and more searches. The more options in this case, the less likely you are to have someone fully navigate the page. Keep topics simple and clear to limit any excessive screen scrolling.
Data storage	All Salesforce organizations have data storage limits. Articles with multiple versions can become complicated with that storage model, as each version may have different attachments and storage needs. Your data strategy here will need to be reviewed.
Data categories	This is the primary function that makes articles searchable outside of just their topic. Just as with most Salesforce products, there is a default organizational limit of 100 data categories. That may sound like a lot, but depending on how many Experience Cloud sites you are planning and for how many different audiences, you may quickly hit that limit.
Article approvals	Should people who have permission to create articles be able to publish straight to the Experience Cloud site, or is there an editorial process? If there is an editorial process, we recommend setting up an approval process for your Knowledge articles. This will ensure that items follow your process and that only approved articles are published to external communities.

Table 10.2: Knowledge strategy considerations

In *Table 10.2*, we mention a few times that there are different limits that you may encounter with Salesforce Knowledge. For more information on these limits, we encourage you to visit Salesforce's resource page on Knowledge scalability: `https://help.salesforce.com/s/articleView?id=sf.knowledge_scalability.htm&type=5`. That page details the limits and also explains that you can request an increase to these limits. If you decide you need to request an increase, you must make sure you have a good explanation of why. Note that increases are not unlimited! You can't just expect that any time you make a request, it will be approved. Use your increased storage requests sparingly, ensure that you have a good business case, and, most importantly, perform regular data cleanup to avoid hitting the limit in the first place.

When you are looking at Knowledge articles, you can use them in more places than just your Experience Cloud site. A prime use case is for service agents to use them in case resolution, allowing them to respond to consumers with a predefined set of instructions on how to resolve a problem versus having to use an email template or manually type them. It helps keep your company's branding on point and the voice/tone of the company's responses consistent. Leveraging Knowledge articles in your support process needs to be part of your overall strategy.

Getting your teams together in a focus session regarding your strategy for Knowledge can be a lengthy process. Make sure you have time planned in your schedule to accommodate these key decisions. Depending on your business partners, we typically recommend a month-long process. You won't be meeting every day, but this is something that requires space to think through scenarios and create content. It may also help some people to start generating content they themselves would want to place in articles. That view of how their sample content would fit within the confines of what they defined can be the key to progress. We wish you luck in your strategy adventure, and we encourage you to think about your Experience Cloud users as you begin creating a Knowledge base to serve them.

Let's fast forward to the other side of Knowledge strategy, known as the act of implementation. The good news is that the implementation of Knowledge is rather straightforward. The longest parts are the strategy and content creation. Just like you experienced with cases, there are two sides to Knowledge setup. In this section, we are going to take you through some of the basic setup steps that will happen within **Salesforce Setup**. We will explore the exposure of Knowledge on the Experience Cloud site in the next section. To start, you need to navigate to **Salesforce Setup**. Next, you will search for **Knowledge** in the top-left search bar. You are looking for **Knowledge Settings**. Take a look at *Figure 10.17* for reference:

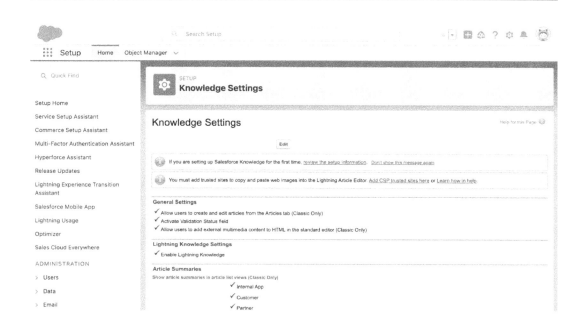

Figure 10.17: Knowledge Settings inside of Salesforce Setup

Notice in *Figure 10.17* that there are two callout information boxes. If this is your first time here, we highly recommend you click on the links to their help articles. These will give you detailed instructions on what each option means for setup. A lot of the options will be default enabled if you are using a new Salesforce instance. If you have a legacy instance, you may not have the latest features enabled.

Once you have the base settings enabled, the next item is article configuration. In the **Object Manager** section of **Salesforce Setup**, you want to search for **Linked Article**. In *Figure 10.18*, we are showing you what the **Linked Article** setup landing page looks like after you have located the object via **Object Manager**:

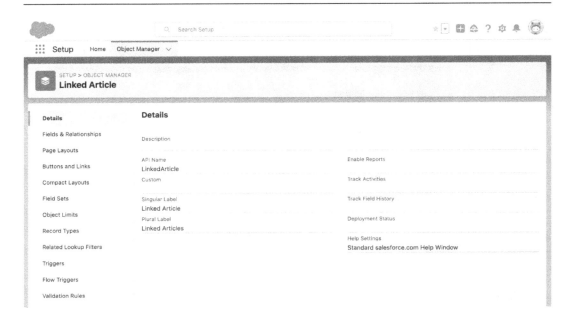

Figure 10.18: Linked Article configuration

In the **Linked Article** configuration, you will be able to add any additional fields, set up approval processes, and define internal layouts. For our purposes with *Delivery International*, the standard fields are all that are required. If you want to learn more about your Knowledge configuration setting possibilities, we recommend looking for a Trailhead course or a Service Cloud-focused book. Let's take our basic setup and head on over to enable this in our Experience Cloud site.

Enabling Knowledge in Experience Cloud

Enabling Knowledge in Experience Cloud is just like case enablement in terms of how each template can be slightly different. You also have the option to curate customized experiences on your site. Let's take a moment to go back to the beginning of the chapter and repeat a screenshot you have seen now as the default support landing page in most of the templates we have reviewed. We'll place the previously shown *Figure 10.7* here to prevent you from having to find it again:

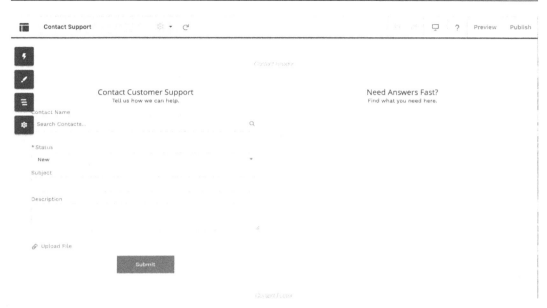

Figure 10.19: Partner Central – default Contact Support page

The component you see on the right-hand side of the page is a Knowledge component. What you want to do is hover over the **Need Answers Fast?** title. You should see a blue lightning bar that pops up over it saying **Case Deflection**. Remember: it is called **Case Deflection** because the goal is to have self-service eliminate easy service tickets that might come in by helping people before they enter a case. This allows your service representatives to focus on more complicated challenges.

Click on **Case Deflection**. That will then bring up options to configure that component. Check out the following screenshot to see what your screen should now look like since you opened the configuration:

Figure 10.20: Case Deflection configuration

In your configuration options shown in *Figure 10.20*, you have a few sections that you can modify. **General Settings** is going to cover the basics of title and subtitle information. From there, you can progress into configuring what the component looks like if it is in an empty state. This means that nothing has been entered by the user yet on the support topic, so it is simply suggesting items either based on a default topic you have selected or through whatever topics are trending across the site.

Next, you will be looking at **Content Types**. By default, **Articles** will be selected, and you have the option of adding discussions to the mix. For an initial go-live of the product, we recommend you keep it simple by sticking with **Articles** as your single selection. Discussions can be great, but if you don't have the time to moderate them, they can lead to a negative consumer experience.

Head on over to set up **Deflection Metrics**. What you are doing here is selecting what prompts people can use to indicate how helpful an article was in solving their challenge or inquiry. You can customize the language so that it is within the brand's voice/tone guidelines for your company. If you don't have such guidelines, Salesforce has some prepopulated recommendations that you can roll with. Once you have made those final choices, you can simply exit the configuration settings. When you do, it will look as though nothing has changed on your page. You may say, *Where in the Astro did my work go?* and be tempted to throw your laptop into the San Francisco Bay in a panic. But don't worry; the component will start to populate once you get articles that match the **Empty State** criteria in which you entered the component. Until then, it will appear blank for you in setup. With those simple steps, you have now enabled the basics of Knowledge articles inside of Experience Cloud. Congratulations! Remember: the biggest hurdle in Knowledge articles is the content management strategy and curation of content. Those are both things that require strong business partnerships and constant maintenance.

Summary

Service Cloud is an incredibly powerful tool to support your users as they ask questions, troubleshoot issues, or perform self-service. While Salesforce can integrate with many applications, it works best with products designed for its experiences, and leveraging Service Cloud for service portals hosted on Salesforce Experience Cloud is no exception.

Now that you understand the native use of Service Cloud and its standard object architecture, you can better combine it with the web interfacing of Experience Cloud. Knowing how Service Cloud works explains how the three primary Experience Cloud templates that leverage native Service Cloud architecture should behave while helping you understand considerations for how you set up internal components. Additionally, you should also have a high-level understanding of how to implement, curate, manage, and use Knowledge bases to solve client questions via case deflection.

In this chapter, we reviewed the following topics:

- How to set up cases
- How to enable service assets in Experience Cloud
- A Knowledge base setup strategy
- Enabling Knowledge in Experience Cloud

Even though Service Cloud has some security considerations to it and we briefly touched on article security in this chapter, we haven't yet reviewed security across all the different aspects of Experience Cloud. We'll explore security in the next chapter, *Chapter 11, Security – Authentication, Data Sharing, and Encryption.*

Part 4:
Site Launch

In this part, you will prepare your site for launch requires security checks and a good monitoring plan. Once you launch your site, we will teach you how to maintain and moderate it.

This part has the following chapters:

- *Chapter 11, Security – Authentication, Data Sharing, and Encryption*
- *Chapter 12, Monitoring Your Site – Salesforce Native Reporting*
- *Chapter 13, Site Launch, Maintenance, and Moderation*

Security – Authentication, Data Sharing, and Encryption

While cyber-attacks are definitely on the rise, most data breaches aren't committed by people who growl, *"I'm in"* as a bunch of neon green letters stream down a page to "hack" into "the mainframe." Data breaches mostly happen when someone at a corporation is sloppy, not paying attention, or deceived by an outside party. Make no mistake, hackers absolutely exist, and good ones can definitely code their way around vulnerabilities in your system architecture to get what they're after. However, the true culprit behind data leaks is usually people within their own organization making preventable mistakes in a hurry.

Good **Information Security** (**InfoSec**) practices start with the right mindset: designing for caution and prioritizing safety first. With anything externally-facing such as a digital site, you need to be especially thoughtful about the security mechanisms protecting yourself and the people who depend on you. Securing your users' data is just as important as guarding your organization's internal data. Your Experience Cloud strategy needs to cleanly tie into the security and sharing rules of your Salesforce CRM. Perhaps you haven't built the CRM side just yet. Don't worry, these same practices will help you inform that strategy. When considering security, user maintenance and authentication must be a part of your plan. In addition, it's important to ensure that a user experience can't be maliciously used to attack your site or CRM.

Our fictional company, *Delivery International*, is thinking about its security needs as it moves forward with Experience Cloud. They have had Salesforce Sales Cloud for a bit, but they know they have to re-assess its current security setup to handle Experience Cloud. They need to do a review of their existing Salesforce sharing model and determine what needs to stay, what needs to go, and what needs to be introduced into their model to accommodate a safe, secure Experience Cloud site. They know they need to review their existing Salesforce contact setup to ensure Experience Cloud end users can safely tie into things such as **Single Sign-On** (**SSO**). Additionally, they need to consider what their options are for extra security layers and review how to set up native tools such as **Lightning Locker**. They also need to set up **Content Security Policies** (**CSPs**) to ensure adherence to their own enterprise standards. Finally, they need to review items requiring encryption, such as sensitive forms of information such as usernames or **Personally Identifiable Information** (**PII**).

In this chapter, we're going to look at security from the following angles:

- Defining your Experience Cloud data sharing model

- Authenticating users on your Experience Cloud site

- CSP and Lightning Locker to combat XSS and clickjacking

- Encrypting your data and protecting your users

- The trickiest aspect of all of this will be getting your head around the mechanisms Salesforce uses for sharing access and records. So, let's get that out of the way first.

Defining your Experience Cloud data sharing model

One of the hardest parts of Salesforce to understand and stay on top of is the nature of record sharing and object visibility, as it is done declaratively… but can also be influenced or even overwritten by coding practices. The essence of Salesforce Security is **profiles** and **roles**, but they extend out to **permission sets** and **sharing rules**. Additionally, developers can write Apex code to respect sharing or not, meaning Apex code can override native Salesforce user security mechanisms in certain situations. Every now and then, Salesforce gloms these things together into a license-granted setting buried somewhere deep in Salesforce Setup or custom metadata.

For Experience Cloud purposes, we will stick with the declarative tools, as those should be the basis for your security design. At a high level, let's review how profiles, roles, permission sets, and sharing rules work, while looking at the concepts of **Field Level Security (FLS)**, **licenses**, and **organization-wide defaults**. Understanding the functionalities explained in *Table 11.1* will set the basis for how access works, although there are a few more idiosyncrasies Experience Cloud introduces in Builder.

Security mechanism	What it does and when to use it
Profile	A profile controls high-level app and object access, in addition to FLS. It also grants user permissions, such as **Marketing User**. Use this as the basis of all access, as every user requires a profile.
Permission set	Permission sets are essentially mini profiles you can layer on top of a user's existing profile assignment. You will also often see managed packages or Salesforce products grant permissions with permission sets or permission set groups. Use these only when you wish to assign granular permissions but don't want to change someone's profile.

Security mechanism	What it does and when to use it
FLS	FLS is a layer that allows administrators to determine which fields can be read, edited, created, or deleted by users.
	Use FLS when you want to grant or restrict access to specific fields on an object a user can view.
Role	Roles are a user hierarchy within Salesforce that determine a user's access to records within objects. Those at the top of the hierarchy can see the most data.
	Use roles to set record visibility based on organizational hierarchy. Note that roles are not mandatory in Salesforce.
Sharing rule	Sharing rules disregard Salesforce roles and organization-wide defaults, allowing you to set specific sharing rules based on the data within a record. Sharing rules can also be assigned to sharing rule groups made of specific users.
	Use these when you have record-based criteria that controls when a record should be shared.
License	A Salesforce license is usually associated with a certain kind of Salesforce product and dictates what a user can see and do within a product.
	Use these when a Salesforce product requires specific licensure to access, such as authenticated users in Experience Cloud.
Organization-wide defaults	This is the default access level for an object across the organization, set to **public** or **private**.
	Use these defaults as a base line, then tailor permissions based on the level of privacy needed.

Table 11.1: Salesforce user access mechanisms

While we mentioned that some of the mechanisms in *Table 11.1* can technically be coded over, the proper way to set up access in Salesforce is through the use of profiles, roles, permission sets, and sharing rules.

Experience Cloud introduces a wrinkle into the standard Salesforce object and record visibility model because authenticated Experience Cloud users can be built off the contact object, and therefore Experience Cloud users live on both the user and the contact object. Consequently, it is very important to consider your contact object's security settings, in addition to the control behind who can enable Experience Cloud users from a contact record.

Delivery International is currently reviewing its Salesforce security policy to prepare for its Franchisee portal. Currently, *Delivery International* has an organization-wide default of public read-write on their opportunity object, and no sharing rules in place. *Delivery International* wants its franchisees to be able to edit their own opportunities, as well as opportunities people within their franchise might have entered. However, they do not want franchisees to be able to access other opportunity records that do not belong to people outside of their franchisee organization. How would *Delivery International* accomplish this?

Since we know not everyone should have access to **Opportunities**, we need to change our organization-wide defaults to set up a private sharing model. To do this, we would go to **Setup** | **Sharing Settings** and select **Opportunities** from the dropdown:

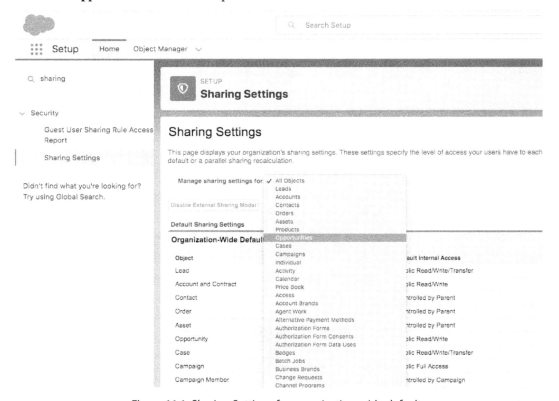

Figure 11.1: Sharing Settings for organization-wide defaults

Selecting **Opportunities** from the menu will take you to an overview of the sharing settings of the object itself. Clicking **Edit** from this page will take you to the organization-wide default edit page, where you can navigate to set access for default external and internal access. See *Figure 11.2*.

Figure 11.2: Default access levels for standard objects

Now that we've defined the organization-wide default for opportunities, we need to create roles that represent who that information should be shared with. To do this, go to **Setup** | **Roles** and create a new role in the hierarchy tree. Let's call this role `Partnership Leader` in the field shown in *Figure 11.3*.

Figure 11.3: Setting up a new role

From here, you can select basic view and edit permissions specific to **Opportunities**, but note that this setting is only for **Opportunities** from accounts for which they are the record owner, which will likely not be the case in Experience Cloud. To fulfill *Delivery International*'s requirements, you will still need to set up sharing rules. Continue, select **Users in this role can edit all opportunities associated with accounts they own, regardless of who owns the opportunity**, and hit **Save**. Now, let's go back in and make a role underneath our `Partnership Leader` role called `Partner Member`. Select the third **Opportunity access** option and hit **Save**.

Figure 11.4: Role overview page

After we have clicked **Save**, we will now see our role page overview. Here, we can review users, sharing group associations, and group visibility settings. Go ahead and associate these roles with your relevant users, as the role hierarchy requires user assignments.

We're almost there; the last step is to set up a sharing rule. Navigate back to the **Sharing Settings** page in *Figure 11.1*. Click the **New** button in the **Opportunity Sharing Rules** section, which will take you to the screen shown in *Figure 11.5*.

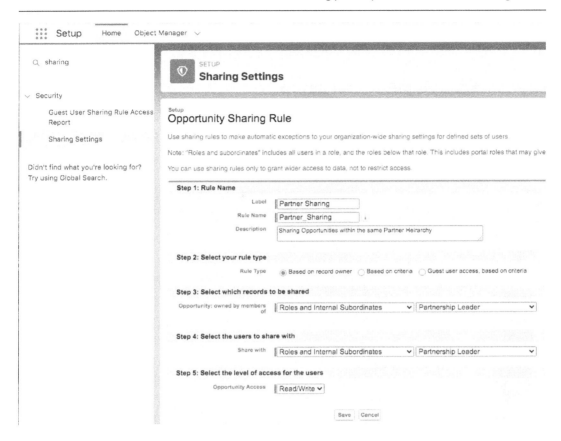

Figure 11.5: The Opportunity Sharing Rule page

From this screen, we can set the criteria for how records should be shared. Since we know we want Opportunities owned by a Partnership Leader Franchisee to be sharable with Partner Members and vice versa, we're going to want to select **Opportunity owned by members of Roles and Subordinates for Partnership Leader**, and ensure that it's shared with **Roles and Internal Subordinates** of Partnership Leader. We know our users need **Read/Write** permissions instead of **Read Only**, so select the appropriate access level and click the **Save** button!

Finally, be sure to test your sharing rules in a lower environment by creating sample records and emulating user access before you publish these changes live. Don't forget to audit all of your Salesforce objects in your sharing model, including activities, files, and libraries! Note also that there are some standard roles that may impact your security model, which come with the pre-baked Experience Cloud templates, such as Partner Central. Some of these roles control who can create and delete new users and overwrite who has access to records in the hierarchy, even overriding the organization's standard defaults. While our illustration shows a stem to stern set up of a hypothetical role, the three standard partner roles (**Partner User**, **Partner Manager**, and **Partner Executive**) could also be used to achieve similar access.

Once you've nailed your Experience Cloud sharing model for authenticated users, it's time to review your guest user profile setup. Let's move over to thinking through this setup.

Experience Cloud guest user setup

You need to decide whether your site will be fully behind authentication or whether there are parts that could be available without having to log in. If some areas of your site do not require authentication, you will have to create what's known in Salesforce as a guest user profile, which grants default levels of access to unauthenticated users.

To set up a guest user, you will first have to ensure guest user access is enabled. Navigate to **Builder | Settings | General** and check **Guest users can see and interact with the site without logging in** under **Public Access**:

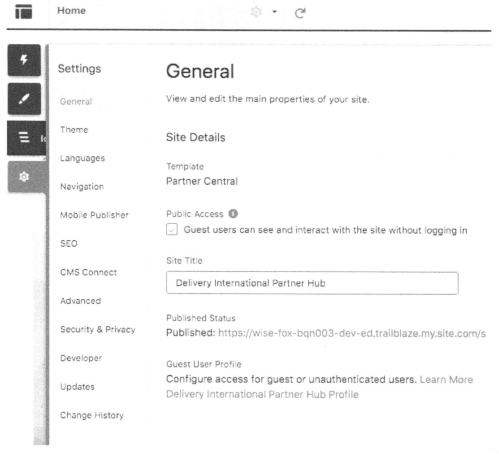

Figure 11.6: Public access setting in builder

After the public access setting is checked, click the link below that says **Delivery International Partner Hub Profile**, which will take you to the profile of the guest user license attached to your Experience Cloud site. Note that if you have entered a different title, then it will say what you entered, not anything containing **Delivery International**. From here, you will get to the standard profile setup page where you can determine page layouts, tab settings, record type settings for your guest user, and more:

Figure 11.7: Guest user profile setup

Note that the guest user license must be associated with the profile to ensure it accommodates non-authenticated usage. Salesforce relies on visibility to operate, so the guest user profile is extremely important for sites that do not require authentication, or sites that have parts that don't require authentication.

If you're looking for a holistic rollup of guest user access, you can also check rule access for guest users by going to **Setup | Guest User Sharing Rule Access Report**:

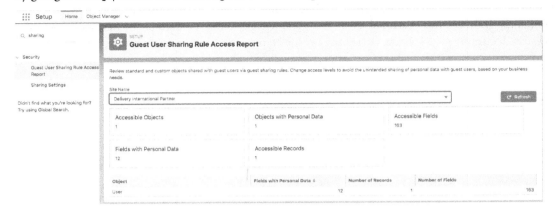

Figure 11.8: Guest User Sharing Rule Access Report

Now that we know the basics for setting up visibility and record sharing for our users, let's move on to how to best authenticate users on your Experience Cloud site.

Authenticating users on your Experience Cloud site

Users can get into your Experience Cloud in a few different ways, whether they're your customers, your internal users, or guest users coming to your site via a Google Search. If you're looking to automate and protect access to your site, let's start with how to set up authenticated users.

Setting up authenticated users

If your user needs to be associated with an account on a partner or customer service Experience Cloud site, you will first need to set up a contact record and parent it under the relevant account record. While you can enable a setting allowing for self-registration and even set up logic for Salesforce to search for a parent account before creating a new one, let's review how to set up an authenticated user in Experience Cloud with account considerations.

First, you will need to ensure that the standard **Enable Customer User** button is on the page layout from the app your users will be using to add folks so that users can click it off the contact record:

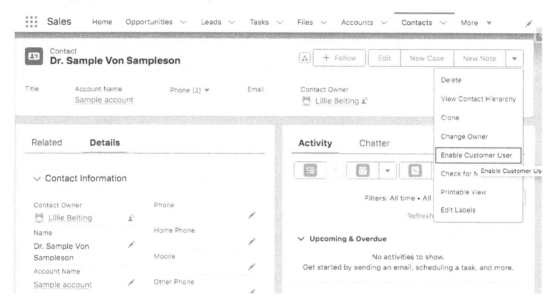

Figure 11.9: The Enable Customer User button

Clicking **Enable Customer User** will open up a user creation record and tie these two records together. Select the appropriate user license on the **User Setup** page and click **Save**. You will then need to assign relevant permission sets at the user level. Saving the user will send out an email to the record on file, prompting a user to set an Experience Cloud password if SSO is not yet enabled. Ensure that the permission sets or profiles you have attached to this customer user are available for your Experience Cloud site by navigating to **Builder | Administration | Members**. If you're on the **Setup** page, you can navigate there by searching for **All sites** and clicking **Workspaces | Administration**.

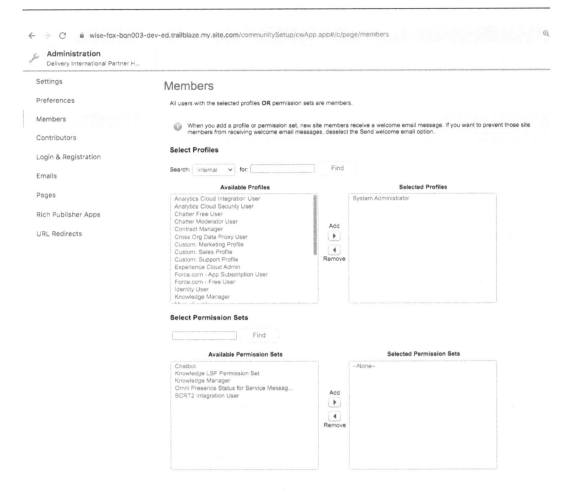

Figure 11.10: UI for adding profiles and permission sets

This page will allow you to add users to an Experience Cloud site by profiles and permission sets, but be advised that it will email new members if the welcome email setting is not deselected. Now that we understand the groundwork for setting up users, let's look at how we would enable SSO for internal and external users.

Connected apps and SSO

Experience Cloud can be placed behind SSO using an **Internal Identity Provider** (**IdP**). You can use both common enterprise IdPs, such as Okta or Microsoft Azure, and third-party social media ones, such as Apple, Google, or Facebook. We strongly caution you to work with your security teams to determine which IdP makes the most sense for your organization, although we generally advise using an internally-controlled enterprise IdP for more granular control over your users' access. A third-party option such as Google or Apple fits better for more relaxed-control environments, such as high volume self-registration sites.

To set up SSO, type in `Single Sign-On` into the Salesforce Set Up search. First, ensure that **SAML Enabled** is clicked:

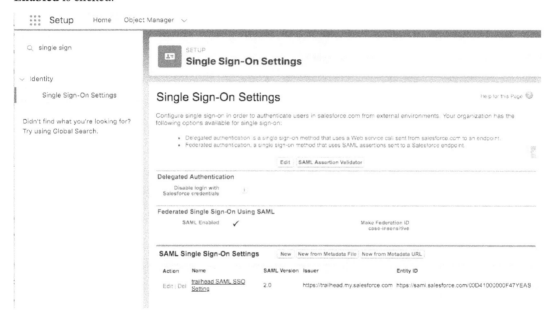

Figure 11.11: SSO setup for Salesforce

Then, you will see the **Load New**, **New from Metadata File**, and **New from Metadata URL** options. The **New** page will prompt a wizard for information, and the **Metadata File** or **Metadata URL** options will pre-populate information based on input. If you are using an internal IdP, you will need to download the Salesforce metadata from setup and upload it into your IdP setup. Please consult your IdP's guide on this, as it may vary by provider.

You will also have to go into your Experience Cloud site's **Builder** settings and enable the option to log in with your username and password, or with the new SSO you just set up, under **Login Page Setup**:

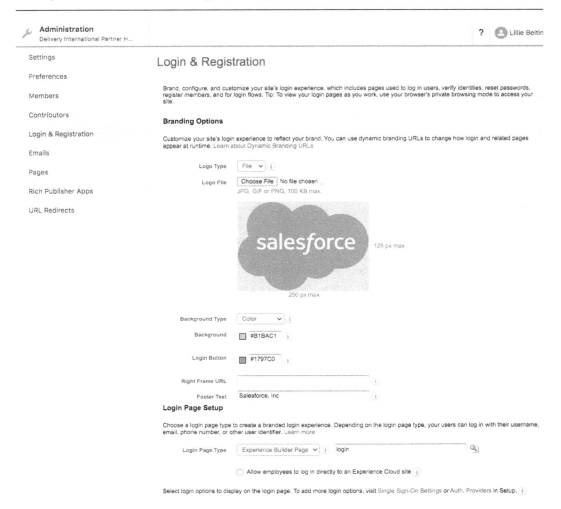

Figure 11.12: Adding SSO to your Experience Cloud login page

For SSO to work, some kind of ID will need to be associated with the user record in question. Depending on how your IdP is set up, this might be a code unique to the active directory that you enter into the **federation ID** field, or it might be ensuring that the value of the username matches with the email address in the SAML call. You will also need to ensure that the profile of your users has permission to use SSO.

SSO setup can vary from company to company, and as always, we encourage you to work with your security teams to ensure that your SSO configuration matches the standards set by the rest of your enterprise. Also, remember that you may need to open a Case with Salesforce to troubleshoot any issues with your connection. Go to **Salesforce Help** and open a Case just to triple check your connections. In the meantime, let's move on to unauthenticated users.

Unauthenticated user considerations

For unauthenticated users, we still have considerations beyond SAML/SSO to keep your users and Experience Cloud site safe. There's another kind of traffic-oriented cyber security weak point you should be aware of called a **Denial of Service (DoS)** or **Distributed Denial of Service (DDoS)** attack. DDoS attacks happen when large amounts of traffic are driven to your site in order to force it to crash. They can take a few formats, such as hitting servers over and over with a bad IP address that has been associated with viruses or spam, but the idea is that all of this illegitimate traffic will block anyone else from using your sites. DDoS attacks can be incredibly complex and this is just a brief overview, so if you're looking for more information on them and how to prevent them, check out Packt's guide at `https://security.packt.com/category/ddos-attacks/`.

You are most likely to experience this kind of attack on unauthenticated sites such as public learning centers, but it's possible that a DDoS attack could happen at the logins of your portals. A way to combat DDoS attacks is to use interstitial pages that put a barrier between traffic and your site to prevent a script from trying to force its way into your site. You can also look at firewall rules, Geo and IP blocking, or rate limitations on calls as mitigation strategies, but ultimately, Salesforce owns the infrastructure that can wholly combat DDoS attacks.

Since we're now familiar with controlling authentication and external traffic as it moves through our sites, let's move on to other kinds of web attacks and how to prevent them.

CSP and Lightning Locker to combat XSS and clickjacking

Security doesn't stop with access or mere record visibility. The very components on your page can put your site at risk if they're not carefully coded, protected, and monitored. There are many methods that malicious parties can use to leverage poor code on your site to work their way into your systems, but most of them broadly involve emulating part of your site code to infiltrate code on the rest of your site and/or extract sensitive information from your users. Even though Salesforce has a lot of declarative "kill switches" to isolate certain attacks that most unmanaged software doesn't come with, we still have to think through our security set up. Lucky for us, the implementation of many of these security best practices is easily configurable using settings within Salesforce. We will review clickjacking later in this chapter; let's start with the CSP.

How to set a CSP

A CSP is an additional layer of security and web standard that dictates how and when content is loaded on your site's pages. The CSP is a list of rules designed to determine what belongs to your site and what doesn't. By clearly delineating what is considered a safe third party versus an unknown one, you can prevent **Cross-Site Scripting (XXS)** attacks, a type of cyber attack that attaches malicious code to your legitimate website while disguising it as browser code. XXS attacks are bad news and can cause a lot of damage, such as keystroke capturing, phishing, malware distribution, and information theft, so it's very important that you set up a CSP. A good CSP creates reporting mechanisms for potential security threats or violations and allows developers to define which domains can load resources, such as scripts or images.

To set up the Salesforce CSP, start by navigating to **Experience Cloud Builder**. Click on the settings icon in the left menu, and navigate down to **Security and Privacy**. In the middle of the page, you will see a box called **Content Security Policy (CSP)**:

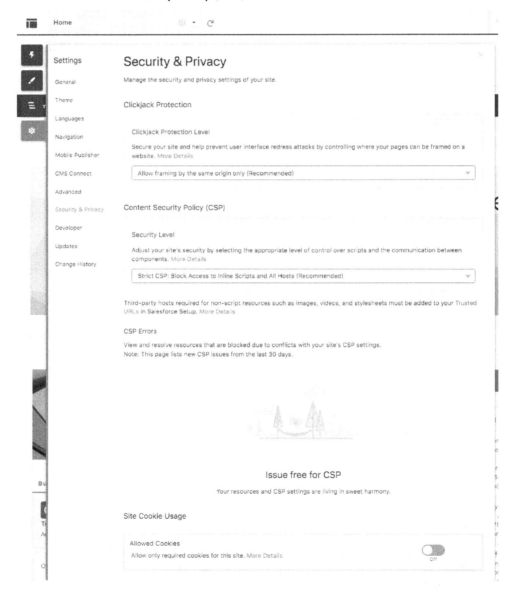

Figure 11.13: The Security & Privacy page

There are two default options for security levels: **Strict CSP: Block Access to Inline Scripts and All Hosts (Recommended)** and **Relaxed CSP: Permit Access to Inline Scripts and Allowed Hosts**. You can also check out any CSP errors or issues that might have appeared over the last 30 days in this view.

Be advised that strict CSP is the default setting for Experience Builder sites, but you can tailor which resources it allows instead of prohibits. If you want to use a relaxed CSP, you will get the following alert:

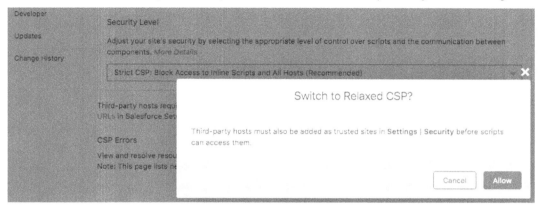

Figure 11.14: Relaxed CSP prompt

Before you can select this option, you will need to go to your **Trusted Sites** page. Note that Lightning Locker will automatically turn on if you select the **Relaxed** option.

To update your trusted URLs, go to Salesforce setup and enter `trusted  URLs` in the search bar, which will take you to the list view for your trusted URLs.

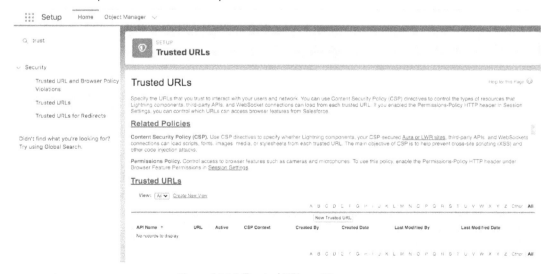

Figure 11.15: Trusted URLs settings page

Click **New Trusted URL**, which will prompt you to enter information about non-Salesforce domains that are allowed to interact with the code on your site:

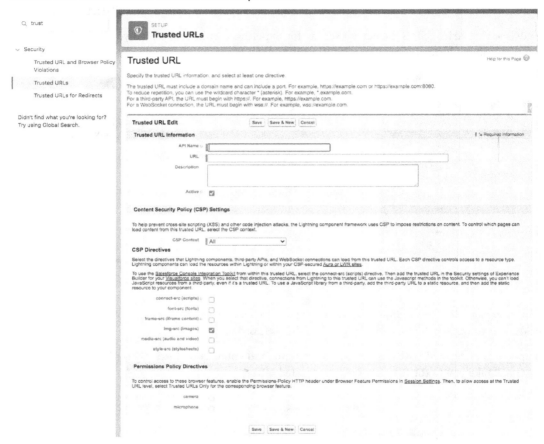

Figure 11.16: Trusted URL setup

After setting up your CSP and trusted sites, the next thing we need to do is set up Lightning Locker.

Setting up Lightning Locker

Lightning Locker is a security layer that essentially dictates how code from different namespaces interacts, allowing for extra security protections when data is sent from a component to an outside source. Lightning Locker is an extra wall of protection on top of a CSP because it insulates components from potential attacks that have made it through other components. Lightning Locker oversees unauthorized API usage, restricts who can access the DOM we discussed in *Chapter 6*, and prevents developers or hackers from publishing to unauthorized frameworks.

Lightning Locker is a default setting in Salesforce, but it can be tailored to your specific needs. As mentioned before, Lightning Locker is enabled by default when you select a relaxed CSP:

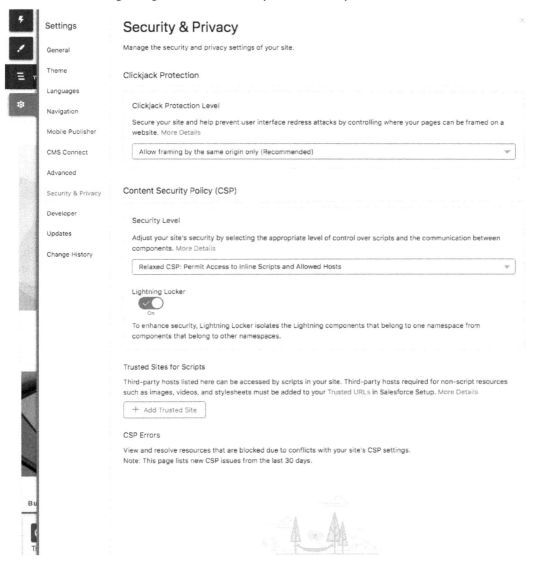

Figure 11.17: Experience Cloud setup of Lightning Locker

Even though Lightning Locker is toggled on by default with the relaxed CSP when it comes to Experience Cloud, there are some customizations you can do to it, although the majority are done through code instead of setup. For more information on how to customize Lightning Locker, visit developer resources:

`https://developer.salesforce.com/docs/atlas.en-us.lightning.meta/lightning/security_code.htm`

Since we've now mastered CSPs and Lightning Lockers, let's review another security method to prevent UI-based attacks.

Enabling clickjack protection

Clickjacking is another UI-based form of hacking whereby someone tricks your user into clicking something that doesn't do what it seems like it should. If you've ever clicked on an ad on an adult site, you're already familiar with this kind of attack.

The first thing you need to do to prevent clickjacking on a Salesforce Experience Cloud site is to install a **Secure Sockets Layer** (**SSL**) certificate – this is essentially a data file that encrypts your connection with web browsers. You may need to work with your internal security team to get certificates if your certificate management is centralized across your company, and it is generally a best practice to have all site certificates managed by a central team if your organization is large enough. You can also generate one through Salesforce if needed by going to **Setup** | **Security** | **Certificate** | **Key Messages**:

Figure 11.18: Certificate and Key Management setting in Salesforce setup

Here, you can either implement a certificate that your security team gave you or generate a new one.

After you've set up your certificates, the next thing you'll want to do is enable clickjack protection for standard Salesforce pages, as well as Visualforce pages. For standard pages, this is a simple setting. Go to **Setup | Session Settings** and scroll down to the **Clickjack Protection** section:

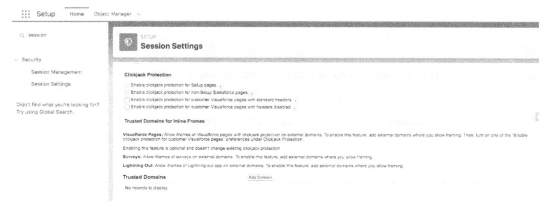

Figure 11.19: Clickjack Protection setup

Here, you can enable your preferred amount of protection. By default, **Enable clickjack protection for Setup pages** and **Enable clickjack protection for non-Setup Salesforce pages** are enabled, but you can select the other two options below those depending on your level of caution and Visualforce page usage. If you have a legacy organization with a significant amount of Visualforce that hasn't yet been migrated, consider using the last two options. On Visualforce pages, you will also need to embed protections within the meta tag on the page's header.

While SSLs and clickjack protection settings are a must in Experience Cloud, it's ultimately the CSP that will prevent attacks. Setting rules that protect the way your site loads and engages with third-party systems is the best defense against third-party attacks. Also, don't forget to check for updates and review your settings. However, another line of defense to protect your users and the data of all parties involves enabling encryption protocols.

Encrypting your data and protecting your users

Encryption is a form of digital security that scrambles transmitted and stored data. This scrambled data can only be unscrambled with a specific digital key. This is a practice known as cryptography. The practice of encrypting your data prevents unauthorized access to sensitive data from both internal users and external users, as you can set who or what has access to the key that decrypts data. Encryption is useful not only for preventing leaks but also for keeping your users from seeing sensitive data such as Social Security numbers or credit card information.

The most common categorizations you will hear about relative to Salesforce will be **data encryption** and **database encryption**, both of which come into play in Salesforce. Data encryption is largely focused on specific records and API messages during transmission, whereas database encryption is concerned with protecting entire objects or fields. While all Salesforce data has some level of encryption across their various products, you can buy additional levels of security such as Salesforce Shield, which allows you to include extra layers of granularity in your security setup. Salesforce Shield is especially useful for organizations with highly regulated or protected information, such as **Protected Health Information (PHI)**.

Data encryption is an extremely vast and complex topic, to the point where people write entire PhD dissertations on it. From a high-level perspective, the advice in this chapter should get you started keeping your information and users safe on an Experience Cloud site. If you'd like to learn more about data encryption, check out Salesforce's security guide resources at `https://developer.salesforce.com/docs/atlas.en-us.securityImplGuide.meta/securityImplGuide/salesforce_security_guide.htm` or take any of Packt's security courses at `https://subscription.packtpub.com/search?query=introduction%20to%20encryption`.

For now, let's look at *Delivery International's* security needs. Anna in quality control wants to make sure that End Consumers can't see the information of other users within Experience Cloud, and Maggie in finance says that encrypting credit card information both within the database and as information is transmitted is non-negotiable for her users. What are our options for honoring these requirements?

HTTPS/TLS and classic encryption in Salesforce

Since Maggie requires that credit card information has data encryption *and* database encryption, we should review a few settings within Salesforce.

The first thing you should know about is HTTPS/TLS Encryption, which is a **Transport Layer Security (TLS)** that keeps information such as credit card numbers safe as it's transmitted between browsers and Salesforce applications. HTTPS/TLS encryption prevents browser attacks and every Salesforce instance comes with an advanced TLS encryption layer by default, but you will need to enable HTTPS on your custom domains.

While Salesforce disabled HTTP-only system-generated domains in 2021, you can check the HTTPS status for a specific domain by navigating to your **Domains** page within Salesforce Setup. Ensuring the domain in question is HTTPS-enabled should assist with Maggie's request for secure transfer.

Next, we need to think about the encryption of the credit card fields themselves. Depending on how Maggie's credit card object model is set up, we may need to encrypt fields across a few different objects to satisfy her requirements. Salesforce standard encryption allows for the encryption of any custom text field of up to 175 characters. It is very easy to set up when creating new fields.

Navigate to **Set Up | Object in Question | Fields and Relationships**. From here, you will see the primitive data types available for a standard creation. Select **Text (Encrypted)** as your data type, which will take you to the details page:

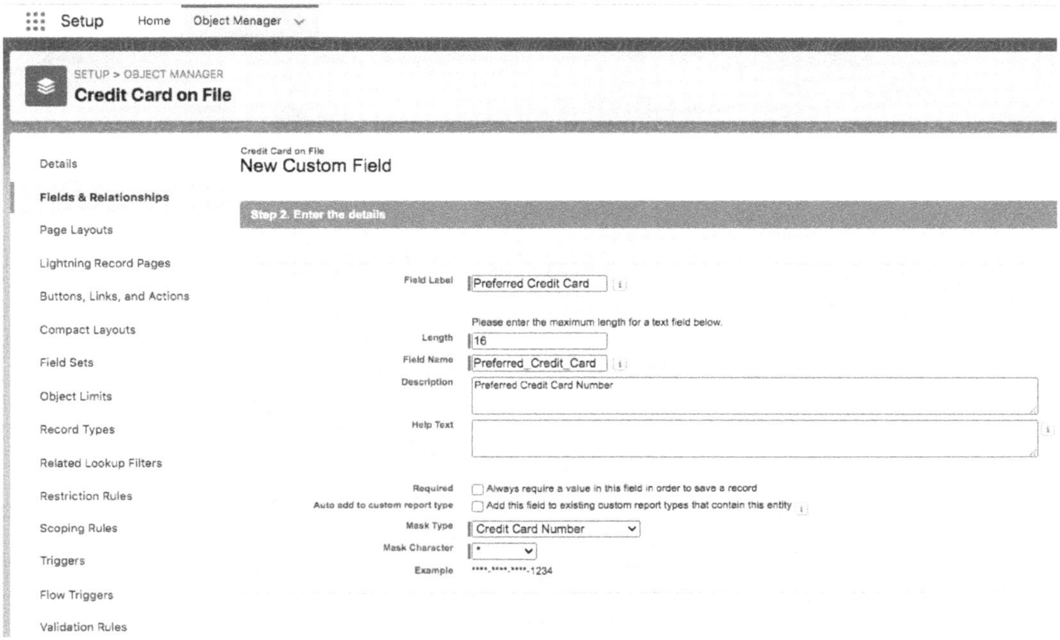

Figure 11.20: Encrypted data field setup

Decide on your mask type and replacement characters, then click the **Save** button. Then, assign the FLS as needed to relevant profiles and determine which page layouts it should live on.

If *Delivery International's* encryption needs become more complex or they find themselves subject to heavy regulation, they may need to purchase Salesforce Shield to stay compliant. Alternatively, depending on the payment processor *Delivery International* uses, all of these encryption policies may already be accounted for in a managed package. Additionally, note that there are two major kinds of encryption relevant to Salesforce Shield: probabilistic and deterministic. The way you are able to report on fields, create SOQL queries, or access them in an API is heavily impacted by the type of encryption you employ, so ensure that you're reviewing all your data extraction needs as you plan.

Now that Maggie's requirements are handled, let's review Anna's.

Protecting your users

Anna's requirement to keep Experience Cloud users from viewing each other's information can be controlled by a few mechanisms inside Salesforce, such as encryption and setting organization-wide defaults to private on relevant objects. However, there is another mechanism inside Salesforce that is specifically designed to insulate Experience Cloud Users, which is kicked off from the **Enhanced Personal Information Management** setting. To access it, go to Salesforce Setup, type in User Management Settings, and ensure that **Enhanced Personal Information Management** is toggled to **Enabled**:

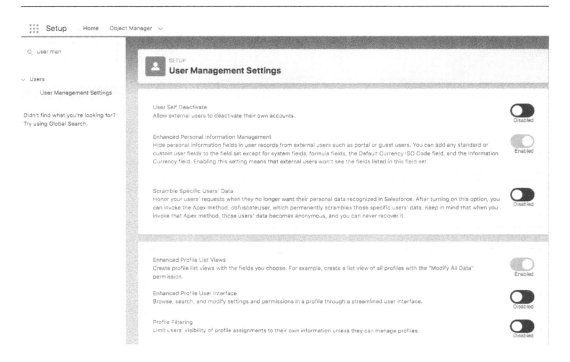

Figure 11.21: Enhanced Personal Information Management

For extra protection, you can also select **Scramble Specific Users' Data**, which will anonymize any data, but be advised that you can never recover that data after selecting this option. However, Enhanced Personal Information Management can mask standard user fields such as alias, SAML federation ID, and username, all of which are controlled by a fieldset that is hyperlinked in the setting. This allows you to decide what constitutes protected information across the board.

Setting up a cookie policy

Additionally, you can set cookie policies for users of your Experience Cloud site to ensure safety and cookie-opt-outs. While most cookie activity on Salesforce is third party, such as the Google and Adobe Analytics tags that can be dropped on a site, there is a native setting in Experience Cloud to reduce extraneous cookie usage.

While Experience Cloud can run without cookies, it may reduce the performance of the site, so it's important to give users the option to keep cookies. To turn on **Allow only required cookies**, go to **Builder | Settings | Security and Privacy** in *Figure 11.15* and scroll all the way to the bottom. There, you will see an **Allow only required cookies for this site** setting.

For a full list of all associated cookies on Experience Cloud that can be adjusted with Apex, review the Salesforce documentation at `https://help.salesforce.com/s/articleView?id=sf.networks_cookies.htm&type=5`.

Setting up encryption and cookie policies makes up the last broad steps of protecting your user information in Salesforce Experience Cloud! Security in Salesforce or any modern web application can be expansive and this is only intended to be an introduction, so validate your security setup internally and with regulation standards where needed.

Summary

While there are many techniques that you can use to protect your users and insulate your data from attacks, the final and most important thing you can do to protect your sites and your Salesforce instance is to test, test, and test some more. If you can automate your regression testing or leverage tools that examine downstream impacts that might compromise your site's security, do it. Often, releases will focus on a specific feature add or element of your site and neglect to check it against existing architecture – therefore, it is on you to ensure that your applications are behaving as expected.

Additionally, keep track of software updates as they come out – and not just ones from Salesforce if you're calling third parties. Keep your eyes open for data leaks, novel technology, or new attacks you might need to protect against. Since hackers are getting cleverer and most "hacking" is social engineering, teaching your users to be mindful of nasty techniques such as phishing will help your end users avoid thoughtless data leaks.

Finally, carefully review what you're pushing in your change sets, environment Git pushes, or any kind of data and/or code update between environment to environment. One of the easiest ways to introduce malware or even just bad code into production is through badly thought-through DevOps practices, so review everything you're about to push before you promote it to a higher environment.

In this chapter, we learned the following:

- Understanding how desired Experience Cloud performance may require security changes within Salesforce CRM and identifying how to implement those changes

- Identifying your login and user authentication strategy to ensure a safe experience

- Learning how to implement CSP and Lightning Locker, with consideration given to clickjack protection

- Knowing when to employ probabilistic vs deterministic encryption and other methods to hide user data

After determining your strategy for safety and compliance, we're almost ready to launch our site. However, before we do that, we need to think about reporting and monitoring our site.

12
Monitoring Your Site – Salesforce Native Reporting

What gets measured gets managed, and a Salesforce Experience Cloud site requires good reporting and analytics to constantly improve your end users' experience. Your stakeholders will want to understand how the investment is achieving the requested **Return on Investment** (**ROI**) goals that were set for the project in *Chapter 1*. Metrics can help create your product roadmap from a data-centric approach.

We will dive into how to enable native Salesforce reporting for your users to view within Experience Cloud and we will help you discern when to create custom reporting, out of the box reports and dashboards, or consider an AppExchange plugin. There are a variety of different web analytics tool plugins for Salesforce Experience Cloud, including an industry standards plugin for Google Analytics to track cross-web property traffic. With these great plugins, you will be able to provide comprehensive reporting across a variety of sources for your marketing teams. All of that does not discount native reporting, so learning which types of reporting match your goals and how to implement them is imperative to effective monitoring of your site.

In *Chapter 11*, we focused on overall security. Here, we will start to dive into security as it relates to reporting. Understanding who can see which data will ensure that your metrics give the intended outcomes. Let's look at what you can expect:

- Experience Cloud out-of-the-box reporting
- Google Analytics and third-party web analytics
- Setting up reporting for your Experience Cloud users

Now that we have an overview, we are going to kick off with native reporting in Experience Cloud, sprinkling in a little taste of Einstein Predictions as we go.

Experience Cloud out-of-the-box reporting

With all good setup items, there are a myriad of ways that native reporting can be handled for Salesforce Experience Cloud. In this section, we will cover three out of the four. We are going to focus on the following:

- Dashboards inside My Workspaces
- Dashboards inside of Salesforce Sales or Service Cloud
- Einstein Analytics configurations

The fourth type of setup is reporting inside of the site itself, for the end users of the site. We are going to cover that in our *Setting up reporting for your Experience Cloud users* section. Let's jump into getting dashboarding set up inside your My Workspaces.

Dashboards inside My Workspaces

The first thing to do is make sure that you have navigated over to the workspace you wish to build reports on from the **All Sites** section of the Salesforce configuration. Once you have navigated there, you will want to click on **Dashboards**.

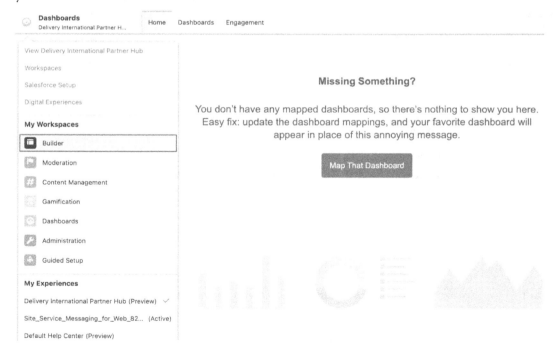

Figure 12.1: Workspace navigation to Dashboards

In *Figure 12.1*, you will see the space under **My Workspaces** for **Dashboards**. When you click on **Dashboards**, you will then see a **Missing Something?** screen if this is the first time you are navigating here. Don't worry though; we will fix that now by clicking **Map That Dashboard**. When you first navigate there, you are going to see that there are lots of items you can fill out.

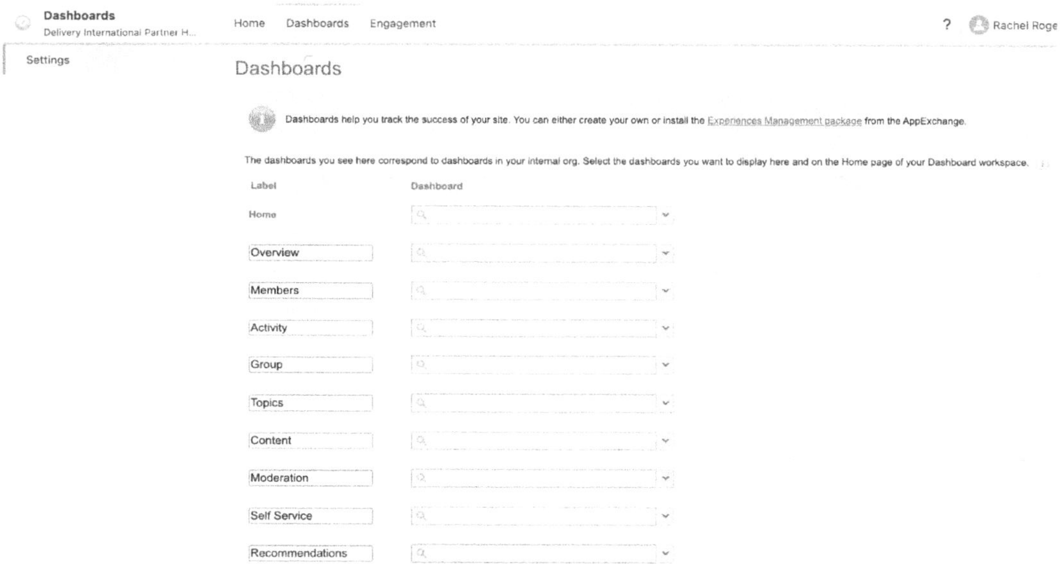

Figure 12.2: Workspaces Dashboard mapping setup

Figure 12.2 showcases some of the options you have regarding which label it recommends that you correlate a dashboard to. There is also a suggestion at the top of the page for you to install the *Experiences Managed Package App*. We recommend that you start by following that suggestion. If you click the link from the info message at the top of the screen, you will see something like *Figure 12.3*.

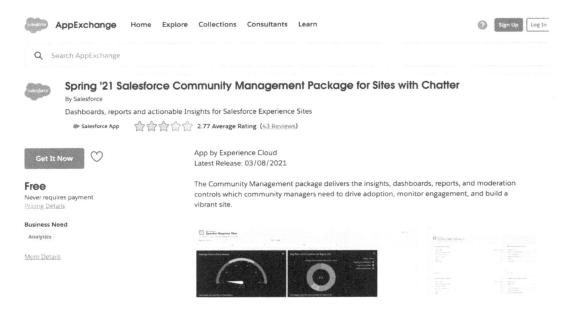

Figure 12.3: Experiences Managed Package app on AppExchange

Figure 12.3 shows you the general information page and highlights that the app is free. It showcases what will be installed in your Salesforce organization should you proceed with the download. If you are unsure whether this will fit your needs, try it out in one of your Salesforce Sandboxes first. A good basis for starting Experience Cloud Analytics is giving your business partners something to react to instead of asking them to dream up metrics. Once you are ready to move forward, click the **Get It Now** button on the left-hand side of the screen.

Sometimes, in the magical land of Salesforce, your login information will not transfer over to AppExchange. So, it is possible that once you click **Get It Now**, you will land on the screen displayed in *Figure 12.4*.

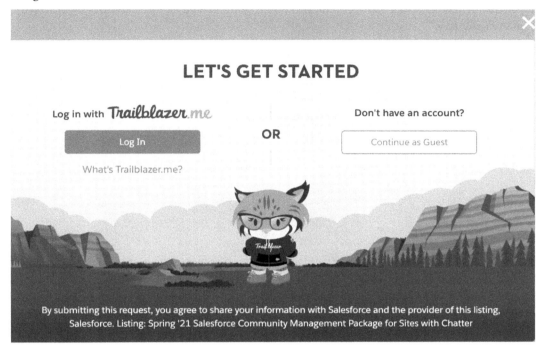

Figure 12.4: AppExchange login screen

In *Figure 12.4*, you can see that there are two options regarding how to log in to the AppExchange. In order to install the instance, you will want to make sure that you pick the **Trailblazer.me** login option. If you choose **Continue as Guest**, then you will not be able to install in an instance as it assumes that you do not have an actual Salesforce instance. Then, you will land on the Trailblazer login screen shown in *Figure 12.5*.

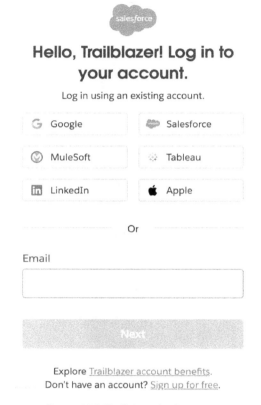

Figure 12.5: Trailblazer login screen

Figure 12.5 shows that you can leverage an existing account. For our purposes, we recommend that you use your Salesforce account. If you do not, you will not see your instance in the AppExchange list for app installment. Note that if this is your first time, you may be required to go through additional verification steps. Please make sure that you complete all steps on the screen in order to get to the screen shown in *Figure 12.6*.

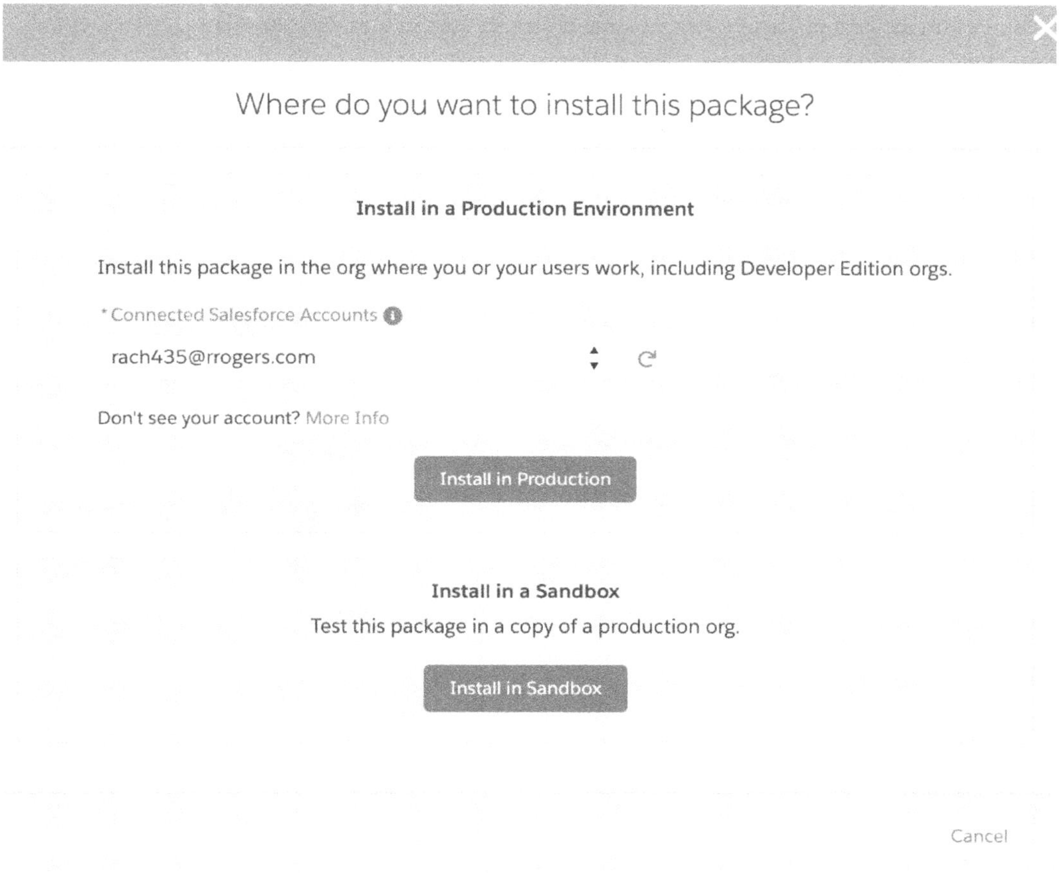

Where do you want to install this package?

Install in a Production Environment

Install this package in the org where you or your users work, including Developer Edition orgs.

* Connected Salesforce Accounts ⓘ

rach435@rrogers.com

Don't see your account? More Info

Install in Production

Install in a Sandbox

Test this package in a copy of a production org.

Install in Sandbox

Cancel

Figure 12.6: AppExchange instance selector screen

Figure 12.6 shows that you are able to install the application in **Production**. If you have multiple production instances, you will see the selector above where you can choose which production instance you would like to put the application into. The best practice is that you install the application in a sandbox first before you make it available in production. Another thing to consider is that if you are in active development and you try to place this application in production, your code base may not be there and your reports could be blank. This is a good item to add to your deployment checklist to ensure that you get it installed in production. You will have a confirmation screen after *Figure 12.6* to confirm that you have read the terms and conditions surrounding your installation. These are standard Salesforce terms and conditions; we recommend that you become familiar with their specifications regarding free applications.

Let's move into the next phase of getting this set up on our site. In *Figure 12.7*, we can see that we now have a choice of whom to install the application for.

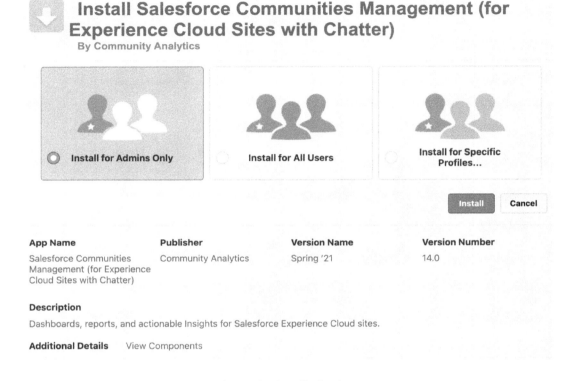

Figure 12.7: Install selections

There are three options for installation in *Figure 12.7*. We recommend that you keep the default selection of **Install for Admins Only**. It gives you the opportunity to make any necessary adjustments. Once you have made your selection, click **Install** and let the magic of Salesforce take over. In the event of the app taking a while to install, Salesforce will give you a warning message letting you know that they will email you when installation is complete instead of asking you to wait around on the installation screen. Once installation is complete, you can find the application in the **Installed Packages** section of your Salesforce setup.

Figure 12.8: Installed Packages

Figure 12.8 showcases what you should now see in the **Installed Packages** section. There is nothing for us to do in this section right now. However, it is the place where you will manage the overall app. So, you can uninstall it or manage licenses for it from this screen.

The beauty of having this app installed is that now, you don't have to worry about mapping any dashboards. Just like magic, they should now all appear when you navigate to **Dashboards** from your Workspaces.

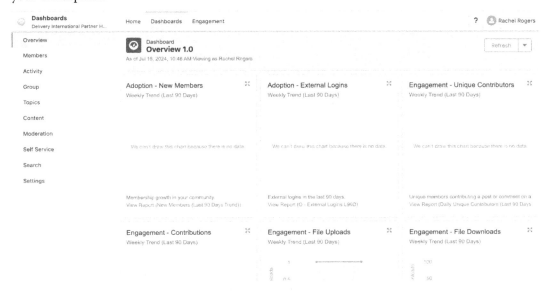

Figure 12.9: Configured Dashboards via the installed Experience app

Figure 12.9 showcases the **Overview Dashboard** that comes with the downloaded app by default. You can see that we haven't really tested our site out yet, so there aren't any metrics populating this Dashboard. However, that doesn't mean that the reports aren't working. They are working, in fact. We just haven't met the filter criteria yet for our items to show on the list. Take a moment to navigate through each of the options on the left-hand side of the screen to familiarize yourself with the data your Experience Cloud site can now report out. If you need a break, now is a good time to pause, as our next step is diving into the world of Dashboards in Sales or Service Cloud.

Dashboards in Sales or Service Cloud

We have now set up the initial Dashboards inside of the Experience Cloud site itself, which is a great first step. However, it is very possible that while you were looking at the security model for your Experience Cloud Site, you decided that access to the workspace for the site would need to be locked down. Locking it down is highly recommended by us until UAT and go-live. So, how will people know the metrics if they cannot access the **Dashboards** tab inside of Workspaces? This is where reporting in Sales or Service Cloud will do the trick.

Since you installed the *Experiences Managed Package App*, the good news is that there is a version of these Dashboards already available inside your Sales or Service Cloud instance. Locate your dashboards by navigating to the **Dashboards** tab in your Sales or Service Cloud instance and click **All Dashboards**. If your Salesforce instance is a legacy version, this may bring up more than what you are looking for. You can head on over to the **All Folders** section. There, you can search for Communities.

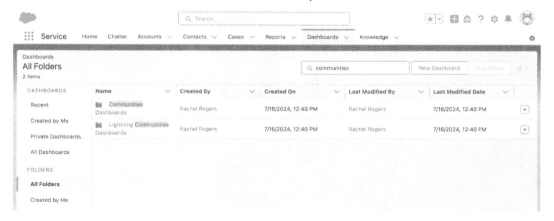

Figure 12.10: Communities folder search

Figure 12.10 shows an example of what you should see when conducting that search. If you have multiple people working in your instance, there may be more than just these two folders that populate. What you are looking to review is the Lighting Communities Dashboards Folder. Click on that to see all the preconfigured Dashboards from within the app.

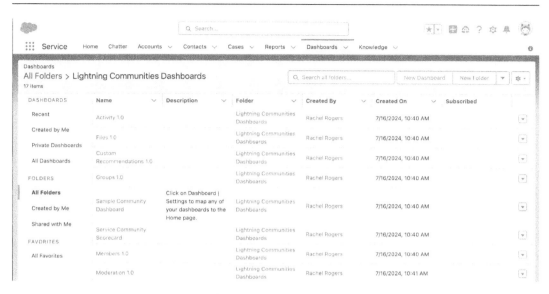

Figure 12.11: Lightning Communities Dashboards Folder

You can see some of the **Dashboards** that are now available to you in *Figure 12.11*. These reports leverage the same filter criteria that you have inside of your Workspace Dashboard space. If you were to update the report/dashboard here, you would also update it in the other view. This keeps your reporting consistent.

You can also venture out and create your own Dashboard. Perhaps after reviewing the preconfigured **Dashboard**s, you found a few of these that you could consolidate into one view for your team versus all the breakouts. You can leverage the existing reports to curate these views or create reports from scratch. We recommend that you hold off on curating customized views until you have actual data to compare these views to. You want to make sure that you aren't consistently interrupting what is being reported. The best way to do that is to ensure that your team understands the basics as Salesforce defines them via these standard **Dashboards** and **Reports**.

We are going to assume that you understand the logic behind the data in the preconfigured reports, so let's talk through how you would curate your own Dashboard. Inside of Salesforce, you are going to want to go to the **Dashboards** object. Once you are on that object, you will see an option for **New Dashboard**, as shown in *Figure 12.12*.

Figure 12.12: Creating a new Dashboard

Once you have clicked **New Dashboard**, as shown in *Figure 12.12*, you will be sent to the **Dashboard configuration** page. The first step is naming your dashboard and determining which folder it should live in. From there, you will be able to select charts or graphs that display the information you have from preconfigured reports. In this sense, a preconfigured report is not limited to only what came from the app that you downloaded. You can pull in any prior report you or others have created as long as you have security permission to view the report.

Figure 12.13: Blank Dashboard canvas

Figure 12.13 showcases a blank Dashboard. You can see on the top right there is a + **Widget** button. Click that to grab a preconfigured report and select how you would like it to be viewed. You can then drag/drop how much space you wish it to take up on your canvas.

There are a lot of options for curating your own Dashboards. We highly recommend that you head on over to **Trailhead** and find a trail. This will give you a sandbox to run through test scenarios on creating Dashboards and Reports with a curated data set. You can see firsthand how they work. There are complex reports with joined objects and custom report types, and there are simple reports with a single object and a summary table. You have plenty of options that will enhance your experience. If you dream of going outside of the *easy* reports instead of Genie, it's time to dive into the world of reporting known as Einstein Analytics. This is an add-on package you may consider, and it offers a lot of extendibility for your reporting warehouse.

Einstein Analytics (CRMA) Configurations

When it comes to Salesforce products, everything that is part of their intelligence suite is labeled **Einstein**. This can make it confusing to know what is included with your base purchase and which items are add-ons. Once again, we are asking the people in charge of Salesforce to stop making their naming conventions so hard to keep track of. You can curate more advanced analytics items by leveraging Einstein Analytics, and you may hear it called **Customer Relationship Management Analytics (CRMA)**. This product can plot trend information over time to show overall consumer engagement. It is more of a visualization layer that allows you to create a storyboard of analytics versus just a bar chart. It does take a particularly heavy amount of JSON to truly customize reporting, so it may not be for everyone. It is not the same drag and drop as the prior reports that we pulled together.

The most impressive part of this application is going to be at the end of this chapter when we will talk about sharing Einstein Analytics Dashboards directly with End Consumers. That alone may be enough of a reason to explore and learn about this add-on product. We encourage you to learn more about how you can leverage this via Trailhead. Search for CRMA in Trailhead's search bar to find hands-on exercises to see how this application may work for your organization.

One unique feature that may cause you to say "Hey, that's not reporting" is the fact that you can now leverage Einstein Bots inside of your instance. Right now, there are up to 25 conversation bots that you can use. Think about empowering your Service Agents by allowing them to ask questions about the data in a conversational format. That is what makes it a new vertical in the reporting world. All the data the bots aggregate is what powers them to answer these questions. To get started, you need to go into Salesforce Setup and search for Einstein Bots.

Figure 12.14: Einstein Bots setup

As illustrated in *Figure 12.14*, the first time you land on Einstein Bots, you will have some legal terms to review. It is important that you ensure that your legal team is OK with the language prior to turning on the Bots. Assuming that you have the green light from legal, to turn them on and start building, simply flip the toggle in the top right to the **On** position. Moving the toggle will bring up a legal screen saying that you must be authorized, on behalf of your company, to agree to those terms. We stress again that it is very important that your legal team agrees to **Artificial Intelligence** (**AI**) consuming your data. You may consider having them send you an email confirming that you are allowed to consent to the terms. Once you get past the legal items, it is time to start curating the bots that will be most helpful to your Service organization.

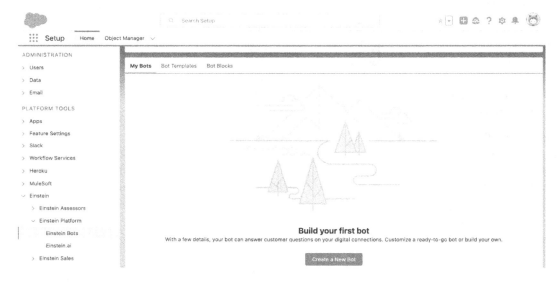

Figure 12.15: Einstein Bots setup

In *Figure 12.15*, we showcase the landing screen for when you go to build your first bot. This may seem like a very exciting time as you venture into the land of AI, and it is! For it to be successful, you need to go into your first build with a clear understanding of what you are trying to solve for your Service Agents. We recommend that you sit down with the head of your service team and understand what the more common scenarios are for service, and at *Delivery International*, Anna in the quality department can help. If you are just starting your build, you may need to wait. This may be one of those items that you circle back to after you have a few months of data under your belt.

We are going to assume that you have the perfect bot scenario identified and have validated that you have enough data in your instance for this bot to be useful. If you are still unsure about what scenario makes the most sense, there are intro templates available when you click to create a **Standard Bot**. To get this AI party started, you will need to click on **Create a New Bot**.

Select bot type

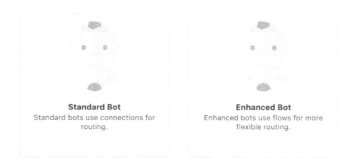

Select a type of bot

You can create either a standard or enhanced bot. Standard and enhanced bots have some differences in routing and functionality.

Standard Bot
Standard bots use connections for routing.

Enhanced Bot
Enhanced bots use flows for more flexible routing.

To learn more about the differences between standard and enhanced bots, visit Salesforce Help.

Cancel   Next

Figure 12.16: Bot type selection

Figure 12.16 showcases the first step of the bot creation process. Standard Bots will allow you to either create something from scratch or leverage an intro template. With an Enhanced Bot, you are going to be creating everything from scratch. If this is your first venture into the land of all things bots, we recommend that you start by choosing **Standard Bot** and select an intro template to get yourself familiar with the process. Since these can vary greatly, we encourage you to follow the on-screen instructions until you have your bot launched.

An item of note is that, as always, you should be trying this out in your sandbox, not production. Following this best practice is going to introduce a wrinkle into testing. You have to remember that your sandbox doesn't see as many entries and data changes as your production instance does because you don't have users in there interacting daily. That means that your bot's accuracy and adaptability may not show its full potential in your test environment. This is a great way to establish a baseline if it works as you had planned, but just know that it will only get smarter. To help calibrate your model in testing, consider seeding your sandbox with sample data.

We have now exhausted our native reporting options for monitoring Experience Cloud and introduced a twist on reporting known as Einstein Bots. As we dive deeper into this chapter, we will go into holistic reporting with your website and dive into the flip side of End Consumer reporting via CRMA. Grab your beverage of choice and let's head on over to third-party analytics!

Google Analytics and third-party web analytics

Since its birth in 2005, Google Analytics has cornered web analytics as the tool of choice. Google Analytics was originally the paid product of a company called Urchin Software Analytics, but Google acquired it, eventually rebranded it to Google Analytics, and made the base-level reporting it offered into a free product. The way Google Analytics works, the data it provides, and the mechanisms by which it compiles and visualizes data have evolved over the years. These days, people use it to check engagement on certain pages of their site, conversion movement on parts, general trends in SEO, and more. As of the publication of this book, **Google Analytics 4 (GA4)** is the current free standard, but there are enterprise versions that may make sense for you to buy if your use case is complex enough.

Thankfully, Salesforce keeps Google in mind when it designs, because it knows that its marketing products need it. Before you install Google Analytics on your site, familiarize yourself with Google Analytics and consider getting certified. You will have to configure Google Analytics to interact with your Experience Cloud site by adjusting a few settings and creating custom dimensions.

Installing Google Analytics isn't too bad, but there is an order of operations within Salesforce. First, you're going to need to dig out your Google Analytics ID, known as a Measurement ID, out of Google Analytics. After you locate an ID that looks something like UA-XXXXX-XX, navigate to the **Settings** sprocket on the left side of Experience Builder and click on **Advanced**:

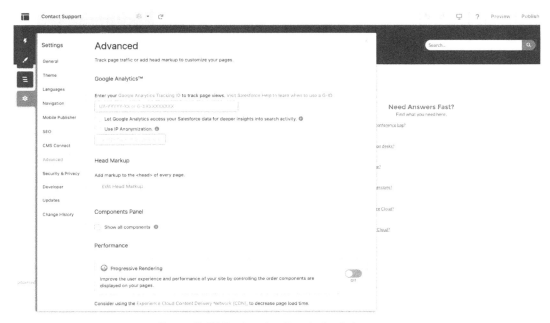

Figure 12.17: Declarative Google Analytics setup

Put your UA code into the box and check **Let Google Analytics access your Salesforce data for deeper insights into search activity**. If your compliance department requires that you mask your users' IP addresses on Google Servers, check **Use IP Anonymization**.

The fun's not over yet; you also must do some security configuration. In the Experience Builder, navigate to **Settings** and then the **Security and Privacy** tab:

Figure 12.18: Content Security Policy setup

In the **Security Level** section on this page, select **Relaxed CSP: Permit Access to Inline Scripts and Allow Hosts**.

Give your setup a day to connect. After the two are integrated, you can start creating custom reports in Google Analytics and Salesforce. You can also install the pre-configured **Google Analytics for Salesforce Communities** managed package into Salesforce for some pre-baked dashboards.

Note that if you use **Google Tag Manager** (**GTM**) instead of Measurement ID in Google Analytics, you will have to work a little magic. Depending on what you're trying to capture, you will most likely have to leverage a custom component with no UI that places your GTM container. *Delivery International* is going to set up Dalbert's best and brightest to talk through how they want to capture information.

Even though Google Analytics is the third-party analytics gold standard, there are other data options you might need to consider. The mortal enemy of Google Analytics is **Adobe Analytics**, and if you work at an Adobe shop, you will have to embed their tracking tags into your Experience Cloud sites using some custom development. When researching third-party tracking or reporting apps, assess whether an AppExchange product exists for easy implementation and research how it could interact with Salesforce.

> **One last word of caution**
>
> If you layer multiple tracking tags on top of each other from any third-party source, they can sometimes fight each other, misfire, and skew your data. Think through how you want your data to flow so you don't shoot yourself in the foot when you're ready to set up your user reporting.

Setting up reporting for your Experience Cloud users

Now that we have reporting covered for your business, let's switch the focus to the people who are leveraging the portals. There are two types of reports that you can enable for your Experience Cloud end users:

- Native Salesforce reporting
- CRMA

Let's go through the native Salesforce reporting.

Native Salesforce reporting

This reporting is included in your purchase. To enable this for consumers, you will need to create custom profiles or permission sets for Experience Cloud. You can enable them to not only view reports but also create and edit reports. Our recommendation is that you curate profiles for your groups instead of permission sets for reporting. If reporting is a main feature of your portal, separating the security into permission sets only creates a greater risk of inaccurately setting up users.

Before you run off and start creating new profiles, let's look at the default switches that must be flipped for the experience. You will need to go into Salesforce setup and type `Digital` into the left-hand search bar. This will bring up the **Digital Experience** section of the setup. The next step is to click on **Settings** under the **Digital Experience** section. Take a look at *Figure 12.17* to see the page you should land on once you click **Settings**.

Figure 12.19: Digital experience settings

In *Figure 12.17*, we scrolled down the **Settings** page to find the **Role and User Settings** options. In this section, there's an **Enable report options for external users** option. You will need to check that box to get reporting to show up as a feature for your consumers. Click **Save** down at the bottom of the **Settings** page once you have selected the option. You have now set up the ability to report on your site. Now anyone who has the profile(s) that you set up for reporting will be able to access reporting inside of the site.

If you have selected a template, such as **Partner Template**, it comes with a preset of pages that support the reporting function. *Figure 12.18* highlights the default pages that you can see inside **Partner Template** for reporting. The data you see displayed in the default view is what you (or the logged-in user) can see. It is important that you curate a few reports for your users so that the section is not blank upon launch.

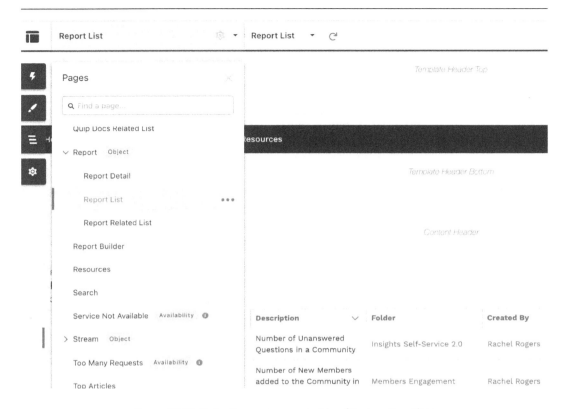

Figure 12.20: Default report pages inside of Partner Template

We recommend creating a folder specifically for reports that you want to display on your digital sites. By creating a folder per site to house reports on that site, you limit the chances of deployed reports failing to function inside that portal. You can control the visibility of those folders with security features. You will also want to ensure that you limit who has the ability to publish to that folder.

CRMA

Let's get into our more advanced reporting options. Earlier in this chapter, we spoke about CRMA. CRMA is the analytics platform that allows you to curate storybook visuals to display all of your reporting needs and trend items over time. This is a great way to use reporting to guide your End Consumers via Experience Cloud. The big thing to note is that this is an add-on option. You will need to see how you are going to implement your Experience Cloud and how much your team wants to invest.

Delivery International is reviewing how they want to handle their portals. They need more information to give to their franchisees to help them expand their business and hit their sales targets. For that population of people, we are going to invest in CRMA, but for the End Consumers, there is no need to get an advanced analytics package. What we want to display to our franchisees is their sales per franchise location.

To set this up, you will need to go to **Analytics Settings**. You will then have to click on **Share Analytics with Communities**. Remember, **Communities** was the legacy name of Experience Cloud before it got the Salesforce rebranding treatment. These settings will simply allow you to pull in Dashboards from CRMA over to Experience Cloud. To configure the Dashboards, you will need to leverage the standard CRMA process. Connect the Salesforce data and curate a dashboard leveraging a JSON code base. We recommend that you start on Trailhead and take a few of the trails/modules they have related to CRMA to get acquainted with how to develop Dashboards. There are a few out-of-the-box templates, but for the most part, this is going to be a custom development item.

When it comes to placing the items onto your Experience Cloud pages, there is a pre-built **LWC CRM Analytics Dashboard component** that you will need to drag/drop onto the page. From there, you will be able to select the Dashboard to display and then configure the Dashboard attributes. The attributes are related to the way you wish the Dashboard to display inside the site. We recommend leveraging the standard component instead of curating your own component. This will save you time in the future by ensuring that it upgrades seamlessly with each automated release pushed by Salesforce.

Summary

Transparency and consistently reporting metrics to your internal and external user communities will ensure a thriving ecosystem of trust and transparency. In this chapter, we took you through native reporting and introduced you to the concepts of leveraging bots, third-party reporting applications, Google Analytics, and CRMA. Here's a reminder of the skills that you should be taking away from this chapter:

- Knowing which native reports come with Experience Cloud for monitoring performance, in addition to which custom reports can be set up within Salesforce

- Learning how to properly implement Google Analytics or other third-party analytics tools into Experience Cloud to capture the data you care about

- Identifying configuration considerations and leveraging guidance in setting up reporting that your end users can see

We are in the home stretch of our journey through setting up Experience Cloud! Up next, we will talk through how to deploy and monitor your site.

13

Site Launch, Maintenance, and Moderation

After significant business preparation, learning about the intricacies of Experience Cloud, designing a perfect experience, and preparing your users for their new site, it's time to go Live with your site! Take a deep breath and make sure to do your prep work. This chapter walks you through a checklist of what you must do before the site launch, including both technical activities, such as preparing environment pushes and setting up users, and change management activities, such as notifying users.

Remember that this preparation also extends to overall business readiness activities. You can't just launch your brand-new digital experience site without ensuring that the right people in the company are along for the journey. Imagine having a perfect service experience but no one there to answer client calls. Delivering a bad client experience like that would be the opposite of everything you have worked so hard to put together.

We will walk you through some final quality assurance practices to make sure that everything matches your brand standards, is tone-appropriate, and navigates like a Fortune 500s portal. Here are the key items we will review:

- Pre-launch activities
- Technical readiness
- Exploring site moderation and users
- Adoption best practices
- Understanding analytics and adopting best practices

Let's get to our pre-launch activities.

Pre-launch activities

The first thing that we need to do before we give the all-clear for site launch readiness is a final **quality assurance** (**QA**) check. Even though you (hopefully) unit tested, did an **end-to-end** (**E2E**) test, and ran **User Acceptance Testing** (**UAT**), remember that UAT might have required significant changes to your development and architecture. If you enabled enhancement requests or fixed bugs, you need to run an additional check. It is great that you have your UAT all buttoned up, but you need to run one final E2E QA task to ensure your new sites work without error.

You might be surprised how many times things are caught in that final E2E test, in addition to how often it will help you determine how to sequence deployment activities. If this is a brand-new site, you can also have it moved to dark production and do the final check live in production before granting external access. The trick before you start moving items is to ensure that you pass technical readiness, which we will review in the next section.

Let's shift focus on maybe the most complicated part of any release: *the people*. You can have a flawless plan for execution using the best technology, but if the people aren't ready, it won't matter. If we think about our *Delivery International* use case, we have quite a large audience that has been involved with us on this journey, who also represent larger populations of people that need to be brought in. There aren't very many "departments of one" in the workforce. Normally, they need time to train their organizations on the new or enhanced processes they have created to support the journey.

Now, let's look at our *Business Readiness Activities* checklist. These are items you will want to sequence with your business partners. You can work on these items at the same time as you check off items in your *Technical Readiness* checklist. Remember, several items on this checklist can inform what your target launch date will be, and you cannot assume the world is ready with you. Answer these questions to confirm or adjust your target date.

Note that the checklist shown here assumes that you are going to deploy Self-Service features. If you have already deployed them or are not deploying them as part of your release, some of these items will not apply to your launch.

Bucket	What's involved?
External Communications	Your organization will typically prepare a series of communications that will go to the target demographic of each site. These communications can take many forms. It is important that you verify the following: • What communications are intended per Target Audience • The sequence of those communications • Whether or not they have been approved for release All of these can impact the date of launch.

Bucket	What's involved?
Internal Communications	Your entire organization will be feeling the shift to a new digital site. Questions will vary as people shift to self-service. It is critical that your internal team understands what the changes are and when they will take place. Communications need to go out prior to the detailed training for jobs that will shift to support the new digital self-service module powered by Service Cloud.
Knowledge Articles Published	Leveraging Knowledge for your End Consumers is a great thing! However, you need to make sure that your business partners have all of their initial content loaded and that there are at least two articles per navigation item. If there are any attachments, you need to ensure that they are downloadable.
Initial Internal User Load	Verify the final list of internal users and what their job functions will be in relation to the new features with the department heads. Have all of those items mapped to the roles, profiles, and any permission sets they will need in order to complete their tasks. If you are setting a site up for the first time, it is a good idea to go ahead and configure the users as the code has been moved up into production. Then, you can verify that the users work as expected prior to launch.
Internal Training	Working inside of Service Cloud or setting up Experience Cloud users may sound like simple items at this point in your journey. Remember that there are a lot of people outside of yourself that will need to be able to complete these same tasks. Having a detailed training plan by role with options for follow-up training is key. Training should also take place as close to launch as possible so that people do not forget how to perform the tasks.

Bucket	What's involved?
External User Load	You need a final agreed-upon list sliced up by Experience Cloud site of who your external users are and how they should be set up. You need to make sure this list details the information needed for the contact creation if these users are not already set up as contacts. You need to account for potentially having to create accounts for these users as well. Take the time to structure your user load list in a format that follows how you would have to execute the load in Salesforce: • Account information • Contact information • User information

Table 13.1: Business Readiness Activities checklist

The information you are going to gather through the *Business Readiness Activities* checklist will be critical in defining a path to success. This list should encompass who needs to be informed and the timing of those communications, in addition to having content ready for the new digital site. These are the keys to aligning with the business and ensuring that when we are "live," everyone is ready and set up for success.

Now that you have started on the business side of the pre-launch activities listed in *Table 13.1*, we are ready to get into the technical readiness aspects. In this next section, we will review all of the physical items you need to get ready in your instance in order to launch.

Technical readiness

Congratulations on getting the business partners aligned for launch! That is no small feat. Let's review the things that are within your wheelhouse. We are going to look at technical readiness through various lenses:

• Deployment sequencing

• Deployment configuration, DevOps, or change sets

• Coordinating with other technical teams

• Modification of inbound workflow routing

• Deployment validation

• Rollback strategy

You may have heard the phrase *plan to fail or fail to plan*. If you plan for the event of potential failure, you will plan for mitigation, thereby ensuring true failure does not ultimately occur. To properly prepare for your go-live, let's review each of these lenses and the steps you will need to take to adequately prepare for them.

Technical Readiness Step	Description and Considerations
Deployment Sequencing	Knowing which order to sequence your release in is critical to a successful launch. Slice your work into pre-work, launch, and post-go-live work. If you have pre-work to do (for example, buying a domain, or setting up an SSL certificate), ensure that's out of the way well in advance of going live. Additionally, you may need to release certain components within your launch before others, so carefully plan the order in which your code and configuration are released. You may also have some post-go-live work that you have to do, such as changing links live in production.
Deployment Configuration, DevOps, or Change Sets	Deployment configuration can take many forms and is heavily dependent on the tool you plan to use for your deployments. Whether it's traditional Git pushes, a DevOps tool such as Copado, or the OG change sets, you will need to set up and test your changes. Work with your DevOps team and developers to properly package and monitor your changes.
Coordinating with other Technical Teams	Experience Cloud pushes are rarely just Salesforce-only; you will likely have to deal with other owners of systems, such as the ERP team in *Delivery International*'s case. You may also have to work with internal IT teams for things such as API management, domain pointing, or even telephony system rerouting. You may also need to whitelist domains or other things in order to ensure that the traffic Salesforce Experience Cloud will produce is allowed into other authenticated systems if that is part of your architecture. Identifying your stakeholders upfront will help you circle back to relevant teams and people to include in your go-live planning. If you have regulatory requirements in your industry, be sure you consult with compliance and audit teams, too.

Technical Readiness Step	Description and Considerations
Modification of Inbound Workflow Routing	If your Experience Cloud build involves heavy changes to internal Salesforce workflows or workflows elsewhere in the business, you will have to plan in advance. You may even have to implement those changes before your Experience Cloud goes live. When launching Service Cloud, remember that any email addresses you want to create cases from will need to be routed over to Salesforce. However, that change is immediate as soon as it is implemented. So do not complete that step until your Service Team is ready to log in and start handling the volume, especially if the email address is already in use by your customers. Where possible, we advise releasing small updates instead of a "big bang" so people can digest change in smaller chunks. If you can get your internal users used to a changed workflow before an Experience Cloud site goes live, do it.
Deployment Validation	After you've pushed your code live, you will need an E2E walk-through to validate your deployment. We recommend a technical walk-through from the developers, in addition to a business walk-through. Document where possible and determine what the criteria should be before an all-clear is issued to your internal users and communications are issued to your clients.
Rollback Strategy	It's always important to have a strategy to pull your release back in the event of unforeseen circumstances. Even though a rollback can be caused by wonky code being released into production, rollbacks can happen because of technical outages, client complaints, or an internal request to remove functionality. Consequently, you should plan what you need to do in the event of a full or partial rollback. Consider how to back up and restore your data, in addition to reverting your code base back to the pre-launch state.

Table 13.2: Technical readiness steps

While you can create templates for technical readiness checks, it's important to tailor your technical readiness to the project before you. Each project can have different stakeholders, considerations, third-party tools, or post-go-live steps, so it's important to capture these as the project goes on and you uncover unforeseen dependencies. Don't wait until the last minute to create a technical readiness plan; create it as the project goes on and share the living document with stakeholders.

Also, depending on when you're ready to push your work live or expose work that's been pushed into production dark, you may have to do this work outside of business hours. Identify the resources involved in your push and ensure they're available to work off-schedule. Unsure of what it means to *push to production dark*? This means that code/configuration is moved to the production environment; however, there is no access granted to that code, meaning no one can access it internally or externally. You may even want to consider pushing it "dark" and giving only internal users access once you verify it is stable. This could help with training before flipping the switch to external users.

Now that you're technically clear to push your site, you're ready to let your users see what you built for them.

Exploring site moderation and users

Once you're ready to open your site, you need to review how you plan to allow your users to access the site. While we touched on your options for user rollout in *Table 13.1*, we haven't talked about some aspects of user management specific to Experience Cloud that are worth considering for ease of use and better client experience.

If you already know which users you need to pre-load, it might be worth provisioning them in advance, as discussed previously. However, if you plan to let your users self-register, allow Experience Cloud users to grant access to other users within their company, or have a specific timeframe when you need to deactivate users, you need to review a couple of other areas.

User self-registration

Allowing users to self-register can be a really good idea in certain circumstances, especially when you can set up logic to match them to potential contacts already in your Salesforce CRM.

To set this up, you will need to enable self-registration and alter the login page. Go to **Workspaces | Administration** and select **Login & Registration** (see *Figure 13.1*).

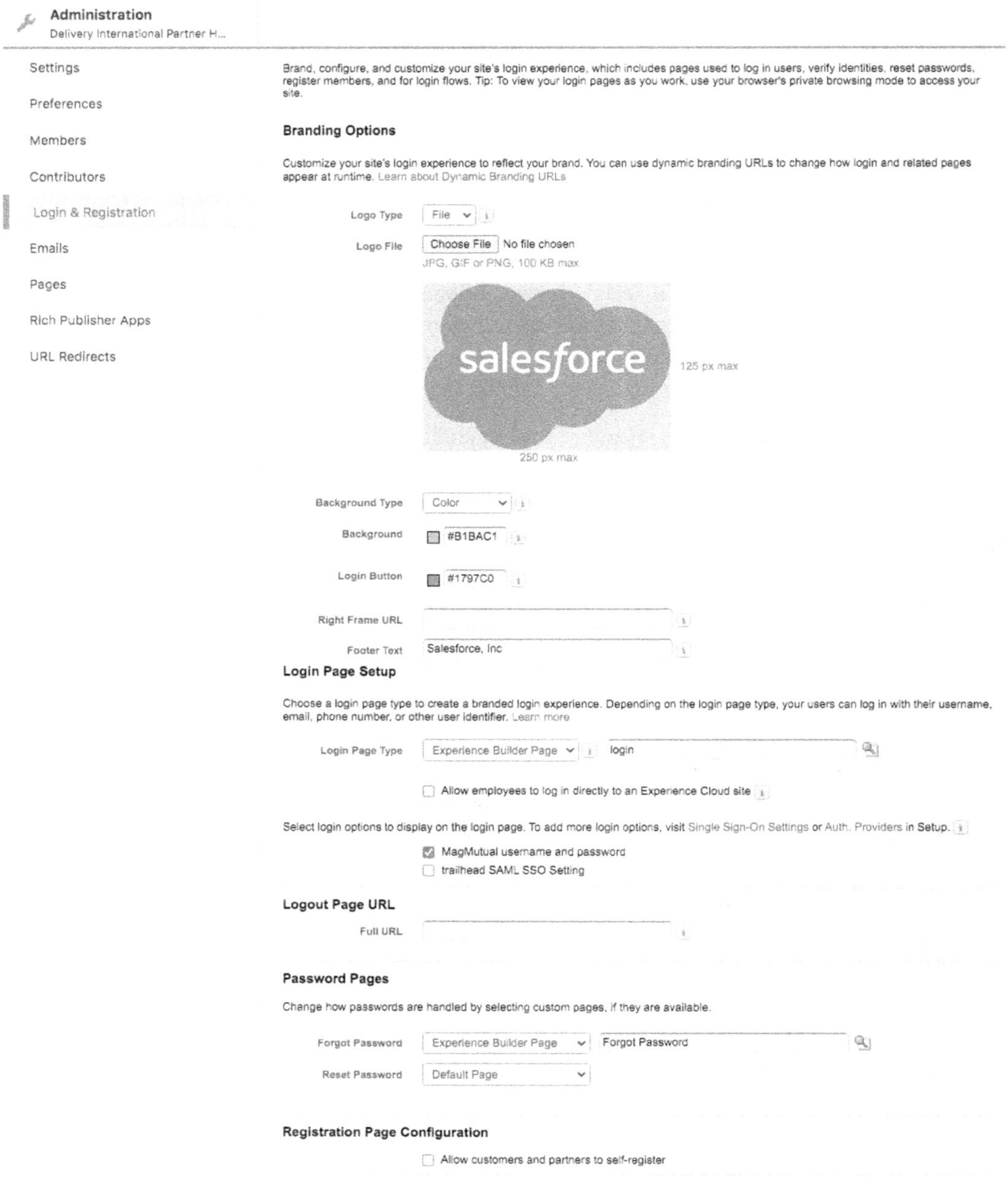

Figure 13.1: The Login & Registration page

Under **Registration Page Configuration**, check **Allow customers and partners to self-register**. There are a few standard components you can use to update the **Login** page, but you can also code on top of them to implement a custom UI.

Note that if you allow self-registration, you may need to review your licensure requirements with your Salesforce AE. Once registered, you can determine a default user role, or even set up special contacts with roles unique to Experience Cloud.

Specialty users

Within authenticated Experience Cloud sites, there are some specific role options beyond just a regular member that allow for delegated management (see *Table 13.3*).

Role Type	Permissions Overview
Member	The most basic level of user who can post and create records based on your access model.
Channel Manager	This person manages your partner accounts and users.
Moderator	A moderator can flag user-created content and users within the site. These people can also set moderation rules to filter out undesired behavior.
Partner Super User (Partner Executive, Partner Manager, Partner User)	Partner super users are a feature in Partner portals that allows users to view and edit the records of people within their account and beneath them in the hierarchy.

Table 13.3: Understanding specialty roles

Delivery International's head of Sales, Kinley, wants to allow her Franchisee users to add employees as users to their Experience Cloud site, while Anna in Quality wants to ensure displeased customers aren't writing inflammatory things in their Chatter sections. To accomplish Kinley's requirements, we know we have to give designated franchisee users the Partner Executive and Partner Management roles. And for Anna, we have to allow her to assign the Site Moderator role to people who watch the site.

User audits

It is best practice to audit both your internal users and external ones. For security purposes and expense reduction, it's worth reviewing who your licenses are assigned to so you can cut access or repurpose licenses. If there's a user who hasn't logged in for many years, it's a safe bet that you can deactivate them to save the license. If you have an SSO or Active Directory configuration, it may be worth creating automation to shut down users' access to a system when they leave or unenroll from your portal.

For license optimization and system improvement techniques, consider using the **Account Role Optimization (ARO)** feature. ARO can minimize the amount of roles assigned to users and improve overall system performance. Note that it is possible to go overboard with optimization and that you need to pay specific attention to your contractual Salesforce language. There is a notion per your agreement that you cannot cycle licenses of the same user within a certain time period. For example, you cannot deactivate a user due to non-use and then reactivate them within 12 months if they are named users. All contracts have variations; make sure you review with legal before you over-optimize.

With users out of the way, let's move on to how to measure our Experience Cloud site.

Understanding analytics and adopting best practices

You may remember from *Chapter 12*, *Monitoring Your Site – Salesforce Native Reporting*, that we installed the native adoption tracking dashboards into our instance. We also covered how you could expand that by leveraging bots and exposing reporting to consumers, Google Analytics, and CRMA. Consequently, we won't be going through any additional installation instructions here. Instead, we are going to focus on best practices for you to consider as you launch metrics. We will also take a dive into how to set realistic expectations for initial results.

Put simply, you need to work with your stakeholders to define what they consider success. Do not try to cover everything at once; start small. Implement web analytics basics and a pick few key activities at your first attempt at analytics. Once you nail the basics, you can start getting more scientific in your analysis by isolating specific data variables and expanding your dataset. If you're working with your stakeholders who aren't sure what to measure, here are a few good starters:

KPI	What it is and how to measure it
User Adoption	This measures how many users are coming through your site and the potential level of engagement.
	This could be metrics such as active users, new users, or user retention, although there are many more.
Content Engagement	This measures how people engage with defined content on your page.
	This could be measured with page views or likes and shares.
System Performance	This measures how the site itself and other downstream systems are responding.
	This could be measured with page load time, API call monitoring, or error rates.
Conversion History	This measures how many people do something revenue-generating.
	This could be lead conversion, opportunity submission, ordering, or others.

Table 13.4: KPI examples

As you grow in sophistication, you can start adding other mechanisms to this list to see how you can impact behavior on your site. You can do things such as sub-sectioning your site by audience, setting up Salesforce campaigns to measure your ROI for conversion optimization, or even leveraging Einstein Analytics for suggestions on how to improve your site! Getting your stakeholders accustomed to making decisions on-site analytics can be extremely beneficial to making informed, meaningful changes to your site.

Analytics are your best insight into how to influence our next topic, adoption best practices.

Adoption best practices

After you've determined the KPIs for the behavior you wish to monitor, you can determine how to better drive engagement. But before you build a dashboard, we hope that you've properly engaged your stakeholders from the beginning of this journey, as they will be your biggest internal advocates for adoption. Data is helpful, but you need the human touch along the way. For complicated or dramatic releases, think about hosting support hours at your company where users can come and ask questions. Ensure your users are properly trained and set training champions or subject-matter experts within impacted departments. It may even be worth keeping a post-production care team, and setting ongoing communication strategies if a release creates friction.

For user retention and adoption on Experience Cloud itself, you will have to incentivize your users. You need to make a compelling case why someone should use this site at all. In *Delivery International's* case, they have centralized management of their franchise agreements in this Experience Cloud portal, so they need to make the experience as easy and helpful as possible to make their franchisees use the portal instead of jamming up support phone lines. From an end-consumer perspective, they need to offer rewards such as coupons or freebies to entice them to order online instead of by phone. All of these can be measured with standard analytics or even external tools such as call tracking numbers.

It's easier to retain users than it is to get new ones. To keep your users engaged, the best thing you can do is ensure the site is monitored, current, and maintained.

Ongoing maintenance

Congratulations on pushing your site live and a smooth release! This is just the beginning of a long relationship with Salesforce Experience Cloud, but getting to evolve your site over time is part of the satisfaction of working on this product.

Here are a few things to consider in your maintenance plan:

Ongoing Maintenance Item	Description
Production Support	Who is going to help users and manage bugs? Production support can take many formats, but it involves the basic day-to-day upkeep of your site.
User retention and management	Related to production support, this involves managing users and removing them from your system. This may be manual or it may be automated, but you will still want to audit it.
New Needs	Your organization will almost certainly want changes to your Experience Cloud site, so you will need to come up with a planning and priority policy to manage expectations.
Third-party tool upkeep	Systems that Experience Cloud is connected to may change down the road, or need to be added to your existing systems. Always be mindful of your API strategy and keep your APIs current.
Salesforce Releases	You need to ensure you are up to date on new features and feature retirement for Salesforce seasonal releases. Use preview sandboxes to check new functionality against your existing architecture, and keep your certifications current if you are certified.
Content Management	If your site is public, you will need to keep your content fresh. Ensure you are connected with your content team and marketing teams and have a content release strategy in place for your site and Knowledge base.

Table 13.5: Ongoing maintenance

Table 13.5 is just a sample of maintenance plans that can come into play, but note that what you may need to keep up a world-class Experience Cloud site could change in the future. It is important to identify who ultimately owns your Experience Cloud sites, in addition to their development and maintenance roadmaps.

Summary

Software development can be extremely stressful and frustrating at times, but a really good release and a really happy user base make it worthwhile. After months of planning and coding, there's nothing better than hearing from your users that you fixed a problem for them and made their lives easier. The best way to create an incredible Experience Cloud launch is to properly understand your product so that you can plan carefully and communicate thoroughly.

This book is intended as a management and implementation guide for Experience Cloud, but there's plenty more documentation on technical specifics. The Salesforce PDF guides on their products can be literally thousands of pages long, so we encourage you to review those guides, developer standards, and the many available courses on Trailhead.

In this chapter, we reviewed the following:

- What activities on the change management and technical readiness fronts must be completed before Go Live

- How to set up site moderators and a support structure

- Native Analytics tools to monitor user adoption and strategies to improve adoption

- How to plan for maintaining the site

Congratulations, you have made it to the end of the implementation guide. If you'd like to test your knowledge or even practice for the Salesforce Experience Cloud Consultant Certification, check out *Chapter 14, Best Practices and Certification Test Preparation*.

Part 5: Certifications

Preparing for your Experience Cloud certification can be challenging and requires pre-requisite certifications. In this final part, you will learn key concepts that relate closely to questions on the exam.

This part has the following chapters:

- *Chapter 14, Best Practices and Certification Test Preparation*

14

Best Practices and Certification Test Preparation

Now that you have a good understanding of Experience Cloud and its management, let's put your knowledge to the test!

There are many different certifications that Salesforce offers. In order to get the Experience Cloud certification, you will have to get the Salesforce Administrator certification. However, the following questions should help you prepare for the Salesforce Experience Cloud Consultant certification. Of course, there are other sources that can help you prepare for your journey. Check out Trailhead, an amazing resource for test question preparation, or our friends over at Focus on Force. It is never a bad idea to review questions from different angles, so study as many different ways as you can if certification is your goal. If certification isn't for you, no worries. There are plenty of people who practice in the field without a certification in every single Salesforce product offering. However, some niche products, such as Experience Cloud, do give you a better competitive advantage in the job market if you have certification.

In this chapter, we will cover the following:

- Understanding the test structure
- Experience Cloud basics
- Sharing, visibility, and licensing
- Administration, setup, and configuration
- Adoption and analytics
- Customization considerations and limitations
- Branding, personalization, and content

Each of these areas will cover specific elements of the test in greater detail. Last but not least, you will find the answers at the end of each section. This allows you to test your knowledge before you see the correct response. Let's move on to reviewing the test structure.

Understanding the test structure

This particular exam consists of 60 multiple-choice questions. The passing score for the exam is 65%. There is also an exam registration fee. We recommend that you head over to Trailhead (`https://trailhead.salesforce.com/`) to figure out the specific cost and test-taking requirements for your country.

Let's break this down by certification category, a few sample questions, and a quick reminder of best practices. We gathered these at the time at which this book was completed, the fall of 2024. It is important to note that Salesforce can and does update test questions relative to each release of the software. In addition, test questions are selected randomly for the exam. In the event that you fail your exam, you can retake the certification, and it is possible that you will see a few different questions from exam to exam. The categories in the following list are based on the summer 2024 release. The good news is that Experience Cloud has been a fairly stable test since the release of Lightning, so you shouldn't expect too much variation. Let's review the test composition:

- Experience Cloud Basics – 8%
- Administration, Setup, and Configuration – 25%
- Sharing, Visibility, and Licensing – 17%
- Branding, Personalization, and Content – 15%
- Templates and Themes – 10%
- User Creation and Authentication – 13%
- Customization Considerations and Limitations – 7%
- Adoption and Analytics – 5%

Per Salesforce's exam website, they recommend you have a minimum of 6 months experience on the Experience Cloud platform prior to taking the exam. We highly advise you to work through a configuration in Trailhead with some examples or look at your client's implementation before attempting the exam. You may also want to join up with a Salesforce user group in your area to get some advice from others on how they have completed an implementation, or how they studied for their certification tests. Having different scenarios will ensure that you have a well-rounded view of the exam.

Note that not every category has been exhaustively reviewed in this book and that questions relating to two test categories, **Templates and Themes** and **User Creation and Authentication**, are mixed throughout the upcoming test bank. This book was intended to hit the most common use cases with deep dives into understanding so that you could practically implement the solution. For some of these categories, we have referred you to Salesforce documentation regarding specific settings. Even as veterans in this field, we still saw questions on the certification exam regarding obscure settings we've never touched in practice, so we tried to include a few of those in the sample questions.

One section of the exam is focused on what they call the Experience Cloud basics. These are the fundamentals for the product at Salesforce. Let's look at the best practices overview and then dive into some sample questions:

- **Choose the right templates**: Select templates that best fit the purpose of your community to ensure usability and engagement.

- **Customize thoughtfully**: While customization allows for a personalized experience, it should not compromise the load time or general performance of the community. Utilize custom development where sensible.

- **Maintain regular updates**: Keep the community software and content up to date to ensure the security, efficiency, and relevance of the information provided to users.

- **Focus on user experience design**: Design for ease of use, intuitive navigation, and accessibility to ensure a positive user experience across all user segments.

- **Train your team**: Ensure that your team is well-trained on the Salesforce Experience Cloud platform to effectively manage and enhance the community.

Nailing the basics is critical to an effective Experience Cloud launch and management strategy. Let's move on to some sample questions:

1. What is Salesforce Experience Cloud primarily used for?

   A) Managing sales pipelines

   B) Creating and managing online communities for customers, partners, and employees

   C) Automating marketing campaigns

   D) Building custom applications

2. Which of the following is a key feature of Salesforce Experience Cloud?

   A) Multi-currency support

   B) Online community creation

   C) Advanced reporting

   D) Custom object creation

3. Which of the following is a template option in Salesforce Experience Cloud?

   A) Partner Central

   B) Marketing Cloud

   C) Sales Cloud

   D) Analytics Cloud

4. What is the role of Salesforce CMS in Experience Cloud?

   A) To manage community themes

   B) To create, manage, and publish content across multiple channels

   C) To track sales metrics

   D) To manage user permissions

5. How does Salesforce Experience Cloud integrate with other Salesforce products?

   A) Using APIs and connectors

   B) Through manual data entry

   C) With built-in reports

   D) Using custom fields

6. Which tool allows users to personalize their Experience Cloud site?

   A) Experience Builder

   B) Salesforce Connect

   C) Lightning App Builder

   D) Data Loader

7. How does Salesforce Experience Cloud support mobile users?

   A) Through a dedicated mobile app

   B) By offering responsive design out of the box

   C) By integrating with the Salesforce Mobile SDK

   D) By offering offline support

8. Which Salesforce Experience Cloud feature is essential for creating a user-friendly community site?

   A) Audience Targeting

   B) Experience Builder

   C) Data Categories

   D) Salesforce Connect

9. How can Salesforce Experience Cloud help in partner management?

    A) By providing a collaborative platform for sharing resources and information

    B) By automating marketing campaigns

    C) By tracking sales opportunities

    D) By offering analytics and reporting tools

10. Which feature in Salesforce Experience Cloud supports content delivery to different user segments?

    A) Salesforce Shield

    B) Data Loader

    C) Lightning Flow

    D) Audience Targeting

11. What is the primary benefit of using Salesforce Experience Cloud for customer engagement?

    A) It provides a platform for real-time collaboration

    B) It offers tools for personalized customer experiences

    C) It automates customer service processes

    D) All of the above

12. How can Salesforce Experience Cloud enhance the customer support process? (Choose two.)

    A) By providing self-service options for case submission

    B) By integrating with Salesforce tools only

    C) By enabling real-time collaboration between support agents and customers

    D) By using AI to make websites

13. Which tool is used for managing the overall structure and navigation of an Experience Cloud site?

    A) Experience Builder

    B) Salesforce Connect

    C) Lightning Flow

    D) Salesforce CMS

14. 14. How does Salesforce Experience Cloud support knowledge management?

    A) By integrating with Salesforce Knowledge

    B) By offering content categorization and search capabilities

    C) By providing tools for content creation and publishing

    D) All of the above

15. What is the purpose of reputation levels in an Experience Cloud site?

    A) To reward users based on their activity and contributions

    B) To manage user roles and permissions

    C) To track user engagement metrics

    D) To personalize content for different user segments

16. Which of the following describes the main use case for Salesforce Experience Cloud?

    A) Facilitating customer and partner engagement through community portals

    B) Automating marketing campaigns

    C) Managing employee performance

    D) Integrating with third-party CRMs

17. How does Salesforce Experience Cloud support global organizations?

    A) By offering multilingual support

    B) By providing tools for managing multi-currency transactions

    C) By enabling cross-cloud functionality

    D) All of the above

18. 18. What is the benefit of using templates in Salesforce Experience Cloud?

    A) They provide pre-built designs and layouts for quick deployment

    B) They offer advanced analytics and reporting tools

    C) They enable integration with external systems

    D) They automate user management tasks

19. Which tool allows you to create custom pages within an Experience Cloud site?

    A) Experience Builder

    B) Salesforce CMS

    C) Visualforce

    D) Lightning App Builder

20. How does Salesforce Experience Cloud facilitate content management?

    A) By integrating with Salesforce CMS

    B) By providing tools for content creation and publishing

    C) By offering content personalization options

    D) All of the above

Answer key

Question	Answer		Question	Answer		Question	Answer
1	B		10	D		19	A
2	B		11	D		20	D
3	A		12	A, C		-	-
4	B		13	A		-	-
5	A		14	D		-	-
6	A		15	A		-	-
7	B		16	A		-	-
8	B		17	A		-	-
9	A		18	A		-	-

Answer key 14.1

Sharing, visibility, and licensing

Understanding how to enable a user to see the right items and perform the right functions is a key part of Experience Cloud. You need to make sure that from permission sets to roles to profiles, you have an understanding of how to apply the correct mix to give out the minimum amount of access. Let's recap some best practices before we jump into question review:

- **Regularly review access controls**: Regular audits of user roles and permissions protect your information and ensure that only authorized users can access sensitive information. Review profiles, roles, and permission sets.

- **Utilize Salesforce's built-in security features**: Take advantage of Salesforce's robust security tools such as encryption to secure your community data.

- **Plan your design**: Carefully think through your design against business requirements and user access before creating architecture.

- **Integrate thoughtfully**: When integrating with third-party systems, ensure APIs are used securely and efficiently.

- **Monitor and manage performance**: Regularly check the community's performance metrics and optimize components to reduce load times and improve overall efficiency.

Those best practices will be key to making sure you are not only set up for implementation but also that you keep your Salesforce Experience Cloud up to date on security. Let's jump into some sample questions:

1. What is the primary purpose of Salesforce Experience Cloud?

    A) To manage customer relationships

    B) To create and deploy online communities for customers, partners, and employees

    C) To automate marketing campaigns

    D) To build custom Salesforce applications

2. What is the role of Experience Builder in Salesforce Experience Cloud?

    A) It is used to manage user permissions

    B) It provides tools for building and customizing the user interface of the community

    C) It allows for the automation of business processes

    D) It is a tool for integrating third-party applications

3. How can you enable external users to access Salesforce data in Experience Cloud?

    A) Create custom Visualforce pages

    B) Use standard objects with sharing settings

    C) Configure Salesforce Connect

    D) Implement Lightning Components

4. Which of the following can be used to set up access permissions for different user types in an Experience Cloud site?

    A) Data Categories

    B) Sharing Rules

    C) Content Deliveries

    D) Lightning Flow

5. What is the main advantage of using the Partner Central template in Salesforce Experience Cloud?

    A) It is designed for B2C customer support

    B) It facilitates collaboration between Salesforce partners

    C) It includes tools for content management

    D) It automates marketing processes

6. What type of user license is required for external users to access a Salesforce Experience Cloud site?

    A) Salesforce Platform

    B) Experience Cloud

    C) Customer Community

    D) Salesforce Chatter

7. How can you manage the visibility of different pages for users in an Experience Cloud site?

    A) Using Audience Targeting

    B) Enabling Mobile View

    C) Setting page-level security

    D) Adjusting the community theme

8. How can you allow external users to submit cases through an Experience Cloud site?

    A) Use the Case Submission Form component

    B) Create custom Visualforce pages

    C) Implement a Chatter group

    D) Enable Salesforce Shield

9. Which of the following features can be used to create a mobile-responsive Experience Cloud site?

    A) Mobile Publisher

    B) Experience Builder

    C) Salesforce Connect

    D) Lightning Flow

10. How can you optimize the performance of a Salesforce Experience Cloud site?

    A) Use heavy customizations

    B) Minimize the use of large images and videos

    C) Implement complex data models

    D) Disable **content delivery network (CDN)** integration

11. What is the role of Audience Targeting in Salesforce Experience Cloud?

    A) To manage user roles

    B) To personalize content for different user segments

    C) To create custom objects

    D) To build external websites

12. How can you enable external users to collaborate on records in Salesforce Experience Cloud?

   A) Using Chatter

   B) Implementing Salesforce Connect

   C) Applying custom Lightning Components

   D) Enabling Knowledge Articles

13. What feature in Salesforce Experience Cloud allows users to find content quickly based on relevance?

   A) Search bar

   B) Knowledge search

   C) Global search

   D) Federated search

14. What is the function of Lightning Community templates in Experience Cloud?

   A) They provide pre-built themes and layouts for Experience Cloud sites

   B) They automate data synchronization with external systems

   C) They create custom objects for communities

   D) They manage user permissions and roles

15. How can you integrate a third-party application with Salesforce Experience Cloud?

   A) Use Salesforce Flow

   B) Implement a REST API or Salesforce Connect

   C) Enable Data Loader

   D) Use Salesforce CMS

16. Which feature allows you to send automatic notifications to users in Salesforce Experience Cloud?

   A) Workflow Rules

   B) Chatter

   C) Email Alerts

   D) Notification Builder

17. How can Salesforce Experience Cloud help improve partner engagement?

   A) By automating sales processes

   B) By providing a collaborative platform with access to shared resources

   C) By offering custom reporting tools

   D) By enhancing internal employee communication

18. How can you provide external users with access to Salesforce reports and dashboards through an Experience Cloud site? (Choose three.)

    A) Embedding dashboards using Experience Builder

    B) Sharing reports via public links

    C) Creating custom report pages for different audiences

    D) Using standard Lightning Components

19. What are some best practices for optimizing the performance of an Experience Cloud site? (Choose three.)

    A) Minimize the use of heavy components on pages

    B) Enable **content delivery network** (**CDN**) integration

    C) Regularly monitor and optimize query performance

    D) Use minimal custom code

20. How can you restrict access to certain files or documents in an Experience Cloud site? (Choose two.)

    A) File-sharing settings

    B) Implementing Data Categories

    C) Custom content permissions

    D) Setting up file moderation rules

21. Which tools can be used to design a custom user interface for an Experience Cloud site? (Choose two.)

    A) Experience Builder

    B) Lightning App Builder

    C) Visualforce

    D) HTML/CSS

22. What are some key features of the Partner Central template in Salesforce Experience Cloud? (Choose three.)

    A) Lead management

    B) Deal registration

    C) Partner onboarding

    D) Employee collaboration tools

23. Which Salesforce Experience Cloud feature allows you to control access to objects based on user roles?

   A) Role Hierarchy

   B) Sharing Sets

   C) Permission Sets

   D) Audience Targeting

24. What is the purpose of the Guest User profile in an Experience Cloud site?

   A) To allow anonymous users to access public pages

   B) To manage the permissions of registered users

   C) To control the visibility of the entire site

   D) To track the activities of internal users

25. How can you enable multilingual support in a Salesforce Experience Cloud site?

   A) Use Salesforce CMS

   B) Enable Language Settings in Experience Builder

   C) Configure Translation Workbench

   D) Apply Data Categories

26. Which tool allows you to customize the URL of your Experience Cloud site?

   A) Domain Management

   B) Experience Builder

   C) Salesforce CMS

   D) Audience Targeting

27. What is the benefit of enabling Advanced Sharing in an Experience Cloud site?

   A) It allows for more granular sharing settings

   B) It enables the sharing of content via public URLs

   C) It automates content synchronization

   D) It supports multilingual content

Answer key

Question	Answer		Question	Answer		Question	Answer
1	B		10	B		19	A, B, C
2	B		11	B		20	A, C
3	B		12	A		21	A, C
4	B		13	B		22	A, B, C
5	B		14	A		23	A
6	C		15	B		24	A
7	A		16	D		25	C
8	A		17	B		26	A
9	B		18	A, C, D		27	A

Answer key: 14.2

If you didn't ace it, don't worry. The details can get tricky. The more you practice in Trailhead, the more these items will become second nature to you.

Administration, setup, and configuration

Knowing how to start your implementation is a key step in the overall process. If you remember, we spent the first four chapters of the book talking through the business process, strategy, and the fundamentals of the product. We then jumped into how to select templates and configure some basic items in your Experience Cloud site. Here are a few best practices to keep in mind as you move through this section:

- **Streamline user onboarding**: Where possible, automate user registration and profile setup processes. Use guided screen flows to aid user onboarding.

- **Plan for scalability**: Plan and configure your community for scalability from the start, especially when it comes to licensure. Considering potential growth in user base and data volume.

- **Leverage Salesforce CMS for content management**: Centralize content management to streamline the creation, modification, and retirement of content across multiple channels and communities.

- **Regularly update community features**: Engage your community by regularly updating features, fixing issues, and rolling out new functionalities based on user feedback and analytics.

- **Maintain a clear data structure**: Organize Data Categories and Knowledge articles to facilitate easy navigation and searchability, enhancing the overall user experience.

Let's test our knowledge:

1. Which of the following templates is best suited for creating a customer self-service portal in Experience Cloud?

    A) Partner Central

    B) Customer Service

    C) Marketing Cloud

    D) Commerce Cloud

2. What is the use of Data Categories in Salesforce Knowledge when integrated with Experience Cloud?

    A) To classify and organize articles for easier navigation and search

    B) To set up user permissions for Knowledge articles

    C) To automate case assignments

    D) To track article usage and views

3. Which feature in Experience Cloud allows users to earn points and badges for their contributions?

    A) Chatter

    B) Gamification

    C) Reputation Levels

    D) Audience Targeting

4. Which tools can be used to monitor and manage community activity in Salesforce Experience Cloud? (Choose two.)

    A) Community Management

    B) Salesforce Shield

    C) Experience Builder

    D) Lightning Flow

5. Which of the following tools allows you to manage multilingual content in an Experience Cloud site?

    A) Salesforce CMS

    B) Audience Targeting

    C) Lightning Flow

    D) Visualforce

6. How can you enable **single sign-on** (**SSO**) for external users accessing Salesforce Experience Cloud?

   A) Configure Salesforce Identity

   B) Enable SSO in Setup

   C) Use a third-party identity provider

   D) All of the above

7. How can you track and manage community adoption in Salesforce Experience Cloud?

   A) Using Experience Cloud Analytics

   B) Enabling Chatter feed tracking

   C) Configuring custom dashboards

   D) Monitoring login history

8. Which Salesforce Experience Cloud feature allows for the bulk import of users?

   A) Data Loader

   B) Salesforce Connect

   C) Lightning App Builder

   D) Salesforce Shield

9. How can you monitor and analyze user activity within an Experience Cloud site?

   A) Community Analytics

   B) Salesforce Shield

   C) Data Loader

   D) Lightning Flow

10. Which Salesforce Experience Cloud features can be used to create a customer self-service portal? (Choose three.)

    A) Knowledge Base

    B) Case Management

    C) Community Templates

    D) Lightning Sync

11. How can Salesforce Experience Cloud be used to support marketing initiatives?

    A) By providing a platform for product announcements and promotions

    B) By offering personalized product recommendations

    C) By integrating with Salesforce Marketing Cloud

    D) All of the above

12. Which tool allows you to design and manage email templates within Salesforce Experience Cloud?

    A) Experience Builder

    B) Email Studio

    C) Lightning App Builder

    D) Visualforce

13. How can you manage user roles and permissions in Salesforce Experience Cloud? (Choose two.)

    A) Permission sets

    B) Profile settings

    C) Community roles

    D) Sharing rules

14. Which Salesforce Experience Cloud feature allows you to publish and manage multilingual content?

    A) **Content Management System (CMS)**

    B) Translation Workbench

    C) Data Categories

    D) Audience Targeting

15. How can you streamline the onboarding process for new users in an Experience Cloud site?

    A) Use automated welcome emails

    B) Provide step-by-step guides

    C) Implement self-paced training modules

    D) All of the above

16. What are the benefits of using Salesforce CMS within an Experience Cloud site? (Choose two.)

    A) Centralized content management

    B) Real-time collaboration

    C) Automated content distribution

    D) Integration with external content providers

17. Which Salesforce feature helps you ensure compliance with data protection regulations in Experience Cloud?

    A) Salesforce Shield

    B) GDPR compliance kit

    C) Data privacy settings

    D) Field-level security

18. How can you set up automated workflows in Salesforce Experience Cloud?

    A) Use Process Builder

    B) Configure Workflow Rules

    C) Implement Lightning Flow

    D) All of the above, but Process Builder and Workflow Rules will be retired

19. Which feature can be used to ensure that only authorized users can access sensitive data in an Experience Cloud site?

    A) IP whitelisting

    B) Field-level security

    C) Role-based access control

    D) All of the above

20. How can Salesforce Experience Cloud be integrated with other Salesforce products? (Choose two.)

    A) Using APIs

    B) Enabling cross-cloud functionality

    C) Configuring data-sharing rules

    D) Implementing Lightning Components

Answer key

Question	Answer	Question	Answer	Question	Answer
1	B	8	A	15	D
2	A	9	A	16	A, D
3	C	10	A, B, C	17	A
4	A, C	11	D	18	D
5	A	12	B	19	D
6	D	13	A, B	20	A, B
7	A	14	B	-	-

Answer key: 14.3

Adoption and analytics

We've talked extensively about the importance of a good user experience and why setting up a site to be tailored to the specific needs of a user is critical in ensuring the adoption of your Salesforce Experience Cloud site. Additionally, knowing what to measure and monitoring your site are key components to developing a healthy user experience over time.

Here are a few best practices to keep in mind:

- **Utilize analytics to drive engagement**: Regularly analyze community data and 3rd party analytics to understand user behavior and preferences. Use insights from reports and dashboards to make informed decisions about community management and content strategy.

- **Encourage user participation**: Implement features such as discounts, points, and upvotes to motivate users to participate and contribute to the community.

- **Offer comprehensive support and resources**: Ensure that users have access to adequate support and training materials to encourage adoption, such as Knowledge FAQs, user guides, and live help options.

- **Promote community through multiple channels**: Where relevant, increase visibility and adoption by promoting your site through emails, newsletters, social media, and other corporate channels.

- **Gather user feedback**: Regularly gather and analyze user feedback to improve the community. Implement changes based on this feedback to continuously adapt to user needs.

Let's move on to the questions:

1. Which of the following features allows for the customization of the user interface in Experience Cloud?

    A) Salesforce Shield

    B) Experience Builder

    C) Lightning Connect

    D) Chatter

2. How can Salesforce Experience Cloud be used to support customer service operations?

    A) By enabling automatic email responses

    B) By integrating with Salesforce Marketing Cloud

    C) By providing self-service portals for case submission and tracking

    D) By offering custom reports

3. What type of license is required to access the Partner Central template in Salesforce Experience Cloud?

    A) Customer Community

    B) Partner Community

    C) Employee Community

    D) Salesforce Platform

4. What is the purpose of the Community Management tool in Salesforce Experience Cloud?

    A) To manage Salesforce Connect settings

    B) To create custom fields

    C) To manage CRM objects

    D) To monitor and moderate community activity

5. What are the key features of the Salesforce CMS when integrated with Experience Cloud? (Choose three.)

    A) Content creation and management

    B) Multilingual support

    C) Chatter integration

    D) Personalization of content based on user profiles

6. Which metrics can be tracked using Community Analytics in Experience Cloud? (Choose three.)

    A) User engagement

    B) Page views

    C) Case resolution time

    D) Content popularity

7. How can you increase user adoption of a new Experience Cloud site? (Choose two.)

    A) Provide interactive tutorials

    B) Implement a rewards system for active users

    C) Disable certain features to simplify the interface

    D) Restrict access to advanced functionality

8. Which feature in Salesforce Experience Cloud helps in analyzing user engagement?

    A) Community Insights

    B) Salesforce Reports

    C) Experience Analytics

    D) Chatter Metrics

9. How can Salesforce CMS help with content strategy in an Experience Cloud site?

    A) By offering data-driven insights into content performance

    B) By allowing real-time content updates

    C) By providing tools for content creation and management

    D) All of the above

10. Which tool allows you to create custom reports and dashboards in Salesforce Experience Cloud?

    A) Experience Builder

    B) Salesforce Reports and Dashboards

    C) Lightning App Builder

    D) Visualforce

11. How can Salesforce Experience Cloud support business growth?

    A) By providing a scalable platform for customer and partner engagement

    B) By automating sales and marketing processes

    C) By offering insights into user behavior and preferences

    D) All of the above

12. How can you analyze the effectiveness of a knowledge base within an Experience Cloud site? (Choose two.)

    A) By monitoring article views

    B) By tracking search queries

    C) By analyzing case resolution time

    D) By surveying users

13. Which feature allows for real-time collaboration among users in Salesforce Experience Cloud?

    A) Chatter

    B) Lightning Sync

    C) Salesforce Connect

    D) Workflow Rules

14. What is the benefit of integrating Salesforce CMS with Experience Cloud?

    A) Centralized content management and distribution

    B) Enhanced content personalization

    C) Streamlined content creation processes

    D) All of the above

15. Which tool provides insights into user engagement in an Experience Cloud site?

    A) Experience Analytics

    B) Community Management

    C) Salesforce Reports

    D) Lightning App Builder

16. What are some best practices for driving the adoption of Salesforce Experience Cloud? (Choose two.)

    A) Providing training and support

    B) Regularly updating the community with new features

    C) Limiting access to key features

    D) Removing customization options

17. How can you track the impact of content published on an Experience Cloud site? (Choose two.)

    A) Using Community Analytics

    B) Monitoring user feedback

    C) Implementing real-time content tracking

    D) Analyzing search queries

18. Which Salesforce Experience Cloud feature can be used to measure customer satisfaction?

    A) Surveys

    B) Reports

    C) Dashboards

    D) Community Management

19. How can Salesforce Experience Cloud support customer engagement?

    A) By offering personalized experiences

    B) By providing self-service options

    C) By enabling real-time collaboration

    D) All of the above

20. What is the advantage of using Salesforce CMS in Experience Cloud?

    A) It allows for the centralized management of content

    B) It enables real-time content updates

    C) It supports multilingual content

    D) All of the above

Answer key

Question	Answer	Question	Answer	Question	Answer
1	B	8	C	15	A
2	C	9	D	16	A, B
3	B	10	B	17	A, B
4	D	11	D	18	A
5	A, B, D	12	A, B	19	D
6	A, B, D	13	A	20	D
7	A, B	14	D	-	-

Answer key: 14.4

Customization considerations and limitations

Salesforce Experience Cloud isn't limited to templates that come out of the box. For organizations with highly specific design needs, you can extend Experience Cloud with custom code using standards such as Aura, LWRs, or LWCs. Before you make the move to custom development, it's important to consider out-of-the-box options and the trade-offs involved with going fully custom. Let's review some best practices:

- **Test extensively**: Before deploying customizations to production, conduct thorough testing in a sandbox environment to identify and fix any potential issues.

- **Use declarative tools before code**: Whenever possible, use Salesforce's built-in declarative tools such as Process Builder and Flow before resorting to custom code.

- **Monitor custom code**: Regularly review and optimize custom code to prevent it from becoming a security risk.

- **Stay informed on updates**: Keep up with Salesforce's release cycles and updates to adapt to changes as needed.

Remember that customization can become incredibly complex, so always heavily plan for maintenance before implementing a customization. Let's look through some test questions:

1. Which tool can be used to create custom pages in Salesforce Experience Cloud?

   A) Visualforce

   B) Salesforce Connect

   C) Salesforce Shield

   D) Data Loader

2. Which of the following should be considered when customizing a Salesforce Experience Cloud site?

   A) Site performance impact

   B) User accessibility

   C) Mobile responsiveness

   D) All of the above

3. Which of the following is a limitation of customizing Experience Cloud sites?

   A) Limited access to Salesforce APIs

   B) Restriction on third-party integrations

   C) Custom code can impact site performance

   D) Inability to use custom objects

4. What is the impact of extensive use of custom code in an Experience Cloud site? (Choose two.)

   A) Enhanced user experience

   B) Potential for inefficient API calls

   C) Potential performance issues

   D) Increased scalability

5. What should be considered when creating custom components for an Experience Cloud site? (Choose two.)

   A) Browser compatibility

   B) Impact on site performance

   C) Restrictions on third-party integrations

   D) Security implications

6. Which customization option allows for advanced configuration of an Experience Cloud site?

   A) Lightning Components

   B) Data Loader

   C) Salesforce Shield

   D) Lightning App Builder

7. What are the potential risks of customizing an Experience Cloud site with third-party integrations?

   A) Data security vulnerabilities

   B) Increased maintenance costs

   C) Compatibility issues with future updates

   D) All of the above

8. What is a key consideration when adding custom JavaScript to an Experience Cloud site?

   A) Ensuring compatibility with all browsers

   B) Testing on various mobile devices

   C) Maintaining performance standards

   D) All of the above

   Which tool is essential for customizing the user interface of an Experience Cloud site?

   A) Experience Builder

   B) Lightning Flow

   C) Salesforce Connect

   D) Data Loader

9. What should be considered when integrating third-party services with Salesforce Experience Cloud?

   A) API limits

   B) Security risks

   C) User experience impact

   D) All of the above

10. How does extensive customization impact the upgrade process for Salesforce Experience Cloud?

    A) It simplifies the upgrade process

    B) It can complicate the upgrade process due to dependencies

    C) It has no impact on the upgrade process

    D) It speeds up the upgrade process

11. What is the limitation of using standard components in Salesforce Experience Cloud?

    A) They cannot be visually coded over

    B) They do not support mobile devices

    C) They can only be used with Salesforce data

    D) They require extensive coding skills

12. Which feature must be considered when deploying custom code on Salesforce Experience Cloud?

    A) Execution governors and limits

    B) API version compatibility

    C) Cross-browser testing

    D) All of the above

13. What is a common challenge when customizing Salesforce Experience Cloud for global audiences? (Choose two.)

    A) Finding images that can legally be used in another country

    B) Implementing multi-currency support

    C) Managing multiple language translations

    D) Making sure your website appears in searches in another country

14. How can you mitigate the risk of performance issues due to customization in Salesforce Experience Cloud?

    A) Regularly review and optimize custom code

    B) Limit the use of third-party integrations

    C) Use only native Salesforce components

    D) All of the above

15. What are the limitations of using custom Lightning Components in Salesforce Experience Cloud? (Choose three.)

    A) They cannot interact with standard components

    B) They may not be supported in all Salesforce releases

    C) They require a higher level of technical expertise to develop

    D) They are all built with HTML

16. What should be considered when implementing a custom theme for an Experience Cloud site?

    A) Brand consistency

    B) User experience

    C) Ease of upkeep

    D) All of the above

17. What is the impact of not properly testing customizations on different devices and browsers in Experience Cloud? (Choose two.)

    A) Reduced user satisfaction

    B) Bad download times

    C) Lower user adoption rates

    D) None, Experience Cloud works with all browsers

18. How can you ensure that customizations do not adversely affect site security in Salesforce Experience Cloud?

    A) Conduct regular security audits

    B) Implement robust testing protocols

    C) Use only vetted third-party integrations

    D) All of the above

19. Which factor should not be considered when deciding between using standard and custom components in Salesforce Experience Cloud?

    A) Ease of maintenance

    B) Development time

    C) Cost implications

    D) Standard objects

Answer key

Question	Answer		Question	Answer		Question	Answer
1	A		10	D		19	D
2	D		11	B		20	D
3	C		12	A		-	-
4	B, C		13	D		-	-
5	A, B		14	B, C		-	-
6	A		15	D		-	-
7	D		16	A, B, C		-	-
8	D		17	D		-	-
9	A		18	A, C		-	-

Answer key: 14.5

Branding, personalization, and content

The beauty of Salesforce Experience Cloud is its ability to quickly stand up sleek, modern digital experiences on top of a turnkey integration with Salesforce. As with any modern website, you will need to come up with a content management strategy, in addition to tailoring your site for specific users. Let's take a look at some best practices before we review some sample questions:

- **Consistent branding**: Ensure that the community branding aligns with your overall corporate branding guidelines to maintain consistency across all platforms.

- **Dynamic content delivery**: Utilize Salesforce CMS to serve content based on user behavior, preferences, or roles to increase engagement.

- **Regular content updates**: Keep the content fresh and relevant. Plan regular reviews and updates to keep the community informative and engaging.

- **Personalize user experiences**: Use data about users to personalize the UI and content, making the experience more relevant and engaging for each user.

- **Optimize for SEO**: If managing a public site, ensure that the community is optimized for search engines to increase visibility and attract new users organically.

When it comes to websites and digital applications, content is king. Let's review some sample questions:

1. Which tool allows you to customize the look and feel of your Salesforce Experience Cloud site?

   A) Salesforce CMS

   B) Experience Builder

   C) Visualforce

   D) Lightning Design System

2. How can personalization be achieved in the Salesforce Experience Cloud?

   A) Using Audience Targeting

   B) Applying CSS styles

   C) Integrating with Salesforce Marketing Cloud

   D) All of the above

3. What should be considered when designing the branding for an Experience Cloud site?

   A) Color scheme

   B) Font choices

   C) Logo placement

   D) All of the above

4. How can Salesforce CMS enhance the user experience in an Experience Cloud site?

   A) By providing a range of templates for content creation

   B) By enabling content to be personalized for different audiences

   C) By allowing easy updates and management of content

   D) All of the above

5. What are the benefits of using custom themes in the Salesforce Experience Cloud?

   A) They ensure a unique visual identity

   B) They can be easily updated

   C) They allow for greater flexibility in design

   D) All of the above

6. Which Salesforce tool allows you to manage content distribution across multiple channels within an Experience Cloud site?

   A) Salesforce CMS

   B) Experience Builder

   C) Data Loader

   D) Salesforce Shield

7. How can you use Salesforce CMS to improve content relevance on your Experience Cloud site?

   A) By using data-driven insights to tailor content

   B) By creating audience-specific content channels

   C) By regularly updating content based on user feedback

   D) All of the above

8. What is the role of branding in Salesforce Experience Cloud sites?

   A) To distinguish the site from competitors

   B) To enhance user engagement

   C) To ensure consistency across all digital assets

   D) All of the above

9. How can you ensure content consistency across multiple Experience Cloud sites?

   A) By using Salesforce CMS to centralize content management

   B) By implementing uniform content guidelines

   C) By conducting regular content audits

   D) All of the above

10. What are the advantages of integrating Salesforce CMS with Experience Cloud for content management?

    A) It simplifies the management of multimedia content

    B) It provides tools for real-time content collaboration

    C) It allows for seamless content syndication across channels

    D) All of the above

11. How can personalization be enhanced in Salesforce Experience Cloud using Audience Targeting? (Choose three.)

    A) By delivering customized content to different user groups

    B) By using dynamic content blocks in emails

    C) By segmenting users based on their interactions

    D) By profiles

12. What is the importance of responsive design in Salesforce Experience Cloud sites?

    A) It ensures accessibility on all devices

    B) It allows for segmentation of data

    C) It makes coding easier

    D) All of the above

13. How can Salesforce Experience Cloud be used to create a visually appealing user interface?

    A) By utilizing pre-built themes

    B) By customizing layouts with Experience Builder

    C) By integrating third-party design tools

    D) All of the above

14. What is the best practice for managing the content lifecycle in Salesforce Experience Cloud? (Choose three.)

    A) Establishing a regular review and revision schedule

    B) Using Salesforce CMS to track changes and updates

    C) Setting content to expire

    D) Implementing approval workflows for content updates

15. How does Salesforce CMS contribute to the personalization of user experiences in Experience Cloud? (Choose two.)

    A) By allowing the creation of content variations based on user profiles

    B) By enabling targeted content delivery based on user behavior

    C) By adding an additional layer of content management into Salesforce

    D) By connecting to `site.com`

16. What are the key considerations when implementing branding guidelines in Salesforce Experience Cloud? (Choose two.)

    A) Cobranding your site with Salesforce

    B) Balancing brand identity with user experience

    C) Aligning brand visuals with company values

    D) Using JPEG instead of PDF

17. How can dynamic content features enhance the user experience in Salesforce Experience Cloud?

    A) By automatically adapting content based on user interactions

    B) By updating content in real time as user preferences change

    C) By providing personalized recommendations based on user behavior

    D) All of the above

18. Which of these is NOT an impact of effective content management on user engagement in Salesforce Experience Cloud? (Choose two.)

    A) Decreased user satisfaction

    B) Higher rates of content interaction

    C) Improved user retention

    D) More user registrations

19. How can user feedback be used to refine content strategies in Salesforce Experience Cloud? (Choose two.)

    A) By reviewing analytics

    B) By implementing changes based on user ratings and reviews

    C) By analyzing user comments and suggestions

    D) By checking login rates

20. What role does A/B testing play in content optimization in Salesforce Experience Cloud? (Choose two.)

    A) It helps identify the most effective content variations

    B) It determines the most aesthetically pleasing images

    C) It facilitates the improvement of user engagement metrics

    D) It is the only metric that explains user engagement

Answer key

Question	Answer		Question	Answer		Question	Answer
1	B		10	D		19	B, C
2	D		11	A, B, C		20	A, C
3	D		12	A		-	-
4	D		13	D		-	-
5	D		14	A, B, D		-	-
6	A		15	A, B		-	-
7	D		16	B, C		-	-
8	D		17	D		-	-
9	D		18	A, D		-	-

Answer key: 14.6

Final thoughts

We hope that these questions have helped you think about the intricacies of Experience Cloud, in addition to some of the "gotchas" that Salesforce often sneaks into some of their exams. These should give you a good idea of how Salesforce certification questions work.

Salesforce Experience Cloud is a living product that changes with each release. This book is a good introduction, but it will never replace hands-on usage and study of the product. Keep watching and reading about Salesforce Experience Cloud to get the best out of it, and don't forget to check forums and release documentation for updates.

Don't be strangers either! The Salesforce Ohana is built on a culture of helping others. Feel free to reach out to us on LinkedIn, X, or the Trailhead communities. Mention that you have the book and what your questions are. We're happy to assist you on your journey or connect you with resources that can help. We hope Salesforce Experience Cloud continues to serve you and your users for years to come.

Index

packtpub.com

Subscribe to our online digital library for full access to over 7,000 books and videos, as well as industry leading tools to help you plan your personal development and advance your career. For more information, please visit our website.

Why subscribe?

- Spend less time learning and more time coding with practical eBooks and Videos from over 4,000 industry professionals

- Improve your learning with Skill Plans built especially for you

- Get a free eBook or video every month

- Fully searchable for easy access to vital information

- Copy and paste, print, and bookmark content

Did you know that Packt offers eBook versions of every book published, with PDF and ePub files available? You can upgrade to the eBook version at packtpub.com and as a print book customer, you are entitled to a discount on the eBook copy. Get in touch with us at customercare@packtpub.com for more details.

At www.packtpub.com, you can also read a collection of free technical articles, sign up for a range of free newsletters, and receive exclusive discounts and offers on Packt books and eBooks.

Other Books You May Enjoy

If you enjoyed this book, you may be interested in these other books by Packt:

Salesforce Sales Cloud – An Implementation Handbook

Kerry Townsend

ISBN: 978-1-80461-964-3

- Find out how Sales Cloud capabilities solve common sales challenges
- Determine the best development methodologies
- Design and build core sales processes, including demand generation and sales productivity
- Implement best practices for testing and training with accurate data
- Build a release plan by understanding the types of post-go-live support
- Explore territory management and model additional processes with Sales Cloud
- Understand common system integration use cases
- Harness the power of AppExchange solutions for sales

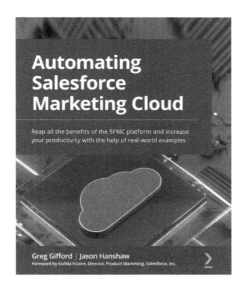

Automating Salesforce Marketing Cloud

Greg Gifford, Jason Hanshaw

ISBN: 978-1-80323-719-0

- Understand automation to make the most of the SFMC platform
- Optimize ETL activities, data import integrations, data segmentations, email sends, and more
- Explore different ways to use scripting and API calls to increase Automation Studio efficiency
- Identify opportunities for automation with custom integrations and third-party solutions
- Optimize usage of SFMC by building on the core concepts of custom integrations and third-party tools
- Maximize utilization of employee skills and capabilities and reduce operational costs while increasing output

Packt is searching for authors like you

If you're interested in becoming an author for Packt, please visit authors.packtpub.com and apply today. We have worked with thousands of developers and tech professionals, just like you, to help them share their insight with the global tech community. You can make a general application, apply for a specific hot topic that we are recruiting an author for, or submit your own idea.

Share Your Thoughts

Now you've finished *Mastering Salesforce Experience Cloud*, we'd love to hear your thoughts! Scan the QR code below to go straight to the Amazon review page for this book and share your feedback or leave a review on the site that you purchased it from.

https://packt.link/r/1-835-46634-6

Your review is important to us and the tech community and will help us make sure we're delivering excellent quality content.

Download a free PDF copy of this book

Thanks for purchasing this book!

Do you like to read on the go but are unable to carry your print books everywhere?

Is your eBook purchase not compatible with the device of your choice?

Don't worry, now with every Packt book you get a DRM-free PDF version of that book at no cost.

Read anywhere, any place, on any device. Search, copy, and paste code from your favorite technical books directly into your application.

The perks don't stop there, you can get exclusive access to discounts, newsletters, and great free content in your inbox daily

Follow these simple steps to get the benefits:

1. Scan the QR code or visit the link below

https://packt.link/free-ebook/978-1-83546-634-6

2. Submit your proof of purchase

3. That's it! We'll send your free PDF and other benefits to your email directly

www.ingramcontent.com/pod-product-compliance
Lightning Source LLC
Chambersburg PA
CBHW080623060326
40690CB00021B/4792